Günter Bischof/Dieter Stiefel (Eds.)

Images of the Marshall Plan in Europe

Transatlantica
Günter Bischof, Editor

Volume 3: Günter Bischof/Dieter Stiefel (Eds.)
Images of the Marshall Plan in Europe

Günter Bischof/Dieter Stiefel (Eds.)

Images of the Marshall Plan in Europe

Films, Photographs, Exhibits, Posters

Hannes Richter, Digital Editor

StudienVerlag
Innsbruck
Wien
Bozen

These essays are dedicated to Charles S. Maier, Harvard University

This publication is supported by the Schumpeter Gesellschaft in Vienna, the University of New Orleans, the ERP-Fonds – Austria Wirtschaftsservice, the Austrian Federal Ministry of Science and Research, the Federal Province of Vorarlberg and the Cultural Department of the City of Vienna.

E-Mail: order@studienverlag.at
Internet: www.studienverlag.at

Corporate design by Kurt Höretzeder
Layout: Studienverlag/Walter Methlagl
Cover: Studienverlag/Karin Berner
Photo: Gailtal Valley drainage project 1951
(ECA-Hilfe für die Entwässerung des Gailtales. Zwischen Kirchbach und Weidegg: Landgewinnung für den Ackerbau durch Drainage von Sumpfwiesen. Bauführer Ingenieur Herbst fährt mit Motorrad das Gebiet ab.)
Signatur US 21592, Austrian National Library - Picture Archive

Distributed in North America by Transaction Publishers, Rutgers – the State university, 35 berrue Circle, Piscataway New Jersey, 08854-8042, USA, www.transactionpub.com

This book is printed on acid-free paper.

Bibliographic information published by Die Deutsche Bibliothek
Die Deutsche Bibliothek lists this publication in the Deutsche Nationalbibliographie;
detailed bibliographic data is available in the Internet at http://dnb.ddb.de

ISBN 978-3-7065-4826-7

Table of Contents

Günter Bischof *

Introduction

Selling the Marshall Plan—Selling America

"Truth also needs propaganda."
– Karl Jaspers[1]

The Marshall Plan was one of the capstones in President Harry Truman's containment strategy of the Soviet Union after World War II. It has been called "the other half of the walnut" of Truman's military containment strategy announced during the Greek crisis of spring 1947. Secretary of State George C. Marshall announced the European Recovery Program (ERP) on 5 June 1947, during the Harvard commencement, only a few weeks after Truman's speech to Congress.[2] The Marshall Plan—an economic reconstruction plan for Europe (actually Western Europe since the Soviet Union refused to participate and forced its satellite regimes in Eastern Europe to reject the benefits of such a generous U.S. aid program)—was launched in 1948. The Marshall Plan was one more step in the finalization of the Cold War division of the European continent into two halves, preordained by the Yalta agreements of February 1945 and now controlled by the two postwar hegemonic powers, the United States and the Soviet Union. This deepening separation between Soviet and U.S. spheres of influence in Europe had been growing ever since the ideological clash sharpened after George Kennan's famous "long telegram" and Stalin's "election speech" of February 1946 and after four-power control had been breaking down in the German occupation in the course of 1946.[3]

With the coming of Korean War in June 1950 and the implementation of NSC-68—the most important U.S. document of the Cold War—a revised U.S. national security strategy was launched, based on a bigger emphasis on nuclear weapons and an invigorated alliance politics, but also a new "crusade for truth"—the winning of "hearts and minds" by way of psychological warfare and propaganda. This new U.S. national security strategy emphasized both "hard" and "soft" power equally. The Korean War and NSC-68 also transformed the Marshall Plan from an economic to a predominantly military aid program.[4] The new emphasis on propaganda—an aspect of what today is called "public diplomacy"—also intimately affected the Marshall Plan. The "public diplomacy" side of the Marshall Plan is the principal theme of this book.[5]

Marshall Plan scholarship has long concentrated on the "hard power" side of "the most successful aid program in history."[6] Scholars have studied the strategic

---

* I would like to thank Hugh Wilford in Long Beach, California, and Dieter Stiefel in Vienna for providing valuable feedback for this introduction.

mission of the Marshall Plan as part of U.S. containment strategy.[7] They have looked at the economic benefits of the Marshall Plan both for the Western European *and* the U.S. economies.[8] Recently, scholars have also studied specific industries like tourism and have shown how investments in hotels and ski lifts increased the flow of tourists, with tourist dollars helping to close the "dollar gap."[9] What has been called "the politics of productivity" has garnered much attention in the community of Marshall Plan scholars.[10]

More recently, researchers have also concentrated on the role of the Marshall Plan as a crucial first step towards postwar European economic and political integration and on the role the U.S. played as a midwife in this process. European integration, launched as a crucial goal of Marshall's strategy, has brought peace and prosperity to a continent whose previous history had been defined by war and bloodbaths.[11] In the fall of 1949, Paul Hoffman, the charismatic director of the European Cooperation Agency (ECA) in Washington, flew to Paris to address the Organization of European Economic Cooperation (OEEC). He presented the OEEC countries with a ten-week deadline to deal with their intra-European trade problems and integrate their economies into a single common market.[12] Scholars have also studied the role of the Marshall Plan in nurturing the reconstruction of postwar European science.[13] Researchers recently have began to study the "Marshall Plan myth": its (non-)transferability to other times, continents, and economic crises.[14] Many individual country studies have been done on each and every of the sixteen participating nations in the European Recovery Program and the relative impact that U.S. aid had on these individual economies as well as on the Western European economy as a whole.[15]

The "soft power" strategies of the Marshall Plan have only recently become the focus of scholarship. The public diplomacy programs of the Marshall Plan are increasingly seen as a long-neglected, yet crucially important, part in "selling" the Marshall Plan and its benefits to the respective constituencies in both the United States and Europe.[16] First the plan for a massive economic aid program had to be sold to tight-fisted and reluctant American taxpayers.[17] The late 1947/early 1948 campaign to advertise the necessity of massive U.S. economic aid to Europe spawned one of the most brilliant and successful public media campaigns in U.S. history. Three special committees were set up to send the United States' political leaders out to cross the country and rally the American public to accept the necessity of a multi-billion dollar program of American taxpayer money to rebuild Western Europe and stop the expansion of communism from Eastern to Western Europe. George C. Marshall, the charismatic Secretary of State, exhausted himself criss-crossing the country with his numerous trips to inform Americans about the vital necessity of the European Recovery Program that would come to carry his name.[18] This government and media blitz rallied the nation in support of the ERP. The great scare produced by the "Czech Coup" of February 1948—and the imminent danger of the further spread of communism in Europe and around the world through subversive means—was the final straw that rallied Congress to pass the Economic Cooperation Act legislation on 3 April 1948 that would open the spigot of U.S. aid for Western Europe.[19] Within days of the passage of the Marshall Plan in

Congress, ships were loaded in U.S. ports, and an avalanche of American products (machines and raw materials such as cotton, food, and fertilizers) began to flow into Western Europe.[20]

Once the economic aid programs began to flow into Europe in the second half of 1948, the need to sell the ERP to the Western European recipient constituencies became imperative, too. Vigorous information campaigns selling the Marshall Plan in Europe were required by the congressional legislation. Elaborate public relations campaigns were designed to utilize all modern mass media (often pioneered by the Americans) in the service of selling the Marshall Plan. The *Voice of America* radio programs (initiated in 1942 to sell the war against the Nazis and Japanese militarists to Americans and to the world) and Radio Free Europe (since 1950) were directed towards selling *the* new global specter to the world: communism and the threat of it spreading.[21] The positive side of Western European economic reconstruction, the benefits of U.S. power and American liberal values of free markets and democracy, as well as popular American mass culture, were touted *vis-à-vis* the Europeans, along with the negative message of the imperative to contain Soviet communism which was threatening Western civilization. In fact, Marshall Plan public diplomacy was also a direct response to communist propaganda charging that the ERP was "American imperialism" and militarizing Europe ("the Marshall Plan is war").[22] Soon films, pictures, posters, pamphlets, magazines, balloons, parades, and lectures, as well as stationary and traveling exhibits on trains and ships, were added to the full spectrum of the vast advertising campaign that sold the benefits of the Marshall Plan and American generosity to the participant nations.[23] David Ellwood, one of the keenest scholars on the campaign to sell the Marshall Plan, has called it "the largest international propaganda operation ever seen in peacetime."[24]

The blitz of Marshall Plan propaganda lasted over a period of four years (1948-1952), as long as U.S. ERP aid flowed into Europe (albeit U.S. psychological warfare against the Soviet Union intensified under the Eisenhower Administration[25]). It was all encompassing from the cities to the countryside; no European could escape its principal messages of the benefits of following the U.S. model of economic productivity for one day triggering a haven of consumer plenty in postwar Western Europe, too. Other principal messages were what might be termed the "export of American exceptionalism," namely the superior American value system, especially when compared to unattractive Soviet "peace" offensives of the era. Moreover, the need for Western European integration to buttress the working and intellectual classes of the continent against the allures of communism was paramount in the mind of American Marshall Planners as well. Never before in history had the benefits of a major political and economic program been advertised so comprehensively and successfully.[26]

The "soft power" Marshall Plan public diplomacy/propaganda campaign had a slow start, but swung into full gear by 1950 at a crucial moment of the Cold War. It was the moment, as noted above, when what has been called "the American national security state" was established in Washington. Begun in 1947, the Truman Administration established the National Security Council, the Central Intelligence

Agency (CIA), and the new structure of the U.S. Defense Department and adopted Kennan's containment strategy to fight the Soviet Union in the Cold War. The new U.S. "hard power" constellation was completed in 1950 with the implementation of NSC-68 during the throes of the Korean War. During the Korean War, the U.S. defense budget quadrupled from $12 billion in 1950 to $50 billion in 1952. The Czech Coup, Joseph Stalin's Berlin blockade, Mao Zedong's victory in the Chinese Civil War and the rise of "Red China," and the detonation of the first Soviet atomic device in 1948/49 were shocking events to the U.S. Cold War establishment. The decision was made to develop a hydrogen bomb—a much stronger and more easily deliverable atomic device. The United States made a firm commitment to strengthen NATO and send U.S. divisions to the Cold War frontier in West Germany along with General Dwight D. Eisenhower as the first American NATO commander.[27] These events unleashed the militarization of the United States to fight the Cold War.

This strengthening of U.S. "hard power" during the era of the Marshall Plan (1948-1952) came with a new commitment to unleash U.S. "soft power" by way of an intense psychological warfare "campaign for truth" to be waged both by overt and covert means.[28] As one State Department official put it, "*In the contest for men's minds, truth can be peculiarly the American weapon*" (emphasis mine), and added: "a highly skilful and substantial campaign of truth is as indispensable as an air force."[29] While Congress was somewhat reluctant to spend money on blatant propagandizing, "If you dressed it up as warfare, money was very easy to come by."[30]

During the years of President Eisenhower, this propaganda campaign against evil communism became a "spiritual crusade" for the hearts and minds of Europeans. Eisenhower perceived the Cold War, with its spiraling nuclear arms race and deepening state of permanent national insecurity, as an unending process of managing apocalyptic threats.[31]

The principal arm for the CIA's truth campaign in the "cultural Cold War" in Europe was what has been called Frank Wisner's "mighty Wurlitzer" organ, "capable of playing any propaganda tune he desired."[32] The Office of Policy Coordination (OPC) was directed by Wisner, the former Office of Strategic Services (OSS) agent in the Balkans. OPC was first under the State Department and since 1950 had been under CIA supervision; it unleashed a host of covert operations programs. The OPC programs subverted both U.S. and Western European institutions in the gargantuan struggle for winning the "hearts and minds" of Western Europeans in the effort to lure them away from communism and neutralism.[33]

The OPC's International Organizations Division was led by Thomas Braden. It ran very sophisticated operations funneling tens of millions of dollars by way of both "pass-through" front and dummy foundations (such as the Farfield Foundation), as well as through bona fide philanthropic ones (such as the Ford and Rockefeller Foundations) to U.S. and European organizations, institutions, and universities to fight communism. Under the aegis of NSC-68, funding for CIA psychological warfare operations was quadrupled by 1952 from the $34 million spent in 1950.[34]

The "intellectual Cold War" was fought with particularly fierce intensity. The CIA set up the Congress for Cultural Freedom (CCF) in Europe in 1950 to lure fellow travelers, leftists, and liberal intellectuals away from the "God that Failed"—

communism. As a propaganda front with global tentacles, the CCF mirrored the Kremlin's Comintern/Cominform. The CIA covertly funded the CCF and its ambitious programs of scholarly conferences, arts congresses, intellectual journals, and magazines such as *Encounter*, *Preuves*, *Der Monat*, and Friedrich Torberg's Austrian *Forum*. The principal argument always pushed the benefits of a liberal, democratic, and capitalist world in the U.S. image and under Washington's hegemony *vis-à-vis* the false appeals of communism and neutralism. The CIA secretly funded numerous organizations—some wittingly, some unwittingly—to carry the messages of the superiority of American values and anti-communism into the world. The American labor unions and members of students', women's, artists', intellectuals', journalistic, Catholic, and African-American organizations were recruited into the covert CIA crusades. Nary a segment of U.S. civil society was left untouched by the CIA's subversive covert operations campaign. This being said, recent scholarship has pointed out that the CIA never controlled these intellectual discourses in Western Europe and the United States. Artists and intellectuals were as leery about American "mass culture" as they were about the threat of communism. Hugh Wilford has reminded us that American intellectuals served neither as "so many ventriloquist dummies" of the CIA, nor could the Agency control their anti-communist zeal, often exceeding that of the professional spies.[35]

Marshall Plan propaganda, it must be stressed here, was part and parcel of this anti-communist crusade answering the massive onslaught of Soviet Cold War and anti-Marshall Plan propaganda.[36] In an ingenious clause of the European Recovery Program's legislative setup, five percent of counterpart funds were set aside to be spent on administrative programs, including "public diplomacy" programs, to "sell" the Marshall Plan in Europe. Additionally, each country mission in recipient countries maintained its own information offices to sell the Marshall Plan nationally. The Western European city folks and peasants, workers and public servants, all were targeted to know that it was American taxpayers' money that brought machines, food, and raw materials to the starved Europeans, in the process improving their lives. Along with the U.S. products came the U.S. message of democratic values, increased productivity, and European integration and the dream of consumer plenty in Western Europe.[37] The "counterpart funds" were national investment accounts generated by the local sale of the U.S. products shipped through the Marshall Plan to Europe. It was the Marshall Plan's two-pronged strategy that sparked Western European economic recovery. U.S. machinery, food, and raw materials were transferred to the participant countries in Western Europe free of charge to fill the "dollar gap" in their massive balance of payments deficits and to accelerate economic recovery. The sale of these products on national markets paid in the national currencies generated the "counterpart funds" that were then reinvested in the national economies as cheap, long-term credits that would benefit these economies long after the end of the Marshall Plan (in the case of Austria, until today through the *ERP-Fonds* in Vienna).[38]

Five percent were diverted from these "counterparts" for both the *overt* public diplomacy campaigns of the Marshall Plan and the *covert* OPC programs. Five percent might sound like very little. In fact, given the size of the Marshall Plan grants and the counterpart funds accumulating from the sales of U.S. products in Western Europe, the 5 percent amounted to approximately $200 million a year. The OPC liberally dipped into these funds. The unvouchered 5 percent funding amounted to a gigantic slush fund of tens of millions of dollars for the OPC— "candy" as the CIA agents called it—more than they could spend and for which they did not have to account. Wisner had an understanding with Averell Harriman, the U.S. Marshall Plan administrator in the Office of the Special Representative in Paris, to use these "5 percent counterparts"; nobody asked questions. As Richard Bissell, the brilliant deputy administrator of the ECA in Washington put it: "Whether anyone anticipated that these miscellaneous [administrative] costs would include overt activities is difficult to say. This was most definitely a gray area."[39]

Unfortunately, the exact financing of the films, photos, and traveling exhibits is the least know aspect of the Marshall Plan. This may be a result of the loose administration of the 5 percent counterparts, used in part for the CIA's covert activities. With Wisner's OPC freely and frequently diverting "5 percent counterparts" to play his "mighty Wurlitzer" around Western Europe, the diversion of these funds to the CCF and various other CIA fronts established in the crusade against communism shows up rarely in the literature.[40] The CIA files documenting these diversions are kept closed, and they show up only spottily in the Marshall Plan records, or have not been studied systematically. While the essays in the pages of this book prodigiously document Marshall Plan public policy programs, particularly in Austria, Germany, Norway, Greece, and, to a lesser degree, Italy, we may assume that many of these effective public diplomacy programs were financed from information programs in each country mission. But surely unrecorded OPC activities played a role, too, in funding some of these activities. In the occupied countries Germany and Austria, the U.S. Army set up massive public information programs (in Austria the Information Services Branch). With the advent of the large psychological warfare programs, in 1950 the State Department took over the coordination of public diplomacy in the United States Information Services (USIS). In 1953, the Eisenhower Administration set up the United States Information Agency (USIA) to fund and direct the public information programs worldwide, including the photographers who so prodigiously documented the Marshall Plan in Austria and elsewhere.[41]

The funding of the labor programs are murkier, for the consummate "labor attachés" Irving Brown and Jay Lovestone operated all over the Marshall Plan area with AFL/CIA funding, as well as covert OPC and Marshall Plan 5 percent counterpart funding. Even though scholars have researched the Marshall Plan labor programs well, the funding sources remain unclear.[42] On the other hand, the CIA funding of the intellectual Cold War through the CCF is much better researched, while the exact amount of contributions by way of Marshall Plan 5 percent counterpart funding is not known either.[43]

The CIA also covertly funded the idea of the European integration movement which came to play such a central goal in the mission of the Marshall Plan. The "conduit for American assistance" became the American Committee of United Europe (ACUE), set up in the summer of 1948 by Allen Dulles and directed by senior figures of the CIA. It worked closely with the senior figures in the European

Cooperation Administration (ECA). The CIA responded to requests for assistance from senior pan-Europeanists such as Austrian Count Richard Coudenhove-Kalergi and Winston Churchill. The CIA did not act as a "puppet master," but responded to discreet requests from prominent European leaders and old friends for help. Many were European federalists enthralled with American federalism. Thomas Braden's International Organization Division eagerly responded with covert financing through its usual unofficial channels to European requests coming from, for example, Coundenhove-Kalergi's European Movement and Jean Monnet's Action Committee for a United States of Europe. Intelligence historian Richard Aldrich concludes how these informal networks of the CIA's "liberal conspiracy" originated as part of "a pattern of human friendships created by members of the intelligence and resistance community during the Second World War."[44] The CIA had to manipulate no one, but simply responded to urgent requests for help from European friends to support the idea of European federalism and thereby a key concept of the Marshall Plan. Sixteen European nations working together was trumpeted by all media as part of the arsenal of Marshall Plan public diplomacy.

The onslaught of the ECA's own education and information programs to sell the Marshall Plan to the Europeans was enormous and produced much overlap. The ECA Information Division in Washington set the strategic goals of Marshall Plan public diplomacy. Harriman's Office of the Special Representative (OSR) in Paris spared no expense in building up an information branch and coordinating country missions. After a slow start, 180 of 600 Americans employed in the OSR were generating the propaganda that sold the Marshall Plan to Europeans. Top-notch professionals such as *Washington Post* journalist Alfred Friendly and Roscoe Drummond from the *Christian Science Monitor* were hired to run the Office of Information in Paris. To make the campaigns highly professional, top advertising agencies were consulted such as J. Walter Thompson and the Advertising Council. ECA country missions developed their own information programs suited to the respective national contexts and local cultures (and sometimes duplicating Army or State Department programs already at work).

State Department cultural diplomats often criticized ECA information offices for their "stereotyped" messages ignoring specific cultural contexts. "Fast media" (radio, film, and press) campaigns were designed to stress productivity, rearmament, and European integration, as opposed to "slow media" (high culture and education exchange programs) with their more general information. The film section, headed by the likes of Lothar Wolff and Stuart Schulberg, and the top talent of directors hired to produce some 250 documentary and feature films, newsreels, and cartoons made the Marshall Plan appealing to Western Europeans who had a love affair with the cinema after the war. Millions saw these movies. The ECA estimated that some 10 million Europeans were reached through fairs and exhibits. Veritable poster wars were unleashed against communist propaganda, and "it was difficult at times in Paris to find a bare patch of space on walls, fences or posts," notes Greg Behrman.[45]

Did the American propagandists reach their European targets? Did they change hearts and minds? The ECA conducted its own polls and found that in 1950,

75 percent of Europeans approved of the Marshall Plan. Only in France, where communist anti-Marshall Plan propaganda was particularly strong, were disapproval ratings higher: 40 percent of Parisians opposed the Marshall Plan. Moreover, apparently the special Labor Information Branch was not so successful either in reaching European workers.[46] After five years of Nazi occupation, the French were leery of direct and shrill propaganda. Many French and Western European intellectuals on the left were neutralists and disliked the Manichean U.S. anti-communist propaganda. Critics considered the U.S. propaganda aimed at communists sterile. The French government was reluctant to unleash propaganda campaigns on the Marshall Plan, though this was expected by the Americans. This probably was true in other countries, too. The success of Marshall Plan propaganda was measured in polls conducted by the ECA or the Gallup organization. One Gallup Poll showed that 88 percent of the French were "aware" of the Marshall Plan. Success was also measured in terms of the millions of visitors that saw the exhibits and films, as well as communist counter-propaganda and vicious reactions to U.S. activities (traveling exhibits were regularly boycotted, assaulted, and sometimes even broken up).[47] Obviously, there is still much work to be done in measuring the precise impact of Marshall Plan propaganda on various national publics in the way Brian Angus McKenzie has studied in great detail Marshall Plan public diplomacy in France and Hans Jürgen Schröder in Germany and Austria.

Was the Marshall Plan "conceived to create a consumers' Europe"? Victoria de Grazia is quick to answer her question with a resounding no. The priorities of U.S. aid were "to boost productivity by investing in industrial retooling and infrastructure such as power stations, electric grids, port facilities, and railroad bridges." During the years of the Marshall Plan, argues de Grazia, "national levels of consumption were not to exceed the prewar benchmark of 1938." American-style consumer plenty—what Eric Hobsbawm calls the "golden age" of the postwar era—slowly began to settle in Europe only in the late 1950s and beyond.[48] David Ellwood suggests, however, that mass consumption was sold through the notion of growing "prosperity" flogged in many Marshall Plan films.[49] Wolfgang Kos argues that the Americanization of daily consumption in food, drink, clothing, and popular culture in postwar Austria—beginning with the Marshall Plan but culminating in the 1960s and 1970s—amounted to a "voluntary reeducation" (*freiwillige Umerziehung*). U.S. "reeducation" efforts (in Austria "reorientation"), of course, tried to impose U.S. democratic governance and capitalist mass production on the defeated and occupied Germans (and Austrians). The "Americanization" of postwar Austria came by way of rational organization of daily life with technical help such as the affordable refrigerator and electric stove, particularly in individual households.[50] The Marshall Plan did not unleash the forces of the voluntary Americanization of daily life single-handedly, but it surely produced the prosperity in individual households that eventually made the dream of an American consumer paradise in postwar Europe feasible.[51]

* * * * *

All but one of the essays in this book were first delivered during the conference *Images of the Marshall Plan: Film, Photographs, Exhibits, Posters* on 19/20 May 2008 in Vienna, Austria. The first section of this volume addresses U.S. perspectives on the Marshall Plan. Victoria de Grazia questions the "folk wisdom" of the Marshall Plan constituting the moment of initiation of Western European consumer affluence. The Americans wanted to rebuild European infrastructure and raise the standard of living, but restrict consumption. They did not want Europeans to aspire to U.S. consumption levels. That would come later in the 1950s and 1960s. Marshall Plan films were designed to sell American best practices, promoting U.S. aid in a non-ideological way and with restrained film narratives to Europeans. George M. Fujii's essay is an original contribution to this volume submitted after the Vienna conference. Fujii analyses the highly effective campaign launched by the Committee for the Marshall Plan (CMP) in 1947/48 to educate the American public about the Marshall Plan and build popular support for the massive and expensive program. The CMP brought together a broad coalition of business, labor, farm, and women's groups, along with veterans, religious groups, and internationalists to support the Marshall Plan as an instrument of public policy. This broad coalition between civil society and domestic politics effectively also sold the "Marshall Plan ideology" to Americans, namely a vision of a prosperous and stable America based on liberal principles that was now engaging in this massive economic intervention in European affairs through foreign aid.

Section II presents some case studies of how the Marshall Plan operated and how public diplomacy worked in different participant countries. David Ellwood gives a very broad vision of the film program—"the greatest international propaganda/information program ever seen in peacetime"—launched throughout the participant nations as part of Marshall Plan public diplomacy. The Marshall Plan film program was supposed "to inform, to educate, and—in the end—to convert," posits Ellwood. It was an invitation for the Europeans to emulate the United States: "*You Too Can Be Like Us*." Hans Jürgen Schröder presents broad goals of U.S. Marshall Plan propaganda in general and the specific mission in still-occupied West Germany, where U.S. propaganda was also engaged in "reeducating" the Germans after Adolph Hitler. Schröder recounts the various film media and their specific visual languages utilized to sell the message of the Marshall Plan in Germany: newsreels, documentaries, re-orientation films, feature films, cartoons, and productivity films. Helge Danielsen and Helge Pharo note how the various political camps in Norway responded to the Marshall Plan, not all positively. They present an enlightening case study of a display of Norwegian consumer goods produced with the help of Marshall aid in Oslo's leading department store, Steen & Strøm. The exhibit was very popular. It showed how American aid helped Norwegians overcome postwar rationing by making the availability of attractive consumer goods feasible again. To Norway, the ERP offered increased access to goods that had not been available during and after the war. Stelios Zachariou's case study of Greece stresses how Marshall Plan aid was mainly used for the purchase of military hardware to fight and win the long and brutal postwar civil war against the communists. Modernization came to Greece via the generosity of the Marshall Plan and was effectively demonstrated to Greeks through media such as the famous movie *Story of Koula* and a traveling exhibit onboard a ship that traveled around the Aegean Sea to various islands showing the benefits of the Marshall Plan.

Section III is dedicated to the "selling" of the Marshall Plan in Austria through film, photographs, and traveling exhibits. With her essay on the Soviet zone in four-power occupied Austria, Barbara Stelzl-Marx analyses Austria's unique situation. Austria was the only participating country where U.S. Marshall Plan aid benefited Austrians living under Soviet occupation. Stelzl-Marx summarizes the Soviet economic exploitation of Austria and the vigorous Soviet propaganda campaign against the "imperialist" and "militaristic" Marshall Plan. Ramon Reichert analyzes in depth the specific narrative techniques used by famous directors such as Georg Tressler in Austrian Marshall Plan movies. Christoph Höllriegl's essay concentrates on the extensive film collection of the Austrian Trade Union Federation—some 1,242 USIS 16mm films.[52] These films were screened into the 1960s all around Austria. In the Austrian countryside, this was often the only form of modern entertainment people experienced. He looks at the visualization of the Marshall Plan in Austria, particularly as presented in prominent themes such as improving the productivity in Austrian industry and business. Höllriegl places his analysis of this vast collection of Marshall Plan films, documentaries, and newsreels in a sophisticated context of modern theoretical media discourses.

Photo archivists Herbert Friedlmeier, Hans Petschar,[53] and Michaela Pfunder present an overview of the broad themes and messages contained in the huge picture collection of the United States Information Service, donated to the Austrian National Library in 1977. The USIS documented all aspects of Austrian life after World War II. With the coming of the Marshall Plan to Austria, more than a quarter of its staff resources were used to document the blessings of Marshall Plan aid in the reconstruction of postwar Austrian industry and agriculture through numerous series of "picture stories/narratives." The USIS photographers also documented top Marshall Plan administrators on their inspection trips of Marshall Plan sites all over Austria, as well as the "Train of Europe" with its Marshall Plan traveling exhibit coming to Austria.

Section IV presents a couple of case studies on the memory of the Marshall Plan—a topic on which ERP scholarship is now beginning to focus.[54] Dieter Stiefel presents a fascinating case study of the publication of *Ten Years of the Marshall Plan in Austria* (*Zehn Jahre ERP in Österreich*) published by the Austrian government in 1958. It documents in great detail the vital contributions across the board that Marshall aid played in the reconstruction of all sectors of the postwar Austrian economy. In the spring of 1959, the Austrian ambassador personally presented a copy of *Ten Years of the Marshall Plan in Austria* to President Eisenhower in the White House as a symbolic thank you gift from the Austrian people to the American taxpayers. At the same time, a brilliant media campaign was launched in newspapers across the United States centering on this theme of Austrian gratitude to the American taxpayers for Marshall aid. U.S. newspapers noted with astonishment that such gratitude was very unusual in international affairs. Next in this section, Linda and Eric Christenson present a case study of the making of their television documentary on the Marshall Plan for the fiftieth anniversary of the ERP in 1997, which was shown on Public Broadcasting Stations across the United States. Broader surveys of the memory of the Marshall Plan for individual participant countries as well as for Europe and the United States at large should, indeed, be a major item on the Marshall Plan agenda.[55]

* * * * *

The editors and conference participants would like to thank the Austrian Marshall Plan Foundation for their generous funding of the Vienna conference as well as this book project. The occasion was the celebration of the tenth anniversary of CenterAustria at the University of New Orleans. Conference participants and friends of CenterAustria were treated to a lavish buffet in the offices of the Austrian Wirtschafts-Service/ERP Fonds as well as a memorable traditional *Heurigen* evening. Eugen Stark and Wolfgang Stoiber, the executive directors of the Österreichische Marshallplan Jubiläumsstiftung,[56] acted as the generous and circumspect hosts for the Vienna conference, taking particularly good care of all the international visitors. Former Finance Minister Ferdinand Lacina, the president of the Austrian Marshall Plan Foundation, has warmly supported this project as well and opened the conference. Anton Fink from the Marshall Plan Foundation's board has been an enthusiastic supporter of CenterAustria over the years and also attended the meetings. Chargé d'Affaires Scott Kilmer brought his greetings from the U.S. Embassy in Vienna, along with Karin Schmid-Gerlich from the Cultural Office of the U.S. Embassy. Austrian colleagues and Cold War scholars Siegfried Beer, Reinhold Wagnleitner, Peter Berger, and Oliver Rathkolb chaired the sessions and gave valuable commentaries on the papers. Terry Kline from the Botstiber Foundation in Philadelphia also graced the meetings with his presence. We are grateful to all of them for their material support and enthusiasm for this project.

At CenterAustria of the University of New Orleans, the team of Gertraud Griessner, Marion Wieser, and Sandra Scherl were most helpful with preparations for the conference. Hannes Richter (our remote CenterAustria fellow in Berlin) edits our home page and helps us sell the activities of CenterAustria to a global audience.[57] He also was present at the Vienna conference. Susan Krantz, the dean of the College of Liberal Arts at UNO, has been very supportive of all tenth anniversary activities of CenterAustria—the Vienna conference being the conclusion of the year-long schedule of activities and events. Jennifer Shimek from the English Department of Loyola University of New Orleans has done a marvelous job in copy-editing these essays—most of them written by non-native English speakers. She wields an incisive pen and improved the wording and flow of every essay.

At the StudienVerlag in Innsbruck, I have worked for many years now with its contemporary history editor Martin Kofler. He helped me in launching the TRANSATLANTICA series. He has been unfailingly helpful in shepherding this project through the publication process. We would like to thank our volume editor Doris Wimpissinger and the entire staff at the StudienVerlag who helped with the production of this volume. We would like to thank the Austrian Marshall Plan

Foundation, the Schumpeter Society of Vienna, UNO's CenterAustria, as well as the Federal Ministry of Science and Research for their financial support of this publication. A special word of thanks goes to Hannes Richter, located in Berlin, who prepared the digital images and films that are on the DVD contained in the back pocket of this volume. Additional film and picture materials can be accessed via the special website www.marshallplanimages.com maintained by Hannes Richter. Digital media allow an easy dissemination of films, posters, pictures, and images, all of which add enormously to spreading the message of the brilliant visual public diplomacy campaign that played such a role part in selling the Marshall Plan and creating its lasting myth.

Finally, we dedicate this volume to Charles S. Maier. Charlie introduced Günter Bischof as a graduate student to the intricacies of Marshall Plan scholarship and has been a mentor ever since. As the director of the Center for European Studies at Harvard, he generously supported Dieter Stiefel in launching the Schumpeter fellowship program. He is a friend of some of the authors of this volume; his path-breaking scholarship serves as a model and an inspiration to all.

Notes

1 Quoted in Frances Stonor Saunders, *The Cultural Cold War: The CIA and the World of Arts and Letters* (New York: Free Press, 1999), 97.

2 See Walter LaFeber's chapter "Two Halves of the Same Walnut," in *America, Russia, and the Cold War*, 4th ed. (New York: John Wiley, 1980), 50-74.

3 The Marshall Plan's role in the East-West division of Europe is still a matter of great historiographical controversy; see the essay in the "Special Forum: The Marshall Plan and the Origins of the Cold War Reassessed" by Michael Cox and Caroline Kennedy Pipe, "The Tragedy of American Diplomacy? Rethinking the Marshall Plan," *Journal of Cold War Studies* 7 (Winter 2005): 97-134 and the responses by Marc Trachtenberg, Günter Bischof, John Bledsoe Bonds, László Borhi, and Charles S. Maier in the same, 135-74.

4 Still the best discussion of the importance of NSC-68 is Ernest R. May, ed., *American Cold War Strategy: Interpreting NSC-68* (Boston: Bedford Books, 1993); see also Michael J. Hogan, *A Cross of Iron: Harry S. Truman and the Origins of the National Security State 1945-1954* (Cambridge: Cambridge UP, 1998); Arnold A. Offner, *Another Such Victory: President Truman and the Cold War 1945-1953* (Palo Alto, CA: Stanford UP, 2002), 347-81. The transformation of the ERP's premier mission from economic to military aid is stressed by Richard Bissell, Jr., with Jonathan E. Lewis and Frances T. Pudlo, *Reflections of a Cold Warrior: From Yalta to the Bay of Pigs* (New Haven, CT: Yale UP, 1996), 66f.

5 "Soft power" and "public diplomacy," even "Americanization," are more recently coined terms used for what formerly was called propaganda, psychological warfare, shadow war, or intellectual and/or cultural Cold War; they are used interchangeably for the same phenomenon—modern communication techniques of promoting one's own values and worldview while making the enemy look awful. While the State Department tended to handle the overt part, the Central Intelligence Agency (CIA) concentrated on the covert aspects; the Marshall Plan organizations Economic Cooperation Administration in Washington and the Organization for European Economic Cooperation (OEEC) in Paris engaged in both overt and covert propaganda. See Brian Angus McKenzie, *Remaking France: Americanization, Public Diplomacy, and the Marshall Plan* (New York: Berghahn Books, 2005), 3-13.

6 See the commemorative section "The Marshall Plan and its Legacy" on the occasion of the fiftieth anniversary of Marshall's Harvard speech in *Foreign Affairs* 76 (May-June 1997): 159-220.

7 Melvyn Leffler, *A Preponderance of Power: National Security, the Truman Administration, and the Cold War* (Palo Alto, CA: Stanford UP, 1992), 182-220; idem, "The United States and the Strategic Dimension of the Marshall Plan," *Diplomatic History* 12 (Summer 1988): 277-306.

8 Alan S. Milward, *The Reconstruction of Western Europe, 1945-51* (London: Routledge, 1984); Rüdiger Dornbusch et al., eds., *Postwar Economic Reconstruction and Lessons from the Past Today* (Cambridge, MA: MIT UP, 1993).

9 Günter Bischof, "'Conquering the Foreigner': The Marshall Plan and the Revival of Postwar Austrian Tourism," in *The Marshall Plan in Austria*, ed. Günter Bischof et al., vol. 8, Contemporary Austrian Studies (New Brunswick, NJ: Transaction, 2000), 357-401; Simone Telser, "Fremdenverkehr und Marshallplan in Österreich: Wiederaufbau bis 1952," Ph.D. diss., University of Innsbruck, 2009; Christoper Endy, *Cold War Holidays: American Tourism in France* (Chapel Hill, NC: U of North Carolina P, 2004); see also the chapter "The Marshall Plan and Transatlantic Tourism," in McKenzie, *Remaking France*, 111-46.

10 Charles S. Maier, "The Politics of Productivity: Foundations of American International Economic Policy after World War II," *International Organization* 31 (1977): 607-33; idem, "The Two Postwar Eras and the Conditions for Stability in Twentieth-Century Western Europe," *The American Historical Review* 86.2 (April 1981): 327-67; Kurt Tweraser, "The Politics of Productivity and Corporatism: The Late Marshal Plan in Austria, 1950-54," in *Austria in the Nineteen Fifties*, ed. Günter Bischof and Anton Pelinka, vol. 3, Contemporary Austrian Studies (New Brunswick, NJ: Transaction, 1995), 91-115.

11 Geir Lundestad, *"Empire by Integration": The United States and European Integration, 1945-1997* (Oxford: Oxford UP, 1998); Michael Gehler, *Vom Marshall-Plan zur EU: Österreich und die europäische Integration von 1945 bis zur Gegenwart* (Innsbruck: StudienVerlag, 2006); Günter Bischof, "Marshall-Plan und Westintegration," in *Menschen—Regionen—Unternehmen: Festschrift für Franz Mathis zum 60. Geburtstag*, ed. Helmut Alexander et al. (Innsbruck: Innsbruck UP, 2006), 31-48; see also *Die Erfindung Europas: (un)erwartete Folgen des Marshallplans*, documentary, directed by Christian Reichhold, Vienna, 2008.

12 Richard Bissell, the brilliant MIT economist and Hoffman's ECA deputy, crystallized the concept of a liberalization of European trade, which resulted in the European Payments Union; Bissell et al., *Reflections of a Cold Warrior*, 62-64.

13 John Krige, *American Hegemony and the Postwar Reconstruction of Science in Europe* (Cambridge, MA: MIT UP, 2006).

14 Barry Machado, *In Search of a Usable Past: The Marshall Plan and Postwar Reconstruction Today* (Lexington, VA: George C. Marshall Foundation, 2007), 113-35.

15 For example, Charles S. Maier and Günter Bischof, eds., *Deutschland und der Marshall-Plan* (Baden-Baden: Nomos Verlagsgesellschaft, 1993); Hans-Jürgen Schröder, ed., *Marshallplan und westdeutscher Wiederaufstieg: Positionen-Kontroversen* (Stuttgart: Franz Steiner Verlag, 1990); Günter Bischof et al., eds., *The Marshall Plan in Austria*; Michael Hogan, *The Marshall Plan: America, Britain, and the Reconstruction of Western Europe, 1947-1952* (Cambridge: Cambridge UP, 1987); Bernadette Whelan, *Ireland and the Marshall Plan, 1947-1957* (Dublin: Four Courts, 2000); Chiarella Esposito, *America's Feeble Weapon: Funding the Marshall Plan in France and Italy, 1948-1950* (Westport, CT: Greenwood, 1994).

16 For the most extended discussion of Marshal Plan "public diplomacy" and the best case study of "selling the Marshall Plan" in one country, see McKenzie, *Remaking France*.

17 See, for example, Traci Donnellon Howerton, "The Southern Debate over the Passage of the Marshall Plan in Congress, 1947-1948," M.A. thesis, University of New Orleans, 2007.

18 See Forrest C. Pogue's masterful biography, *George C. Marshall: Statesman, 1945-1959* (New York: Viking, 1987), 197-257.

19 Michael Wala, "Selling the Marshall Plan," *Diplomatic History* 10 (Summer 1986): 247-65; idem "Die innenpolitische Durchsetzung des Marshall-Planes: Eliten und öffentliche Meinung," *Zeitgeschichte* 14.3 (1987): 112-34; see the chapter "Selling America" in Greg Behrman, *The Most Noble Adventure: The Marshall Plan and the Time When America Helped Save Europe* (New York: Free Press, 2007), 114-40; Machado, *In Search*, 15-30. See also the Fujii essay in this volume.

20 On 14 April 1948, the victory ship *John H. Quick* was loaded with 9,000 long tons of grains and sailed for Europe; see Berman, *Most Noble Adventure*, 174-77.

21 Arch Puddington, *Broadcasting Freedom: The Cold War Triumph of Radio Free Europe and Radio Liberty* (Lexington, KY: U of Kentucky P, 2000); Walter L. Hixson, *Parting the Iron Curtain: Propaganda, Culture, and the Cold War, 1945-1961* (New York: St. Martin's, 1997), 29-56.

22 McKenzie, *Remaking France*, 25-38 (quotation 25).

23 Hans-Jürgen Schröder, "Marshall-Plan-Werbung in Österreich und West-Deutschland," in *"80 Dollar": 50 Jahre ERP-Fonds und Marshall-Plan in Österreich 1948-1998*, ed. Günter Bischof and Dieter Stiefel (Vienna: Ueberreuter, 1999), 315-42; McKenzie, *Remaking France*, 18-65; Machado, *In Search*, 15-30. See also the Schröder essay in this volume.

24 David Ellwood, "'You too can be like us': Selling the Marshall Plan—American Propaganda during the European Recovery Program," *History Today* 48 (October 1998): 33-39.

25 Kenneth A. Osgood, *Total War: Eisenhower's Secret Propaganda Battle at Home and Abroad* (Lawrence, KS: U of Kansas P, 2006); Ira Chernus, *Apocalypse Management: Eisenhower and the Discourse of National Insecurity* (Palo Alto, CA: Stanford UP, 2008).

26 McKenzie, *Remaking France*, 27ff; Hixson, *Parting the Iron Curtain*, 12ff.

27 Leffler, *Preponderance of Power*; Offner, *Another Such Victory*.

28 Apart from Saunders' *The Cultural Cold War*, Truman's and Eisenhower's Cold War propaganda strategies have become a cottage industry; see Hixson, *Parting the Iron Curtain*; Gregory Mitrovich, *Undermining the Kremlin: America's Tragedy to Subvert the Soviet Bloc, 1947-1956* (Ithaca, NY: Cornell UP, 2000); Scott Lucas, *Freedom's War: The American Crusade against the Soviet Union* (New York: State U of New York P, 1999); Volker Berghahn, *America and the Intellectual Cold War in Europe* (Princeton, NJ: Princeton UP, 2001); Chris Tudda, *Truth Is Our Weapon: The Rhetorical Diplomacy of Dwight D. Eisenhower and John Foster Dulles* (Baton Rouge, LA: Louisiana State UP, 2006); Osgood, *Total War*; usually ignored by American scholars are the two excellent German studies by Bernd Stöver, *Die Befreiung vom Kommunismus: Amerikanische Liberation Policy im Kalten Krieg 1947-1991* (Cologne: Böhlau, 2002), and Frank Schumacher, *Kalter Krieg und Propaganda: Die USA, der Kampf um die Weltmeinung und die ideelle Westbindung der Bundesrepublik Deutschland, 1945-1955* (Trier: Wissenschaftlicher Verlag Trier, 2000).

29 Saunders, *Cultural Cold War*, 97.

30 Hixson, *Parting the Iron Curtain*, 25.

31 Chernus, *Apocalypse Management*, 1-28.

32 Hugh Wilford, *The Mighty Wurlitzer: How the CIA Played America* (Cambridge, MA: Harvard UP, 2008), 7.

33 Ibid.

34 Saunders, *Cultural Cold War*, 97.

35 Wilford, *Mighty Wurlitzer*, 113f. On the Congress of Cultural Freedom, see also Giles Scott-Smith, *The Politics of Apolitical Culture: The Congress for Cultural Freedom, the CIA, and Postwar American Hegemony* (London: Routledge, 2002). Like Wilford, Scott-Smith offers a thoughtful challenge to the iconic Saunders book. He stresses collaboration between American and European intellectual elites and very much portrays the CCF as a cultural counterpart to the Marshall Plan.

36 On the shrill Soviet anti-Marshall Plan propaganda in occupied Germany and Austria, see Schröder, "Marshall Plan Werbung"; see also the essay by Barbara Stelzl-Marx in this volume.

37 McKenzie, *Remaking France*, 27-38; Victoria de Grazia, *Irresistible Empire: America's Advance through 20th-Century* Europe (Cambridge, MA: Belknap, 2005), 345-50.

38 Bissell et al., *Reflections of a Cold Warrior*, 44f.

39 Evan Thomas, *The Very Best Men: Four Who Dared—The Early Years of the CIA* (New York: Simon & Schuster, 1995), 40f; Behrman, *Most Noble Adventure*, 240f; Bissell et al., *Reflections of a Cold Warrior*, 68f (quotation 68).

40 The only exception being Sallie Pisani, *The CIA and the Marshall Plan* (Lawrence, KS: U of Kansas P, 1991), and Siegfried Beer, "The CIA in Austria in the Marshall Plan Era, 1947-1953," in *The Marshall Plan in Austria*, ed. Bischof et al., 185-211; see also Richard J. Aldrich, *The Hidden Hand: Britain, America, and Cold War Secret Intelligence* (Woodstock, NY: Overlook, 2001), 137-41.

41 On the role of the USIA, see Osgood, *Total War*, 253-87. For Austria, the best introduction to the administrative and institutional changes is the model study on U.S. cultural diplomacy by Reinhold Wagnleitner, *Coca-Colinisation und Kalter Krieg: Die Kulturmission der USA in Österreich nach dem Zweiten Weltkrieg* (Vienna: Verlag für Gesellschaftskritik, 1991), 80-102; on the ISB's photo-

graphic section in Austria, see Hans Petschar, *Die junge Republik: Alltagsbilder aus Österreich 1945-1955* (Vienna: Ueberreuter, 1995), 46-49, 171-73. In 1947, the Information Services Branch of the U.S. Army in the occupation of Austria employed sixty-two Americans and 675 Austrians. Forty Austrian photographers and journalists worked in the picture section of the United States Information Service in Austria; these were also the people that documented the Marshall Plan activities in Austria. See also the essay by Friedlmeier, Petschar, and Pfundner in this volume.

42 Wilford, *The Mighty Wurlitzer*, 51-69; Peter Weiler, *British Labour and the Cold War* (Palo Alto, CA: Stanford UP, 1988); Ted Morgan, *A Covert Life: Jay Lovestone, Communist, Anti-Communist, and Spymaster* (New York: Random House, 1999); Gene Sensenig, *Österreichische-amerikanische Gewerkschaftsbeziehungen 1945 bis 1950* (Cologne: Pahl-Rugenstein, 1987); Aldrich, *The Hidden Hand*, 458f. On labor and U.S. covert money tracing the payments from the OPC to Lovestone and Brown, see also Anthony Carew, "The American Labor Movement in Fizzland: The Free Trade Union Committee and the CIA," *Labor History* 39 (1998): 25-42.

43 Saunders, *Cultural Cold War*; Michael Hochgeschqwender, *Freiheit in der Offensive? Der Kongress für kulturelle Freiheit und die Deutschen* (Munich: Oldenbourg, 1998); Giles Scott-Smith, *The Politics of Apolitical Culture*. See also Hugh Wilford, *The CIA, the British Left, and the Cold War: Calling the Tune?* (London: Frank Cass, 2003).

44 Aldrich, *The Hidden Hand*, 342-70 (esp. 343-45); Wilford, *The CIA, the British Left, and the Cold War*, 225-42.

45 Machado, *In Search*, 24-27; Behrman, *Most Noble Adventure*; 238f (quotation 238); McKenzie, *Selling France*, 23f, 32-34 (for the State Department critique of ECA "stereotyping," see 34); on the importance of film as a medium of choice in Marshall Plan public diplomacy, see also the essays by de Grazia, Ellwood, Schröder, Reichart, and Höllriegl in this volume.

46 Machado, *In Search*, 30.

47 McKenzie, *Remaking France*, 30-45, 66-110 (chapter on exhibits and communist attacks).

48 De Grazia, *Irresistible Empire*, 346; see also her essay in this volume making the same argument more elaborately.

49 See Ellwood's essay in this collection.

50 Wolfgang Kos, "Die Ziege in der Küche," in *Die Sinalco-Epoche: Essen, Trinken, Konsumieren nach 1945*, ed. Susanne Breuss and the Vienna Museum (Vienna: Czernin Verlag, 2005), 15f. The exhibit *Sinalco-Epoche* and the catalogue of the exhibit present overwhelming evidence of these Americanization trends in daily life in Austria (and presumably in the rest of "Marshall Plan Europe" as well).

51 On individual country studies of the Americanization of postwar Europe and the anti-Americanism it often produced, see Alexander Stephan, ed., *The Americanization of Europe: Culture, Diplomacy, and Anti-Americanism after 1945* (New York: Berghahn Books, 2006); for a sophisticated discussion of the Marshall Plan and Americanization, see McKenzie, *Remaking France*, 4-13.

52 Two mobile film projection units drove in vans through Austria to play the productivity films in towns and villages; the goal was to familiarize Austrians with the ERP's productivity campaign. Between 1950 and 1954, some 46,000 film demonstrations were made; see Ramón Reichart, "Die Filme des Österreichischen Produktivitätszentrums," in *Österreich Baut Auf: Wieder-Aufbau & Marshall Plan* (Vienna: Technisches Museum, 2005), 132f.

53 Hans Petschar published a lavish selection of pictures on everyday life in postwar Austria from this USIA collection; see his *Die junge Republik: Alltagsbilder aus Österreich 1945-1955* (Vienna: Ueberreuter, 2005).

54 The study of historical memory is now becoming an active subfield of international history scholarship; for a programmatic introduction to this field, see Robert D. Schulzinger, "Memory and Understanding U.S. Foreign Relations," in *Explaining American Foreign Relations*, 2nd ed., ed. Michael J. Hogan and Thomas G. Paterson (Cambridge: Cambridge UP, 2004), 336-52. An introduction to Marshall Plan memory as usable and unusable past, see Machado, *In Search*, 113-35; for Austria, see Günter Bischof, "Der Marshall-Plan und Österreich," in *Österreich Baut Auf*, 63-66.

55 There is a growing literature of anniversary volumes published; on the occasion of the fiftieth anniversary in 1997, see, for example Hans H.J. Labohm, ed., *The Fiftieth Anniversary of the Marshall Plan in Retrospect and in Prospect* (Clingendael: Netherlands Institute of International Relations, The Hague 1997); Hans-Herbert Holzhamer and Marc Hoch, eds., *Der Marshall-Plan: Geschichte*

und Zukunft (Munich: Olzog, 1997); Günter Bischof and Dieter Stiefel, eds., *"80 Dollar": 50 Jahre ERP-Fonds und Marshall-Plan in Österreich 1948-1998*. For the OECD's sixtieth anniversary symposium in 2007 in Paris, see Eliot Sorel and Pier Carlo Padoan, eds., *The Marshall Plan: Lessons Learned for the 21st Century* (Paris: OECD, 2008).

What is needed, however, is also a broader analysis of public discourses about the Marshall Plan from the 1950s to the present. Key to such an analysis would be the repeated calls for a Marshall Plan for the Third World or Eastern Europe after the end of the Cold War. Bruno Kreisky suggested a Marshall Plan for the Third World in the early 1980s; see Ferdinand Lacina, "Der Marshall Plan—Ein Beitrag zur Übergangswirtschaft Österreichs," in *"80 Dollar,"* ed. Bischof and Stiefel, 17-20, and Elisabeth Röhrlich, "Kreiskys Aussenpolitik: Zwischen östereichischer Identität und internationalem Programm," Ph.D. diss., University of Tübingen, 2008, 349-59. Former Austrian Finance Minister Hannes Androsch suggested a Marshall Plan for Eastern Europe to master the 2008/2009 financial crisis; see "Der Krise gemeinsam entgegensteuern!", *Europäischen Rundschau* 37.1 (2009): 3-9 (see 4f). On postwar Marshall Plan discourses for Eastern Europe, see also the de Grazia essay in this volume. In 2005, British Prime Minister Gordon Brown called for a "modern Marshall Plan" for Africa, *The Guardian*, 3 June 2005. On the applicability of the Marshall Plan metaphor for large-scale economic aid projects, see Eric Frey, "The Marshall Plan as a Model: Can Massive Aid Resolve International Conflicts?", Annual Marshall Plan Chair Lecture, CenterAustria, University of New Orleans 2002.

56 Austrian Marshall Plan Foundation, http://www.marshallplan.at.

57 CenterAustria, University of New Orleans, http://www.centeraustria.com.

Section I:

The United States and the Marshall Plan

Victoria de Grazia

Visualizing the Marshall Plan:

The Pleasures of American Consumer Democracy or the Pains of "the Greatest Structural Adjustment Program in History"?

Short of conducting a purely internal, textual analysis of the Marshall Plan films, the remarkable corpus of propaganda cinema made under the European Cooperation Agency's aegis between 1949 and 1953, inquirers need to identify the appropriate historical framework in which to analyze it.[1] What were the goals of the European Recovery Program (ERP)? What was its impact in the short, medium, and long term? Where did the cinematic language of the films come from, and how was it used to convey the ERP's goals, especially in light of the evolution of other dimensions of U.S. postwar global hegemony?

The literature relevant to the economics and politics of the European Recovery Program is immense and contentious. It only becomes more so from the late 1980s onward, spurred by the fortieth anniversary commemorations in 1988, by 1990s debates over the harsh structural adjustment plans introduced to address post-Soviet capitalist transitions and the Asian financial crises, and by more finely detailed research in European archives regarding the ERP's role in promoting postwar U.S. hegemony in Western Europe.[2] Withal, U.S. historiography had recently inclined toward a new consensus, namely that the Marshall Plan inaugurated American-style consumer democracy in Western Europe (however much it was indigenized) and that mass consumption (as opposed to military occupation and other political means) was the foundation of U.S. hegemony.[3]

The view that presents the Marshall Plan as the Ur-moment in the U.S. exercise of soft power has important implications for interpreting the films. One implication is that even if the films were conceived as U.S. government propaganda, it was propaganda of a virtuous sort. Basically, it was information-oriented, with low-key reminders of the American sources of aid, and it conveyed a basically ameliorative and legitimate message about the need to move on, rebuild, and strive for a better life. At worst, the argument goes, the films encouraged audiences who were as varied as French, Danes, Greeks, Turks, and French West Africans to "be just like us." In other words, the message of the films was to encourage local peoples to emulate the desires, wants, and outlook on freedom and democracy associated with U.S. consumer society.[4]

But what if the recently developed "folk wisdom" which holds that the Marshall Plan was the founding moment of Western European consumer affluence is misbegotten? Would that discovery not call into question the facile view that the films as well as other information and propaganda are best understood as enticing European publics to believe in U.S. consumer democracy? By way of response, my first concern here is to examine some recent findings about the Marshall Plan's effects on mass consumption. These strongly suggest that that to speak of the ERP's primary goal or effect as being "mass consumer democracy" is wrong-headed. My second goal is to suggest we need a differently-grounded context for analyzing the films, both in terms of the Plan itself and in light of their promoters' endeavor to connect the global message of the ERP to many different milieus. The remarkable thing about the films is how many local people they employed. In a sense, the film project was a mini-European Works Project Administration for filmmakers, and we need to know far more about how they referred back to their own documentary and feature film traditions and—however obliquely—to the audiences that they conceived as their spectators. In brief, it is necessary to treat the Marshall Plan as a historically specific model of capitalist intervention, defining as precisely as possible what was intended by both mass consumption and democracy—both very broad terms. True, simply placing the so-called cinema of the Marshall Plan within new or at least different historical perspectives is only the start: much needs to be done to bring to its formal analysis the various toolkits provided by film historians.

The first question is whether the Marshall Plan was linked in any direct way to promoting "consumer democracy" in the immediate postwar period.[5] My immediate answer is that the key phrase for speaking of the ERP's goals should be "higher standard of living" rather than "mass consumption," especially not the mass consumption associated with the post-scarcity world of post-Fordism, arising in the mid-1970s. At least since World War I, Western reformers had argued that "misery" was the source of the social conflicts that led to political polarization and war. The failure to ameliorate misery, resulting in the Great Depression and the rise of totalitarian regimes, made the solution to the social question, defined broadly as raising the standard of living, all the more urgent. However, the question of what the "higher standard" meant and how it would be achieved was a contentious issue. Most basically, it meant full employment, shelter, and adequate diet, in addition to some mix of items to improve civility (basic furnishings, kitchen equipment, hygiene, education, recreation, and so forth). The ERP was invested in one way of achieving that goal, by means of what Charles S. Maier aptly called the "politics of productivity." Focusing on the supply-side, this politics pressed for a better deal for workers based not on political democracy, but on more effective negotiation between labor and management over the distribution of enhanced profits from economic innovation.[6] At its core, this vision of modernity resuscitated the pre-Depression virtuous circle of Fordism, meaning advanced technology, high productivity, standardized production, lower unit price, higher wages, and, finally, all other things being equal, growing foreign and domestic markets for mass-produced basic goods within the framework of greatly intensified international commerce. Assuming free trade, political democracy, and worker representation based on non-ideological unions (meaning they were motivated by managerial notions of payouts for productivity rather than notions of justice and re-distribution), wages would rise and so too would workers' "purchasing power," all other things being equal. There was relatively little discussion about the nature of consumption, which was putatively left to market choices and social welfare systems, much less how consumers exercised democracy through market choices. Of course, this model was in sharp contrast with that of social democrats who argued that the standard of living could only be raised by a more fundamental redistribution of wealth, effective representation of labor through the political system, and support for a certain type of consumption which was based on full employment, the social provision of collective goods, and prioritizing the items necessary for household consumption, starting with decent shelter and adequate food. Nor were the so-called liberal and social democratic models of consumption the only alternatives; on the continent, in particular, elites were heavily conditioned by Social Catholics like Ludwig Erhard who, while making strong rhetorical gestures about consumer sovereignty, the consumer's needs and wishes, and freedom of choice, profoundly believed that these liberties would be assiduously guided by carefully negotiated national labor contracts, tight money supply, and conservative good taste.[7]

In fact, the Marshall Plan presumed all kinds of decisions about consumption. Beginning in 1945, U.S. economists warned against encouraging Europeans to desire a standard of consumption similar to that of Americans. The so-called "American" or "high" standard of living set unrealistic goals; it encouraged rising expectations that would unleash rancorous feelings and political radicalization; and it undermined local values, offending religious and other conservative interests. Indeed, American elites themselves were ambivalent about the consumption habits of their own "masses," all the more so in view of the big increase in female wage earners during the world war with their purportedly chaotic spending habits, domestic concerns about weighing new military expenditure against consumption during the Cold War, and discomfort about a global hegemony based on the American victory in what David Riesman dubbed the "Nylon Wars."[8]

More importantly, in terms of the plan itself, the ERP was dead set against sponsoring collective forms of consumption. These included social security, national health, unemployment insurance, and public transportation, as well public housing, recreation, and free schooling—which, in the longer run, would prove very important to European consumer booms in the late 1950s and 1960s. For this purpose, planning goals insisted on achieving recovery, using 1938 as the benchmark for various indices, including calories per day of food consumption. Especially because the European Recovery Program was conceived against the background of America's advanced consumer capitalism—in which the technologies of distribution and marketing were well developed, the consumer occupied a clear-cut role in the economy and culture, and the ERP-sponsored foreign missions to the United States showcased these dimensions—the ERP was sensitive to the economic, but especially political, dangers if the cart of consumption was put before the horse of productivity. The overriding goal was, thus, to structure investment so as to curb government spending on "welfare" measures (also known as collective consumption), focusing on building infrastructure, reviving capital goods manufacturing, modernizing agriculture, and promoting key consumer-goods industries whose destination was the export rather than the domestic market in order to build up international and cross-European trade. It is true that lots of aid went to alleviating food and fodder shortages and could, thus, be regarded as sustaining consumption. If it is true that this aid alleviated famine-creating shortages and assisted agricultural recovery, there is no evidence that retail food prices dropped as a result or that on average people were better or differently fed than in the pre-war years.

"The greatest structural adjustment program in history" was the phrase that economic historians Barry Eichengreen and J. Bradford DeLong used to describe the ERP when they first revisited it in the early 1990s, prompted by debates over intervening with big U.S., German, or IMF assistance and loan programs to promote a more egalitarian, less violent transition to capitalism in Eastern Europe and the former Soviet Union.[9] Sharply contracting consumer demand was a key feature of the 1990s bailout model. It would have been useful if the authors had put more emphasis on this dimension when they made the comparison between the 1990s impositions and the constraints on consumer demand imposed in post-1947 Europe to obtain Marshall Fund aid, Had they done so, admittedly not an easy matter since there has been no overall study of consumption levels for the period from roughly 1948 to 1952, they could have found evidence in several country-level studies that point to the sharp compression of wages, various constrictions on purchases, and cuts in government payouts for collective services as the price of accepting ERP aid.

The best studied place is Great Britain where the United States engaged with the Labour Party to curb state spending on welfare programs which, together with rationing, greatly restrained consumption through the early 1950s.[10] In Denmark, according to Alan Milward's student Vibeke Sorensen, where consumption was relatively high when compared to that of other European countries, the European Cooperation Agency (ECA) pressed the Labour government to reduce consumption in relation to national income.[11] Using fiscal measures, as well as reinstituting wartime restrictions, it was forced to damage its own rural, working-class and urban middle-class base. When the Labor government, in an effort to placate its constituencies, lifted restrictions on the fat content of dairy products (which would have led to more domestic consumption, as well as the need to import more animal fodder and reduce or raise the price of exports), it was met with ECA resistance. If its liberal conservative successor was more inclined to use monetary as well as fiscal measures, it, too, confronted ECA opposition. The upshot was that it cut back on the grain imports financed by Marshall Plan aid.

In France, Irwin Wall argues, the investment priorities set by the Monnet Plan under the terms of the Marshall Plan were as harsh in terms of popular consumption as those imposed by the Five Year Plans within the Soviet bloc. The French government committed itself to raise consumer incomes only with the Second Four Year or Hirsch Plan, which was launched in 1954.[12]

In Italy, the constraints imposed on consumption are harder to discern. Some argue that the United States actually wanted the government to spend more on consumption-inflating projects, rather than to continue the fiscally conservative politics of President Luigi Einaudi, a classic liberal, and Prime Minister Alcide de Gaspari which acted to deflate the economy, pay down the budget deficit, and grow foreign reserves.[13] Industries, which were always loath to raise wages even when there were significant increases in productivity, didn't have to do so. Labor was in a very weak position to negotiate for wage increases after the Left parties were ousted from government as a condition of Marshall Plan aid and the radical trade unions were expelled from major industries. By the early 1950s, an even more perverse logic kicked in, according to the economist Marcello de Cecco. Export-oriented Italian industry which had revived quickly with the reprise of international trade, thus reducing unemployment, began to be hurt by competition as other European countries' industry revived. Because the domestic market was so weak, based as it was on ill-paid workers, under-employed peasants, and an impoverished middle class, surplus capacity drove down wages.

However, to insist that the effect of the Marshall Plan was to compress consumption does not contradict that its implementation signaled a huge rupture in ways of thinking about the economy of wants and desire. There was the very idea of the "gift" of aid on the part of the wartime victor. There was the competition between the ERP and the social democratic and Communist Left, and between the United States and the Soviet Union over which regime of consumption would make for a better society. There was the spectacular effect of the whole effort: the launch of programs and the arrival of U.S. films pushed by Hollywood corporations through cartels and governmental accords. All of this went hand in hand with the revival of markets that had occurred as early as 1946, well before the arrival of Marshall Plan aid.

A major issue for propaganda efforts was, thus, to address a paradox, namely that the Marshall Plan arrived during a crisis and was associated with, if not always causing, the compression of consumption standards. Put another way, American plenty in the form of productive investment had to be disassociated from the "plenty" usually found in celebrations around expectations of change in material culture. In the mass consumption identified with the U.S. way of life, this would take the form of the multiplication of commodities, a total makeover and self-transformation, the celebration of exuberance, and irrational wants. In the plenty associated with the kermesse of traditional consumption is the riotousness of the circus, the mystery of the gift, the Rabelaisian pleasures of a world turned upside down, and the feasting after fasting, with a big expenditure on food consumption. Contemporary socialist propaganda films promote that eschatological vision of redemption with the "new" man and woman of socialist society finding collective joy in state housing projects, party leisure activities, and public celebrations of resistance to Anglo-American imperialism, the successor to the Nazi-Fascist warmongers. One doesn't have to be a fusty Frankfurt school analyst to highlight one element of the complicated (and still not at all systematically studied) meanings embedded in the cinematic language of the Marshall Plan films, namely their narrative *restraint*.

Very schematically, the culture of the Marshall Plan (as evidenced from only a first sampling of a huge production of information about it, including the films) should be regarded as offering a new narrative about material progress. This spelled out a distinctly conservative version of the story told about the development of mass consumption in the United States, namely that it comes out of new machines, greater productivity, and getting back to work and that by dint of hard work, by the men in the factories and the women at home, it will gradually evidence itself in small improvements. Whether focusing on individuals or nations, the films focus on the necessities required for social reproduction, such as employment, work tools (including draft animals), shelter, food, and clothing—and how depressing their absence—with hardly a nod to these as objects of desire, much less that these acquisitions point to a new ethos of consumer gratification or U.S. standards of comfort. In other words, it is true that with the ECA propaganda effort, American officials were reconceptualizing traditional propaganda as mass marketing. ECA Director and former Studebaker Company executive Paul Hoffman regarded it as self-evident that for the local missions to function without a "strong information arm" would be "as futile as trying to conduct a major business without sales, advertising, and customer relations." A half-century's practice at selling products and public policy had taught that information imparted in non-ideological language offered the most effective means of convincing people to trust new social calculations. Hence, the Marshall Plan should emphasize best practice, not politics, the "American assembly line," not "the communist party line," the "full dinner pail," not the "free lunch."[14] This goal did not contemplate social makeovers or conversion scenarios, quite the contrary.

The films' remarkably measured tone is all the more noteworthy if we consider the sense of rupture and restraint that had been circulated through Europe by means of U.S. commercial cinema since World War I. Siegfried Kracauer offers one of the most cogent analyses of the disruptive and normative faces of U.S. culture as it was viewed from his agitated home town of Berlin in the second half of the 1920s. A sociologist and cultural critic, Kracauer was perhaps the most astute observer of the so-called "New Living Culture," and especially of the need for norms, rules, and styles to give meaning to what he called the "spiritual homelessness of the commodity world of the new class." As "the house of bourgeois ideas and feelings in which the middle classes had previously lived collapsed because of the erosion of its foundations, brought on by economic development," people found themselves "without a doctrine to which they could adhere to, without a goal to guide them." He saw advertising as providing a new authority of sorts, especially American-style advertising with its unceasing injunctions about the utility of innovative products to signal new hierarchies in body culture and social status. Elsewhere, he called attention to the norms embedded in Hollywood classical narratives, especially in the concern to play down the cinema's role as vanguard of a new mass culture, given the social upset attendant on that, while upholding its superior entertainment value. The result was a remarkable tension between experimentation to stimulate interest and conformity to broaden access. This tension was especially visible in the most popular forms of cinema, namely slapstick. Comics' antics highlighted the oppressive technologies of work, moral policing, and social discipline "subjects the world to an often unbearable discipline." The same antics, in turn, "dismantle this self-imposed order." [15]

In sum, discipline, disruption, and the imposition of a new discipline characterized the films. The classic example of this is *Modern Times*, Charlie Chaplin's 1936 film which was one of the most widely viewed in 1930s Europe. It shows the assembly line, the authoritarian boss, the acceleration of work tempos that drives

Charlie mad; it shows Charlie resisting but never escaping the rules. Indeed, it shows all possible avenues for a working stiff to make a living, both the legitimate means as a line worker and department store custodian and the illegitimate ones, namely, vagabondage and theft. The film also shows all the institutions that try to contain Chaplin's resistance, namely, the speeded up (and self-feeding) machinery, the insane asylum, jail, and church. In sum, Chaplin shows all of the norms and all of the infractions; he disrupts, but he cannot escape, except by going out of society, only to leave us unsure of his fate. In the end, the Little Tramp has his self-dignity and the gamin as his mate, but little more.

The Marshall Plan might itself be seen in light of Kracauer's view of U.S. consumer culture as disruption: the opening up of possibilities—incredibly subversive, sensual, and playful —and their closing down by means of new norms and regulations. If we consider the ECA films from that perspective, we see that that the propaganda film is unable to exploit the charm of the American cinematic narrative or its European emulators. Far from engaging in the full cycle of disruption, disorder, and restraint, it passes from disruption to restraint: the leitmotif is sober realism rather than populist reveries; the films promise productivity. But their visualization of the economy of desire is distinctly stingy, and their pedantic voiceovers always deep-voiced in the resonant tones of omniscient male pedagogues instruct about the new norms and procedures that should rule this economy of desire.

My favorite example of what we might call "reined in disruption" is *The Story of Koula*, one of a handful of films dedicated to the reconstruction of Greece, where the United States was involved in an arduous, eventually successful operation to restore the conservative monarchy in the face of Communist-led republican insurgents. Filmed in 1951, Charles (Vittorio) Gallo's pseudo-documentary spells out a parable of needing, gifting, getting, and using. The need is for draft animals. The gift is mule power. The getting calls for patient attention to new rules. But to appropriate the gift in a truly socially and economically worthy way calls for a carefully worked out combination of new and old world skills.

Accordingly, as the camera moves amid the stone hovels, olive trees, and dry-as-dust fields of Filavia, a mountain village of northern Thrace, to show the futile labors of the old men, boys, and women in the absence of adult males (victims, it is implied, of the Communist-fomented civil war), the narrator speaks in stentorian tones of the people's inveterate struggle for subsistence. Their biggest need, as he diagnoses it, is powerful draft animals to furrow the rocky land. The story of Filavia's redemption then unfolds. First there has to be a valid application for assistance; whereas the old people are fatalistic and diffident, an enterprising youngster signs up and at the appropriate time is summoned to the port at Xanthi to meet the ship with its cargo of mules. Meanwhile, rules cover the handover of mules from the ship's captain to the dockside consignee, preventing patronage or corruption. Then the mules are assigned by numbers, precluding personal favors, only to permit one violation to show that the rule makers might countenance exceptions dictated by common sense. Thus the hardened farmers can show their humanity, which in turn redounds to the credit of the new system by awarding Koula the mule to the only boy who has come down from the mountain and who, because he is young and hopeful and motivated by a strong personal passion, should be rewarded by winning the mule with which he has fallen in love, regardless of not having the right lottery number. Then there are the rules about using the beasts: there are to be no kicks and slaps because animals, like humans, work more efficiently when treated as individuals, called by name, and cajoled into new routines, as opposed to being treated like anonymous beasts of burden that are cursed, beaten, and starved into submission. But even the animals have to obey rules: there is to be no insubordinate bucking once Koula is harnessed to work and no stalling when the time comes to produce, all the more necessary given the scale of his appetite. To teach him the rules, the boy hitches him up to his tiny, spindly female donkey. The final message comes through: individuals who resolve to choose a better future, combining new machinery with age-old practice and prowess with patience "work together for a little more productivity, a little bit more well-being." So the parable ends. The Marshall Plan—signified by the exoticism of the giant animal, its distant origins, its glossy rump branded U.S.A. in Roman letters—is intended to produce not the high standard of living in itself, but rather the technologies, procedures, and information about how to achieve "a little bit more well-being." In the closing shot, this new well-being is signified with only a hint of playfulness: the boy puts wildflowers in each of the animal's bridles, and as the sun moves lower over the hills of this ancient land with its inveterate labor, the boy takes charge of his own and his family's destiny.

There is no way in which we can ascertain the reception of this film, which was translated into many languages, as well as being reproduced for other audiences (such as in Turkey where it became *Yusef and his Plow*, 1951). So it is uncertain whether it is even worthwhile, except in a broad way, to think of a historian's notion of reception, which would call for investigating to whom it was shown, under what circumstances, on what occasions, or with what other feature or documentary films. Nor do we know much about the leeway given to the filmmakers themselves, except that they worked with a sense that they were not making propaganda in a fascist or communist way; hence only one, perhaps two, mentions of the Marshall Plan or ERP were expected.[16] The director, Gallo, was relatively unknown (and unlike some others) would remain so. Like most of his contemporaries, he was influenced by current idioms of neo-realism, which, in turn, linked back to the modernizing visions of the 1930s that could be found in a wide range of propaganda/documentary films whether from Fascist, Soviet, New Deal, Labourist, or Popular Front sources.[17] It is rare that Marshall Plan films have the "thinginess," much less the *jouissance* which we associate with commercial U.S. films of the period, such as Billy Wilder's *Foreign Affair* (1948), or European commercial comedies, such as Jacque Tati's *Jour de Fête* (1949) whose protagonist is a rural postman taunted to compete with American "vitesse," or Luis Garcia Berlanga's *Bienvenido Señor Marshall* which spoofed the notion that the Marshall Plan would transmogrify a rural backwater, or Vittorio de Sica's *Miracle in Milan* (1951) about the struggle of poor people to fulfill wishes for happiness in the face of cruel capitalists, which employed a Hollywood man, Ned Mann, to do the special effects.

We might also want to compare the narrative restraint of the Marshall Plan film to Soviet bloc propaganda/documentaries of the same epoch. Common sense has it that the Soviet film could permit the eschatological view that the Plan, like Socialist modernization generally, envisaged the creation of the new man and the new woman. At the same time as documentaries could denounce Marshall Plan imperialism, they could generate a view of total material happiness in the making, building the future and combining it with festive celebration. It is unscientific to use the pseudo-documentary *Architects of Our Happiness*, the newsreel from 1950 using footage from the epoch allegedly filmed by the famous director Jerzy Burski, at the heart of Andrzej Wajda's *Man of Marble* (1976) as material for a strict comparison. However, it is useful to look at it within the framework of the whole film, which is also the story of a young filmmaker, Agnieszka, coming of age in the 1970s and making the film to earn her degree, who is looking back at the relationship between reality and the façade of propaganda and what the censor allowed and did not allow. Simply calling attention to the complex circumstances in which Social Realist propaganda was made and disseminated reminds us that the Marshall Plan film was only one small visual artifact in the total arc of cinematic output. But it also underscores the fact that, because of the goals and context, the films were thematically and visually deeply constrained so as not to promise a total makeover (which the Marshall Plan could not and did not want to deliver), nor promote the use of stridently ideological language, which was delegated to other forms of propaganda, notably that of the Catholic Church and conservative and centrist national government official newsreels.

We could thus contrast the succession of scenes of individuals in action in *the Story of Koula*, each one teaching a lesson about self-improvement with the full-scale mobilization which we see in the footage of two films within *Man of Marble*, the first of which is called "Birth of a City" and is censored, and the second, a remake, which is called "Architecture of Our Happiness" and redeems the young filmmaker Burski. In the former, Agnieszka, in quest of the lost memory of early Stalinism, in particular, a Stakhanovist hero named Mateusz Burkit, views "*cinéma vérité*" film footage of the construction of Nowa Huta: bulldozers gutting the flowering hillsides and slogging through the mud, Spartan barracks, even a demonstration in which the workers protest their measly lunch ration by pelting Party officials with moldy dried fish. In the latter footage, carefully constructed to appease the censors, the fictional Burski (Wajda's name appears on the credits of this film as assistant director) has peasants sallying forth from distant villages to become workers at Nowa Huta, the barracks spiffed up as hostels where peasant-workers learn to read and are inspired to sustain improbable work rhythms; the workers' sports club, where Birkut, the hero, meets the gymnast, Hanka Tomczyk, his future wife; President Bierut's visit to the construction site, culminating with the central sequence when Birkut and his team lay 30,500 bricks in a single shift. The film continues with a celebratory sequence, a grand (and very bourgeois) ball celebrating New Year 1950, Birkut elected a Workers' Delegate, Birkut posing as a model for monumental socialist art and inaugurating the Second National Art Exhibit at which the vitality of aesthetic realism is contrasted with the degeneracy of Western abstraction, a festive mass demonstration of Socialism's accomplishments featuring a smiling Mateusz and Hanka, posters of Bierut and Joseph Stalin, and monster puppets with the faces of the "fascists": President Harry Truman, General Douglas MacArthur, and last but not least, a louche Generalissimo Francisco Franco dressed as Carmen. Finally, the closing shots show the protagonists moving into their new apartment, described as "their own handiwork," (as opposed to shelter built by alienated capitalist labor and market forces).

To speak of the narrative restraint of the Marshall Plan films is not to argue that they are not propaganda or that they are less propagandistic. They can be perceived as doing the cultural work for which they were intended. In Western Europe, the goal was explicit, namely to labor for a better standard of living, to demobilize ideologically, and to conceive of the new society as steps toward an order that was doubly secure, both militarily and materially.

Clearly, the Marshall Plan was promoted in order to gain a powerful grip on the collective imagination of Europeans. It promised all of the productivity that a revved-up capitalist war economy could deliver. But propaganda was also designed to suppress the ludic character we associate with consumer wants, the disorder of old styles of consumption, still extant in Europe, the cornucopias of populist tradition. At the same time, the standard of living characterized as appropriate for living better was silently if not explicitly contrasted with other standards of living, that which was associated with liberal collectivism in the shape of the Beveridge Report, state planning in Eastern Europe which by the mid-1950s had delivered reconstruction, as well as all of the home and small-craft means of getting by not contemplated by mass production industry and large-scale infrastructure projects—the ports, dams, canals, railroads, and so forth so often the subject of Marshall Plan films.

Mass consumption in the form associated with "Americanization" comes in the second half of the 1950s, when practically everybody had ceased speaking about the Marshall Plan! U.S. hegemony plays a large part in that development, working on many other terrains that led to the formation of mass consumer society; by widening and deepening markets, supporting new social stratifications around goods and services, and promoting new standards of well-being, governments could promote consumption as a major element of growth. Many events and circumstances helped European mass consumption along: the Korean War (1950-1953) which at the same time as diverting funds and creating shortages returns Germany to being an exporter; the widening of markets that is a legacy of the European Recovery program; the decolonization brokered by the United States, resulting in cheap gasoline, which in turn spurs the boom in individual mobility made possible by the auto and the return of capital to investment in Western Europe; the cheap labor force, disciplined in cooperative trade union structures, gradually being introduced to the set of household goods associated with mass consumer society; the big surge of U.S. private investment; and American tourism.

The year 1959 is a good one on which to end this analysis. It marked the victory of the Conservative Party and Harold MacMillan in the British general elections, on the occasion of which Michael Cummings' *Daily Express* cartoon showed MacMillan relaxing in the company of a television, a washing machine, and a fridge. "Well, gentlemen," he says, "I think we all fought a good fight." The distance from the end of the major flood of U.S. aid is barely seven years, but Western Europe is a different world, one in which references to the Marshall Plan are rare; the European Economic Community, whose legislation hardly refers to the benefits of an economically unified market to consumers, is the harbinger of well-being; U.S. private capital in the form of advertising, consumer industries, and services speaks in its corporate American voice about consumer variety, choice, and freedom; and the left-wing parties of Europe are beginning to organize their constituents to demand what might be called "citizenship goods," namely the new basics, including small-cylinder automobiles which demonstrate that they may still be politically excluded, but for purposes of material life, they have basic rights.

So why did the Marshall Plan become identified as the origin of a mass consumption society in Europe? Perhaps it is only *post hoc, ergo proper hoc* reasoning in which the boom that followed is attributed to what came before. Or perhaps it was a confusion of the grants obtained from the Marshall Plan, often invested in infrastructure, with the aid received from the United Nations Relief and Rehabilitation Administration, CARE, and other relief packages after 1945, which indeed did deliver all sorts of well-appreciated and fondly remembered help.

The myth that the Marshall Plan delivered the goods was also abetted by the terrible fear of an alternative, namely Soviet domination. But that fear was not shared by all. Large groups in Western Europe within the labor rank and file, peasantry, and the Communist left believed that socialism was delivering the goods in a more socially just *and* abundant way than in the capitalist West. Moreover, the working classes, much less rural families, did not begin to have access to the new consumer goods until well into the early 1960s. In frontline states in particular, notably Austria, the scarcity identified with Soviet rule was conflated with wartime penury. A thorough study of the "memory politics" around the Marshall Plan might well uncover the altogether complicated twists and turns in public thinking and public recollection about this heavily-determined moment of the past.

Meanwhile, back in the United States the Marshall Plan was advertised to American taxpayers who were footing the bill as an indispensable contribution to raising the European standard of living. In 1952, the Mutual Security Administration (MSA), which succeeded the ERP, commissioned the film unit in Paris to make a series of twenty-six films under the title *Strength for the Free World* to be broadcast on the ABC television network in the United States. This occurred despite the Smith-Mundt Act that specifically forbade films made by government agencies for foreign audiences or with counterpart funds from being used to "propagandize the American public." The purpose was clear. It was an election year, and, as one official put it, "Our task, to put it bluntly, was to convince American audiences that Marshall aid had been well spent. It had put our NATO partners on their feet again; and now, with the extra support of MSA's (Mutual Security Act) military assistance, Europeans stood shoulder-to-shoulder with us, ready to defend Europe and the Free World."[18] The series aired once again in 1953, the message being that tax dollars were being well spent on remaking Europe in the United States' image. This effort contributed not a little to making many Americans believe that their way of life was the most virtuous on the planet, and in that way, the Marshall Plan in Europe helped to consolidate the humanitarian and progressive virtues of the "Consumer Republic" at home and around the world.

All that said, the myth that the Marshall Plan established European consumer democracy is of a more recent vintage, dating to the early 1990s. Once the Soviet bloc collapsed and European social democracy was also demonized by neo-liberalism, the U.S. model of consumer democracy acquired an air of historical inevitability. Mass consumption became an ahistorical category with analysts losing sight of the fact that the demand for goods can both promote and undercut liberty and democracy. If interventions like the Marshall Plan could guarantee a specific outcome in the face of messy transitions to democracy, then the United States—or the IMF and World Bank—should by all means intervene in order to use them. That was the mindset in which the CNN Cold War Series on the Marshall Plan was produced in the latter half of the 1990s and the framework in which the fiftieth anniversary celebrations of the Marshall Plan occurred in 1998. Events after the turn of the twenty-first century, notably the hardening of the neo-liberal Washington consensus and U.S. military intervention to build regimes in the name of the goodies of mass consumption, would only deepen liberal nostalgia for the good old days of the Marshall Plan, the bountiful images of American good works, and the apparent success of foreign aid

Notes

1 Researchers have to be eternally grateful to Linda R. Christenson and the George C. Marshall Foundation for the unstintingly scrupulous labor dedicated to creating the Marshall Plan Archive and Marshall Plan Filmography, http://www.marshallfoundation.org.

2 A good overview and historiographical essay about Marshall Plan literature through the late 1980s is provided by John Killick, *The United States and European Reconstruction, 1945-1960* (London: Routledge, 2000); see also Barry J. Eichengreen, ed., *Europe's Postwar Recovery* (Cambridge: Cambridge UP, 1995). The main focus of studies, starting with Alan Milward's *The Reconstruction of Western Europe, 1945-1951* (Berkeley, CA: U of California P, 1984), emphasizes the endogenous roots of European recovery and the big return the U.S.-led recovery achieved with a relatively small investment. This view is incorporated by Gérard Bossuat, *L'Europe occidentale à l'heure américaine: Le Plan Marshall et l'unité européenne, 1945-1952* (Brussels: Edition Complexe, 1992).

3 Certainly, my own work, *Irresistible Empire: America's Advance through Twentieth-Century Europe* (Cambridge, MA: Belknap, 2005) has fed the misconception that the Marshall Plan was the pivotal moment in European consumerism. My intention, however, was to show how many other conditions had to change for there to be a mass consumer society in Europe akin to that in the United States. Indeed, the United States' primacy and its conception of the standard of living as part of its hegemonic model rested on premises that were to a large degree construed as exceptional and, thus, though being promoted as universal, could not be replicated elsewhere.

4 The phrase, originally appearing in David W. Ellwood's pioneering work on the films, has taken on a life of its own. His original wording reads, "The Marshall Plan, I would like to suggest, launched the idea of economic growth in the sense we know it on its distinguished European career, and it did so by means of a devastatingly simple yet unprecedented message: 'You too can be like us.'" David W. Ellwood, "From 'Re-education' to the Selling of the Marshall Plan in Italy," in *The Political Re-education of Germany and her Allies after World War II*, ed. Nicholas Pronay and Keith Wilson (Beckenham, England: Croom Helm, 1985), 227.

5 This term was not part of post-1945 language. It was introduced to the historical debate relatively recently and was greatly fostered by the publication of an important historical study on U.S. trends,

namely Lizabeth Cohen's *A Consumer's Republic: The Politics of Mass Consumption in Postwar America* (New York: Alfred A. Knopf, 2003). It is hard to resist the temptation to apply the term to postwar Europe, even when recognizing that it might be an anachronism. See, for example. Sheryl Kroen, "A Political History of the Consumer," *The Historical Journal* 47.3 (2004): 709-36, esp. 728-36.

6 Charles S. Maier, "The Politics of Productivity: Foundations of American Economic Policy after World War II," in *Between Power and Plenty: Foreign Economic Policies of Advanced Industrial States*, ed. P.J. Katzenstein (Madison, WI: U of Wisconsin P, 1978), 23-49.

7 De Grazia, *Irresistible Empire*, 340, 359.

8 Ibid., 350-59.

9 J. Bradford DeLong and Barry Eichengreen, "The Marshall Plan: History's Most Successful Structural Adjustment Program," in *Postwar Economic Reconstruction and Lessons for the East Today*, ed. Rudiger Dornbusch et al. (Cambridge, MA: MIT, 1993), 189-230.

10 Ina Zweiniger-Bargielowska, *Austerity in Britain: Rationing, Controls, and Consumption, 1939-1955* (New York: Oxford UP, 2000).

11 Vibeke Sørensen and Mogens Rüdiger, *Denmark's Social Democratic Government and the Marshall Plan, 1947-1950* (Copenhagen: Museum Tusculanum Press, University of Copenhagen, 2001).

12 Irwin Wall, *The United States and the Making of Postwar France, 1945-1954* (New York: Cambridge UP, 1991).

13 Marcello De Cecco, "Economic Policy in the Reconstruction Period," *The Rebirth of Italy, 1943-1950*, ed. Stuart Woolf (London: Longman, 1974); Anthony Carew, *Labor under the Marshall Plan: The Politics of Productivity and the Marketing of Management Science* (Detroit: Wayne State UP, 1987). See also Federico Romero, *The United States and the European Trade Union Movement, 1944-1951* (Chapel Hill, NC: U of North Carolina P, 1992).

14 Quoted from de Grazia, *Irresistible Empire*, 348.

15 Ibid., 271, 302.

16 Albert Hemsing, "The Marshall Plan's European Film Unit, 1948-1955: A Memoir and Filmography," *Historical Journal of Film, Radio and Television* 14.3 (1994): 269-97. See, for example, Sandra Schulberg and Richard Pena, *Selling Democracy: Films of the Marshall Plan, 1948-1953* (New York: New York Film Festival, 2004).

17 Closer examination of the content of the films suggests the paradox involved in pressing viewing publics with the notion that the ERP was producing a big rupture in traditions given how fearful these same publics (and their rules were) of visiting even more big ruptures on people who had experienced depression, dictatorship, war, and occupation. See, in particular, Amy Garrett, "Marketing America: Public Culture and Public Diplomacy in the Marshall Era, 1947-1954," Ph.D. diss., University of Pennsylvania, 2004; Paola Bonafazio, "Narrating Modernization: Documentary Films in Cold War Italy (1948-1955)," Ph.D. diss., New York University, 2008; Anthony S. Roman, "The Italian Marshall Plan Films: The Handmaiden of Recovery," M.A. thesis, Columbia University, 2008.

18 Cited in Roman, "Italian Marshall Plan Films," 18-19.

George M. Fujii[1]

Selling the Marshall Plan in the United States

Over fifty years since its conception, the phrase "Marshall Plan" lives on as a powerful symbol of an ambitious U.S. foreign aid program that "worked." While the scholarly debates over the Marshall Plan's limitations and consequences continue, the verdict of general audiences and many scholars is clear. They judge this $13 billion program, the equivalent of over $127 billion in 2009 dollars (and over $500 billion in terms of U.S. Gross National Product), to have been a success in its goals of rebuilding war-damaged European economies and stimulating postwar economic development.[2] Politicians and pundits, including U2 singer Bono, continue to issue repeated appeals for new Marshall Plans for worthy causes ranging from tackling climate change, to eliminating poverty and coping with catastrophic natural disasters.[3]

The fondness for the Marshall Plan and its legacy in U.S. popular memory is no historical accident. From 1947 to 1948, the Committee for the Marshall Plan to Aid European Recovery (CMP), an umbrella organization for pro-Marshall Plan groups, waged a highly effective campaign that built a favorable domestic climate of opinion for this massive foreign aid program. This was no easy task. Two previous large-scale internationalist programs, the 1944 Bretton Woods Conference, and the complementary 1945 Anglo-American Financial Agreement—a $3.75 billion U.S. loan to Britain—had failed to live up to the lofty rhetoric of their backers. U.S. taxpayers had, by early 1947, granted or loaned some $9 billion for European reconstruction, with seemingly little to show for their largess.[4] In a July 1947 letter to Herbert Hoover, powerful Republican Senator Robert Taft worried that the proposed Marshall Plan aid might be frittered away like the earlier loan to Britain in a futile attempt to maintain "a higher standard of living in England than was absolutely necessary."[5] Adding to the difficulties of Marshall Plan supporters were challenges from the political left including former Vice-President Henry Agar Wallace, who attempted to capture the mantle of Franklin D. Roosevelt's New Deal. Yet the supporters of the Marshall Plan ultimately triumphed thanks to their broad inclusive rhetoric, their superior organizational network, and a bit of serendipity. The 1948 Czech coup gave their efforts an added anticommunist bounce in the crucial final stages of ratification.

The first public appearance of the CMP came on the morning of Monday, 17 November 1947. Readers of *The New York Times*, *The New York Herald-Tribune*, and *The Washington Post* were greeted with full-page advertisements proclaiming the establishment of a "Committee for the Marshall Plan to Aid European Recovery." These ads listed over 150 prominent citizens as members and called for the support of a million Americans to "help in the fight to sustain those who share with us common ideals of freedom and human dignity." Readers might have recognized several names, such as union leaders William Green and Philip Murray, businessmen Gerard Swope and David Sarnoff, the mayors of New York City and San Francisco, and even the publisher of the *New York Times*, Arthur Hays Sulzberger. The day before this ad appeared, *The New York Times* ran a sympathetic front-page story announcing the CMP's establishment, which reprinted verbatim the text of the Committee's policy statement and most of its membership roster.[6]

Readers could hardly have been unaware of the grave conditions in Europe to which the CMP advertisements referred. The front page of that day's *New York Times* included an article on the arrival in New York City of the Friendship Food Train, which carried thirty carloads of gifts bound for France and Italy.[7] Subscribers to the weekly *CIO News*, the newspaper of the Congress of Industrial Organization (CIO) labor union federation, would have been doubly familiar with the grave situation in Europe. Its 17 November 1947 edition splashed across its cover a full-page photograph of a little European girl who, according to the caption, "like millions of her brothers and sisters gratefully munches a piece of bread." The caption, titled "Our Responsibility," called for Congress "to act on aid abroad" to prevent "further suffering and starvation." It quoted CIO president Philip Murray as he called for U.S. aid to Europe "not merely as a gesture of humanitarianism," but also because "hunger" was "a threat to the peace and security of the world. Murray's language was remarkably similar to that employed in CMP's own advertisements.[8]

These three newspaper advertisements marked the opening salvo in the CMP's campaign to educate the American public and to build a base of popular support in favor of the European Recovery Program (ERP), popularly known as the Marshall Plan. From November 1947 to approval of ERP legislation in March 1948, the Committee for the Marshall Plan waged an extensive publicity campaign that included pamphlets, newspaper advertisements, radio broadcasts, press releases, and telegram campaigns. The CMP raised over $158,000 (over $1.5 million in 2009 dollars), circulated nearly 1.25 million pieces of literature, arranged seven network radio broadcasts, and succeeded in assembling a broad coalition, including prominent businessmen and all of the major veterans organizations, in support of this $13 billion dollar economic assistance program to sixteen Western European nations.[9]

The CMP provided a venue within which the realm of high-level diplomacy and state policymaking mingled with the world of civil society and domestic politics. It brought together a broad coalition of business, labor, farm groups, women's groups, veterans, internationalists, and religious organizations in support of the Marshall Plan as an instrument of public policy and also as an ideology. The "Marshall Plan ideology," as presented by the CMP, offered a vision of a prosperous and stable United States governed by liberal, not socialist, principles represented as contingent on this program of massive U.S. economic intervention in European affairs through foreign aid.

The Marshall Plan and the CMP eschewed the harshly anticommunist rhetoric of the Truman Doctrine in favor of a gentler, more implicit anticommunism. The CMP followed the tone set by Secretary of State Marshall himself in his famous 5 June 1947 "Marshall Plan" address, which assured its listeners that "our policy is not directed against any country or doctrine but against hunger, poverty, desperation, and chaos."[10] This policy shift pleased many liberals who had been dismayed by the strident language of the Truman Doctrine. These liberals could now rejoin the Democratic Party fold and again unite in a common cause with centrist liberals to form Cold War consensus liberalism.[11]

At the same time, the CMP and the Marshall Plan (ERP) helped to divide the Left. A small group of liberals led by Henry Wallace and the Progressive Citizens of America (PCA) rejected the ERP's implicit anticommunism and division of the world into two competing blocs. PCA was a coalition of disaffected liberals, some trade unionists, veteran Communists, and Hollywood artists. The five-year "Wallace Plan," this coalition's alternative to the ERP, blended New Deal ideas of large-scale planning and massive government spending on agricultural and industrial development with an internationalist administrative structure. It envisioned a world food granary, and a massive, new U.N.-administered foreign assistance program for Europe funded mostly by U.S. contributions, but also by funds from other willing nations. In contrast, U.S. State Department officials structured the Marshall Plan, from its earliest stages, as a U.S.-run, funded, and administered program. Will Clayton, undersecretary of state for economic affairs, wrote on 27 May 1947, "[W]e must avoid getting into another UNRRA. *The United States must run this show.*"[12] (U.S. and Soviet officials had quarreled repeatedly over administration of the United Nations Relief and Rehabilitation Administration (UNRRA), which provided relief operations for war-ravaged nations from 1943 to 1947.)

Much of the appeal for the Marshall Plan came from its broad, progressive liberal ideology, which appealed to traditional U.S. values of mutual aid, to economic self-interest (creation of an export market for goods), and to fears of communism. The Marshall Plan was not simply large, bold, and mostly successful. It was also, in the eyes of most Americans—except for a handful of dissidents—generous and benevolent (even if mixed with a dash of national self-interest), an impression created in large part by the efforts of the CMP and other Marshall Plan supporters.[13]

CMP Origins and Leadership

One of the first documented records of the CMP's existence comes from 8 September 1947 when Hugh Moore, president and co-founder of the Dixie Cup Corporation and later CMP treasurer, solicited the advice of seven fellow Marshall Plan supporters as to a suitable name for their new organization. Moore forwarded a list of titles that had emerged during a discussion at a board meeting of the American Association for the United Nations (AAUN), an organization from which several CMP members and staffers would come.

Moore's list of "Titles for Consideration" reflected a deliberate, carefully thought-out concern with the publicity and public relations effects of this seemingly minor detail. Moore's list divided the possible titles into five groups, sharing the common subtitle, "Supporting the Marshall Plan," and variants of the form "Committee to ______ by Aiding Europe." The group included one "Anti-Russian Title"

("Combat Communism"), two "Anti-War Titles" ("Prevent War" or "Avoid War"), seven "Pro-American Titles" ("Defend America," "Protect America," "Safeguard America," Preserve America," "Aid America," "Help America," "Save America"), four "Pro-Peace Titles" ("Promote Peace," "For the Promotion of Peace," "Keep the Peace," and "Insure Peace") and a "Miscellaneous" title ("Committee to Help Europe to Help Itself"). Although the CMP adopted none of these title options, this list offers a fascinating window into five goals the creators of the CMP shared for the Marshall Plan, namely anticommunism, fear of renewed warfare, a belief that the United States was somehow in peril and that the ERP was the answer, a belief in the ERP's peaceful nature, and agreement with the administration on the principle of "self help."[14]

Structurally, the CMP consisted of two membership groups, an Executive Committee and a National Council, and a professional staff based in a main New York City office in the Empire State Building and a satellite Washington, D.C. branch on K Street. The Executive Committee, which met weekly in New York City along with the paid staff, set CMP policy and direction, while the National Council existed to provide funds, lobby friends and neighbors, set up regional committees, and lend prestige to the organization.[15]

Henry L. Stimson, a former secretary of war and secretary of state, nominally headed the CMP as national chairman. His October 1947 *Foreign Affairs* article "The Challenge to Americans" outlined the CMP's official position. In practice, Judge Robert P. Patterson, the Executive Committee chairman and a former secretary of war, along with the rest of the Executive Committee and the staff, directed and executed CMP policy and affairs. Executive Committee members included Alger Hiss, then heading the Carnegie Endowment; AAUN director Clark Eichelberger; Moore; Philip Reed and Herbert Bayard Swope of General Electric; CIO Secretary-Treasurer James B. Carey; David Dubinsky, president of the AFL-affiliated International Ladies Garment Workers Union (ILGWU); and several others, including Allen W. Dulles, Arthur Page, and McKee, as well as the Executive Committee's one woman, Edith Wilk, referred to in the records as Mrs. Wendell L. Willkie.[16] At least two CMP executive committee members, Herbert Lehman and Dubinsky, were also members of the liberal Americans for Democratic Action (ADA).

Key CMP Supporters

The ADA began waging a pro-Marshall Plan campaign even before the CMP's inception, as indicated by a 24 October 1947 statement by Joseph L. Rauh, Jr., secretary of its National Board, that "the ADA is making the fight for the Marshall Plan its No. 1 issue."[17] Indeed, some sections of the ADA, such as the New York State ADA in its 1948 election policy platform, were more enthusiastic for the Marshall Plan than they were for President Truman. The New York State ADA Political Action Policy of 3 April 1948 made "support of the Marshall Plan, without strings" one of six conditions for candidate endorsements. In a contradiction, though, one of the other ADA conditions was "opposition to any attempts to include Fascist

Spain among the ERP recipients." In addition, complaining that Truman had failed to offer "consistent, integrated, or dynamic leadership," the New York State ADA called on the Democratic Party to nominate Dwight D. Eisenhower as its presidential candidate.[18]

The American Federation of Labor (AFL) was also a firm supporter of the Marshall Plan, approving by unanimous vote a resolution in support of the program at its October 1947 annual convention in San Francisco. The CMP also attempted unsuccessfully to recruit economist John Kenneth Galbraith, then at *Fortune* magazine, to be its executive secretary, a post filled by John Ferguson, formerly an assistant to Dean Acheson at the State Department.[19]

Significantly, most of the Executive Committee were also members of the New York-based Council on Foreign Relations, a point that historian Michael Wala emphasizes in his studies of the CMP,[20] although the Council itself did not become officially involved in the CMP's activities. The Committee also enjoyed at least the tacit support of the Truman Administration, which was loath to become directly involved in or start its own domestic propaganda operation.[21] While my research has found no evidence of direct funding for the CMP from either the Council on Foreign Relations or the U.S. State Department, members of these two organizations and of other government agencies did participate in CMP activities, and some joined the CMP. Dean Acheson, for example, played an important role in supporting the CMP by suggesting possible members and by making pro-Marshall Plan speeches across the country.[22]

The CMP National Council

Based solely on the Executive Committee membership roster, the CMP might appear to be just a northeast-centered group of liberals, businessmen, and unionists. The National Council, though, reflected greater diversity, both geographically and professionally. Although the Executive Council ran the CMP, the National Council members, along with sympathetic non-members, raised the funds needed for CMP's expensive publicity campaigns and provided the manpower necessary for regional canvassing and letter-writing campaigns to Congressmen. National Council members also organized various CMP regional committees, in the Northeast (New York, New England, Philadelphia, Baltimore, and New Jersey), a women's division (headed by Mrs. Willkie), and chapters in Des Moines and Hollywood (southern California).[23] The Boston-based New England Committee for the Marshall Plan to Aid European Recovery, chaired by Henry Parkman, raised $7,169.84 in contributions from 1 January to 31 March 1948, and spent $5,398.46 during that same period on publicity activities and staff salaries.[24]

An undated roster of CMP National Council members by state lists 274 names, with by far the largest membership in New York (ninety), followed by large contingents in Massachusetts (twenty-five), Pennsylvania and California (nineteen each), Ohio (fifteen), and Washington, D.C. (fourteen). Twelve of the then forty-eight states, mostly in the mountain West, had no National Council members. Although at first glance the membership roles appear heavily skewed towards the Northeast, in particular New York State, two factors mitigate this apparent imbalance. First, several individuals listing their residency as New York or Washington, D.C. were representatives of national organizations, such as the Brotherhood of Sleeping Car Porters. Second, New York was then by far the most populous state with over 13.4 million residents, according to the 1940 census, followed in size by Pennsylvania with around 9.9 million, Illinois with around 7.8 million, California and Ohio with around 6.9 million, and Texas with 6.4 million. Massachusetts had about 4.3 million residents, and the District of Columbia had about 663,000 residents. Factoring in these statistics, the CMP was comparatively underrepresented in Illinois (nine members), and notably in Texas (two members, although eight individuals donated over $500 to the CMP, largely due to local lobbying efforts in Houston by Will Clayton).[25]

At the 11 December 1947 CMP Executive Committee meeting, public relations consultant Harold L. Oram noted "representation in Chicago was limited and that he was anxious to have any suggestions as to improving that situation."[26] The result was a canvassing of Chicago CMP members as reported by Laird Bell, a Chicago lawyer and member of the local CMP and Council on Foreign Relations, in a 14 January 1948 plea to CMP Executive Director John H. Ferguson to send Senator Vandenberg out to sway local opinion. Bell wrote that a meeting of several Chicago CMP members concluded that the region was "dominated [...] by papers either hostile or lukewarm, both in Chicago and downstate," with the latter region "strongly Republican and with [...] a good deal of latent hostility to the Plan."[27] He concluded that it would be counterproductive to attempt to recruit new members in Chicago at that point. Therefore, other than in a few specific regions, CMP membership generally reflected the population distribution of 1947/1948 America.[28]

Sorted by profession, the National Council included politicians, among them Minneapolis Mayor Hubert Humphrey; businessmen of all sorts, such as IBM's Thomas Watson, candy maker Russell Stover, and the Radio Corporation of America's David Sarnoff; university administrators and distinguished faculty, such as University of California president Gordon Sproul, Harvard president James B. Conant and philosopher John Dewey; Hollywood moguls, such as Eric Johnston and Darryl Zanuck; various union leaders, including Teamsters president Daniel J. Tobin and Brotherhood of Sleeping Car Porters president A. Philip Randolph; farmers' organization leaders; Walter White of the NAACP; newspaper owners (of the *New York Times* and *Herald Tribune*); and religious and ethnic leaders, such as Charles P. Taft, president of the Federal Council of Churches of Christ in America, Stephen S. Wise, president of the American Jewish Congress, and Clarence A. Pickett, the executive secretary of the American Friends Service Committee.[29] (Notably absent from this list was Henry Luce of *Time/Life*, who apparently was never asked to join and apparently never sought to join).

One insight into the thoughts of National Council members comes from a July 1947 *Atlantic Monthly* article written by Eric Johnston, previously president of the U.S. Chamber of Commerce and from 1947 to 1948 president of the Motion Picture Association of America (MPAA), on the subject of "Partnership Capitalism" and U.S. foreign policy. By "partnership capitalism" Johnston meant a wedding of "American capital and know-how" with "the capital, the manpower, and the resources in other countries," in a "mutual and cooperative" fashion. According to Johnston, the United States gave the world two distinctive contributions, namely, "the concept of the dignity of man" and the technique of "mass production," yet mass production depended on "mass markets." Johnston added that the United States could not for long "survive as an island of plenty in a world ocean of want," thereby justifying a policy through which the United States would "help others produce so that they may in turn buy from us." This general idea that U.S. prosperity depended on international markets and the related fear that continued economic inequality would lead to revolutions and upheavals, would recur in subsequent publicity materials for the Marshall Plan, both by the CMP and other groups.[30]

CMP Staff and Finances

The final component of CMP's structure was its professional staff, which ran day-to-day affairs. Also pivotal to the CMP's efforts was noted public relations consultant Harold L. Oram (of the Oram Group) who advised the Committee to take out full-page advertisements in leading newspapers and conduct telegram campaigns in order to create the impression of mass popular support. The Oram Group provided its services to a variety of liberal causes that would come to include the American Friends of Vietnam, and the firm still is in business, with a client list that includes the University of California Press.[31] By the end of 1947, the CMP employed a staff of fifteen with a payroll of $5,527.15 (over $54,000 in 2009 dollars) and spent $40,214.02 in expenditures for its two offices. By 8 January 1948, the CMP had raised $84,400, mostly from donors. The donation receipts reveal a surprising range in the size of donations, with a number of individuals donating only $1 or $5, while corporations, organizations, and other individuals (notably Edwin W. Pauley and Nelson and John D. Rockefeller) donated $500 or more.[32] One small donor was a Miss Lila J. Hood, "County Extension Home Economist, Agriculture & Home Economics, Waterloo, Iowa," who donated $1.40 to the Committee.[33]

The financial figures for CMP's total period of active operation, from 30 October 1947 to 9 April 1948, are even more impressive. The CMP took in over $168,000 in funds (over $1.5 million in 2009 dollars) and spent nearly $166,000, of which around $60,000 went to the cost of printing and mailing publications, just over $26,000 for contract services (promotion, publicity, and other services), about $12,000 in telephone and telegraph costs, nearly $8,000 for advertising, and nearly $7,000 in travel expenses. In addition, the CMP's publicity agency, the Phoenix News Bureau, obtained seven free radio network broadcasts for CMP worth $60,000. The CMP also sent several of its Executive Committee members and other ERP supporters around the country to serve as speakers for local meetings, forums, and radio broadcasts, including Patterson, William Green of the AFL, Reed, Charles Taft, Alger Hiss, and Mrs. Willkie.

Clearly, then, the CMP had the resources necessary to wage an effective information and publicity campaign. It quickly built a robust infrastructure capable of projecting its message out to the American public through a variety of mediums.[34] Public backlash and Congressional criticism of earlier U.S. government publicity campaigns contributed to a lackluster State Department pro-Marshall Plan publicity campaign. Harold Stein, the head of CMP's Washington office, recalled in August 1952 that "[o]n the whole, State's role was not very satisfactory. Everything seemed to be one dimension too big. The stuff they developed was so elaborate that Fran [sic] Wilcox complained that they couldn't leaf through it. The President's message was too long; no impact."[35] Michael Wala largely concurs with Stein's judgment, arguing that "the State Department's efforts to promote the Marshall Plan were weakened by internal uncertainties, incompetent officers, legal barriers, and accusations of using propaganda."[36] This essay, though, disagrees with Wala's claim that the CMP was effectively "an external propaganda agency acting on behalf of the European Recovery Program (ERP)."[37] While retired and current government officials played leading roles in the CMP, the CMP had a higher degree of autonomy, particularly in its tactics and techniques, than Wala suggests.

The Pamphlet War

What, then, was the message, and the ideology conveyed therein, of the Committee for the Marshall Plan and its supporters? What were the competing viewpoints put forth by Marshall Plan opponents? A small war of pamphlets raged during the critical period from late 1947 to mid-1948 when ratification of the Marshall Plan hung in the balance. The CMP's first efforts were reprints of newspaper articles, followed by a series of pamphlets that included *Dollars Can Help Save Europe*, *A Statement of Purpose*, *Four Essentials of a European Recovery Program*, and *The Marshall Plan is Up to You!*. From 28 January to 15 March 1948, the CMP released weekly fact sheets titled "Facts about the Marshall Plan" that were designed to highlight favorable press coverage and counter attacks by critics. Finally, children's book author Munro Leaf volunteered his services to the CMP, producing the illustrated pamphlet, *Who is the Man Against the Marshall Plan?* Leaf is best known for his 1936 book, *The Story of Ferdinand,* the tale of a gentle bull that wanted to sniff flowers rather than fight in the bull ring, which was made into a 1938 eight-minute Disney short animated film), as well as his ___ *Can Be Fun* series, covering topics such as the metric system, grammar, and patriotism (in his 1964 book, *Being an American Can Be Fun*). Because it dealt with Spain and appeared in print during the Spanish Civil War, *The Story of Ferdinand* generated a swirl of controversy. As Leaf put it, "It was attacked by everybody! It was called 'Red propaganda,' a bitter satire of pacifism, on one hand, and a pro-Fascist tract on the other." Leaf's work for the CMP was not an aberration, though, for he would produce a similar pamphlet in 1951 for the Committee on the Present Danger.[38]

A number of non-CMP pamphlets also supported the Marshall Plan. Several of these pamphlets, such as Livingston Hartley's *The Marshall Plan or Else ...* and the ADA's *Toward Total Peace: A Liberal Foreign Policy for the United States*, took an explicitly anticommunist line. Other pamphlets took a gentler stance, including those from church organizations explaining why Christians should support the Marshall Plan, such as *The Churches and the European Recovery Program*. Generally written in plain language, widely distributed, and inexpensive (five cents for the CPUSA pamphlets or even distributed freely), these pamphlets offered a way for the general American public to learn about the ERP.

Stop Stalin Now! (Or Not ...)

Our survey of publicity materials begins with one that never appeared in public, the CMP's proposed *Stop Stalin Now!* full-page newspaper advertisement. After the CMP staff produced a full-page mockup of *Stop Stalin Now!*, the Executive Committee rejected it as too harshly anticommunist, reflecting the general absence of overtly anticommunist rhetoric in other CMP publications. The proposed ad was modeled on a similar *Stop Hitler Now!* advertisement produced by the Committee to Defend America by Aiding the Allies (CDAA) that had run in major newspapers on 10 June 1940 and that President Roosevelt himself publicly praised in a subsequent news conference.[39] *Stop Stalin Now!* warned that "WE MUST STOP STALIN NOW through the European Recovery Program." If Stalin controlled Europe, the ad warned, then "we shall have no other business, no other aim in life, but primitive self-defense. We shall exist only under martial law—or the law of the jungle." However, if "confronted with strength," then the Russians would "modify their policy of cheap aggrandizement" and "accept a peaceful settlement." *Stop Stalin Now!*, then, sought to play on two dangers its authors perceived that Americans feared, namely the risk on the one hand of state tyranny (similar to F.A. Hayek's fears of "serfdom," or fears of a "garrison state") and alternately, anarchy, with both options anathema to U.S. liberalism. The reference to the "law of the jungle" would stir up fears about what Michael Hunt has termed Americans' "nagging preoccupation with the perils of revolution, most acute among a propertied elite," including the Bolshevik Revolution in Russia. Conversely, *Stop Stalin Now!*'s contention that Stalin only understood strength, eerily echoes American diplomat and Russia expert George F. Kennan's assessment of Russia as capable of understanding "only the 'logic of force,'" an idea that led to the doctrine of containment. The CMP Executive Committee's rejection of *Stop Stalin Now!* then suggests discomfort on some level with deploying the "red card" of overt anticommunism. Other groups were not as circumspect.[40]

In *The Marshall Plan or Else ...*, Livingston Hartley, director of the Washington office of the CDAA from 1940-1942, outlined the bleakest possible scenario if Congress did not approve the Marshall Plan.[41] Although providing a more sophisticated argument than did *Stop Stalin Now!*, Hartley, like Johnston had earlier, employed the metaphor of an ocean to describe the consequences of U.S. inaction. According to Hartley, the Marshall Plan would "create a dyke against any westward sweep of the Communist tide." Failure to erect said dyke would result in "an economic collapse of Western Europe unparalleled in the history of the Western World." As "the Communist tide" swept westward through France and Italy, soon thereafter Germany—"an alien instituted island of democracy in the midst of a Communist sea"—would fall.

Hartley then saw U.S. difficulties as spreading out worldwide. Following the collapse of Western Europe, Hartley portrayed subsequent setbacks in the Middle East, "since power talks so eloquently in this part of the world," and then in South America. Hartley argued that problems here were inevitable given that South Americans considered France and Italy "the cultural centers of their civilization," and that South Americans, according to Hartley, had "long been accustomed to dictatorships, revolutions, and the rule of 'strong men.'" Ultimately, without the Marshall Plan, concluded Hartley, U.S. culture would become militarized, costs and taxes would snowball, and the strong possibility would persist of "an eventual atomic war with the Soviet bloc." Thus, in a clear, direct, and straightforward way Hartley articulated the logic of containment policy and deftly linked it with the Marshall Plan, using an approach rather different from that of the CMP, or indeed, of the Truman Administration. While Hartley's rhetoric might convince centrist liberals and conservatives, the article's sharp division of the world into two opposing camps would alarm leftist liberals, such as Henry Wallace.[42] In effect, Hartley had inverted earlier CDAA anti-fascist rhetoric into his call for supporting the Marshall Plan as a bulwark for anticommunist action.

The ADA, the emerging voice of centrist Cold War liberals, was also unafraid of employing similarly strong, stark rhetoric, albeit with a few nods to more utopian liberal goals such as "the creation of a world government." In *Toward Total Peace*, the ADA warned that Congressional rejection of the Marshall Plan and refusal of further funds for foreign aid "would cause more widespread misery in Western Europe than the Nazi occupation." The political consequences of inaction included Communist expansion across Europe resulting in either Soviet power across Europe or "prolonged civil strife," with even more alarming results if communist control of European colonies followed. However, if the Marshall Plan, "the climax of our foreign policy," was approved, then "a heavy blow" would be struck at "the Leninist certitudes which dominate the Politburo" by minimizing "the appeal of Communism." Therefore, the ADA, although still expressing the hope that Soviet policy might change, accepted the division of the world into two separate and competing spheres of influence, while still including some calls for a strengthened United Nations.[43]

Much in the ADA's vision as articulated in *Toward Total Peace* reflected a continuation of Wilsonian ideals, particularly in the ADA's continued adherence, at least in principle, to an eventual "world government" through a "steady strengthening of the United Nations." This ADA policy statement corresponded to what N. Gordon Levin, Jr., described as Wilson's view that the United States had a "historic mission to bring Europe into a peaceful international order based on world law," and that "the bi-partisan Cold War consensus" represented the "complete triumph" of "Wilsonian values" with an international and multinationalist U.S. foreign policy opposed to both communism and imperialism.[44]

The Marshall Plan is Up to You!

How, then, did the Committee for the Marshall Plan go about selling the Marshall Plan to a skeptical American public facing inflation and domestic shortages, and still jittery about the situation overseas, particularly in Europe? To answer this question, we turn first to *The Marshall Plan is Up to You!*, the CMP's "community activity" booklet. The language and tone of this pamphlet differs greatly from that of any of the other pamphlets surveyed in this essay, except for Leaf's *Who is the Man Against the Marshall Plan?* The friendly, chatty, and colloquial language of *The Marshall Plan is Up to You!* comes across from the pamphlet's opening sentences: "We'd like to have an over-the-fence chat with you about something that's not just important but *crucial* to your children's future as well as your own. That something is the Marshall Plan." The contrast with Hartley's opening line—"What Congress does about the Marshall Plan will have far-reaching consequences on many sectors of American life"—is striking. Both pamphlets convey the same basic information in these passages, but with markedly different phrasing, notably the difference between Munro's use of the more casual second person versus Hartley's use of the more formal and detached third person.[45]

After a section on what the Marshall Plan "boils down to" and its cost, *The Marshall Plan is Up to You!* "explodes some myths." Countering grumblings about the cost of the program, the pamphlet proclaims that "it's not being a sucker to help put out a fire in your neighbor's house so your own house won't burn down," thereby concisely making Hartley's "Communist tide" argument without the communism, while referring to Roosevelt's fire hose metaphor for wartime Lend-Lease. In another contrast with Hartley's pamphlet and *Stop Stalin Now!*, *The Marshall Plan is Up to You!* argued that "It [ERP] is not aimed against Russia," echoing, and quoting the public line from Marshall's 5 June 1947 speech launching ERP that the Soviet bloc was welcome to participate in the program.[46]

CMP officials were aware of popular skepticism towards giving Europeans additional foreign aid after the failure of earlier measures.[47] The references to "not being a sucker" in *The Marshall Plan is Up to You!* are a response to these concerns. Dean Acheson's CMP correspondence file, for example, includes a clipping of a 1948 *Chicago Tribune* political cartoon, titled "Beginning to Get Suspicious," which opposed further aid to Europe. The cartoon depicted a drunk European, resembling Churchill, dressed in ragged clothes, with two empty bottles labeled "UNRRA" and "Loan to Britain" in his pockets, with his stovetop hat, labeled "Plea for Aid," extended to a skeptical Uncle Sam, who—sniffing the European's alcoholic breath—asks "SA-A-Y-Y-Y, Sure You're Gonna' Get a Cup O' Coffee With This One?" Further reinforcing the cartoonist's message was his decision to stage this scene outside the "Idle Hour Bar," from which emanated the wafting sounds of a drunken chorus singing "Ain't Gonna' Work No More No More." Combating this stereotype of the lazy, undeserving European would prove to be a major challenge for pro-ERP publicity materials.[48]

The Marshall Plan is Up to You! also urged its readers to use nontraditional, even somewhat subversive, means to build support for the ERP, such as the suggestion to "gossip constructively" about the program, using "simple, human terms," since "like atomic energy, conversation has a chain reaction." Beyond mere words, the pamphlet suggested a variety of creative ways with which to publicize the Marshall Plan, from musical jingles, such as "It's a bargain for you and me, It's the Marshall Plan to keep us free," to "live actors or dummies in tattered clothes, eating skimpy diets and being too weak to work efficiently" (to illustrate hunger in Europe), to even dramatizations, using national costumes, of the sixteen participating nations, with descriptions of each country's needs. Finally, the pamphlet concluded with a bit of guilt, noting that "when the war was on, there were very few buckpassers on buying bonds, rolling bandages, giving blood, on fighting and dying—and those few were regarded as beneath contempt. The Marshall Plan is a very real part of the war."[49]

Therefore, the pitch of *The Marshall Plan is Up to You!* was rather different from that of *Stop Stalin Now!* or Hartley's pamphlet, which drew upon American fears of the specter of communism. Instead, *The Marshall Plan is Up to You!* sought to appeal to patriotism and civic values, through its references to buck-passing and to community action to save a neighbor's burning house. The pamphlet presented the Marshall Plan as "a common sense investment" to safeguard "our war-time investment of blood and dollars." The repeated references to money, "buckpassing," and "investment" are intriguing, since this rhetoric seems calculated to appeal to wartime "patriotic citizen consumers," who followed government dictates to buy war bonds and restrict purchases.[50]

As Lizabeth Cohen elaborated in *A Consumer's Republic*, during the war "the consumer embodied the loyal, self-sacrificing citizen on the home front." However, according to Cohen, a tension existed during this period from 1947 to 1948 between the wartime "citizen consumer" impulse and the postwar "purchaser consumer" alternative, in which manufacturers urged mass consumption of durable goods and other consumer products in order to stimulate and create "postwar prosperity built around mass consumption." Therefore, consumers were urged to save now and spend later. *The Marshall Plan is Up to You!* sought to restrain this emerging "purchaser consumer" impulse as it charged that "our own heavy demand for goods has already led to inflation. A sound policy of conservation [...] will keep the Marshall Plan from aggravating our inflation," a concern raised by critics.[51]

Finally, *The Marshall Plan is Up to You!* explicitly targeted other aspects of the domestic front by using a hypothetical "Mrs. Allen, a housewife in Wichita, Kansas" as its example of how "everybody can do something" to support the Marshall Plan. Mrs. Allen, according to the pamphlet, could "inform herself on the issue," then "talk it over with her husband," her neighbors, and the League of Women Voters, as well as discuss it at the local Parent Teacher Association (P.T.A.) meeting. Therefore, *The Marshall Plan is Up to You!* sought to embed the Marshall Plan into the fabric of U.S. society as a whole, with a special appeal to the domestic front.[52]

Who is the Man Against the Marshall Plan?

Munro Leaf, the children's book author, produced the second of the CMP's pamphlets to adopt a friendly, colloquial, and straightforward tone, in his *Who is the Man Against the Marshall Plan?* A highlight of Leaf's pamphlet is his stick-figure drawings interspersed throughout the text, which give a cartoonish feel to the production. Again, like *The Marshall Plan is Up to You!*, Leaf's *Who is the Man Against the Marshall Plan?* employed a remarkably gentle, not overtly anticommunist, tone towards ERP opponents. "In this country," the pamphlet opened, "the man against the Marshall Plan is nearly always as well meaning and patriotic an American as any of us," merely uncritical and unthinking in his beliefs. Leaf then proceeded systematically to demolish ten arguments against the Marshall Plan. To answer the charge that "the rest of the world takes us for a bunch of 'dumb sucker' Santa Clauses," Leaf's pamphlet noted that the United States gave over $50 billion to its allies during the war, and then called the Marshall Plan "a first step toward accepting the responsibilities of world leadership." The Marshall Plan, then, was a logical extension of wartime Lend-Lease aid. To counter the charge "We can't afford it," *Who is the Man Against the Marshall Plan?* argued that the $6 billion Americans collectively "bet on the horses *last year* alone plus only a part of what our girls spent in the same time on lipstick, powder and other cosmetics would more than cover the cost" of the Marshall Plan. Again, like *The Marshall Plan is Up to You!*, Leaf's pamphlet called on Americans to resist the allure of "mass consumption" and abstain from indulging in a few luxuries. Indeed, Leaf repeatedly criticized American spending patterns in the pamphlet using facts and figures such as the fact that Americans spent $1.5 billion on jewelry the previous year, as part of his retort to charges that the Marshall Plan would raise the cost of living.[53]

Leaf's favorite type of evidence in *Who is the Man Against the Marshall Plan?* was statistics. For example, he addressed the "widespread and willingly believed lie" of lazy Europeans by noting that these "lazy" people had already brought production up to or even above pre-war levels. When addressing the anti-Marshall Plan argument that the cost of the ERP would weaken the United States, Leaf puzzled how citizens of a country "twice as strong and wealthy as it was before the war" could make such "a strange argument."[54]

Who is the Man Against the Marshall Plan? then shifted to address four anti-Marshall Plan arguments that *The Marshall Plan is Up to You!* did not address: 1) "we have the Atom Bomb ... Just let 'em start something!", 2) "it's a Wall Street Plot", 3) "Let 'em go bust!", and 4) "We Can Live Alone!" Munro used an ideological argument to counter reliance on the atomic bomb, arguing that "when free men are so outnumbered that only atom bombs can save them from slavery, then none of us will be free much longer." Implicit in this statement was an argument that totalitarian forces could not be fought solely with "the most destructive explosives, the deadliest mass-killing poisons, the greatest air power," and "the biggest army and navy"; rather, some sort of U.S. counter-ideology along with generous economic aid was essential. The "Wall Street Plot" reference obliquely alluded to Henry Wallace, who charged in a speech at the 1947 United Electrical, Radio, and Machine Workers of America (UE) union convention, printed as the pamphlet "Let's Come Out Fighting!," that "When Roosevelt died Wall Street moved in." Wallace had decried the influence in the Truman Administration of former investment bankers such as Secretary of Defense James Forrestall, Secretary of Commerce W. Averell Harriman, and Undersecretary of State Robert Lovell.[55]

Leaf then argued that isolationism, or what he termed the "Let Europe go Communist" so they will "find out it's no good" and "do things our way" argument posed grave dangers for U.S. interests. According to Leaf, it took "more than courage and determination to keep yourself strong enough even to want to have a voice in your government," thereby calling for active U.S. participation in European affairs. Leaf's arguments echoed those of Marshall Planners in the State Department, such as George Kennan, in arguing that U.S. financial and material aid to Europeans would be the best way of strengthening its anticommunist friends there.[56]

Religious denominations also weighed in favor of the Marshall Plan, with the Federal Council of the Churches of Christ in America, whose president, Charles Taft, was a CMP member, publishing the pro-Marshall Plan pamphlet *The Churches and the European Recovery Program*. Taft's open support for the Marshall Plan was in stark contrast to the views of his brother, Robert A. Taft, the powerful Republican Senator from Ohio and contender for the 1948 Republican presidential nomination, who was a leading critic of the program. Senator Taft feared that, like the earlier loan to Britain, the Marshall Plan would do little to aid Europe, would raise prices at home, and would even destroy "the freedom of the individual, freedom of States and local communities, freedom of the farmer to run his own farm and the workman to do his own job."[57]

In contrast, *The Churches and the European Recovery Program* stated its support for the ERP in the "conviction" that the program would be "one of history's most momentous affirmations of faith in the curative power of freedom and in the creative capacity of free men." The ERP would unite economic and political "ways and means" with "essentially moral and spiritual" motives and objectives. The pamphlet urged that European reconstruction go beyond merely providing tools and supplies and "appeal to the consciences, arouse the wills, and enlist the best efforts of men of good will on both sides of the Atlantic." "American aid" would be "an act of faith." Finally, after encouraging support for the United Nations and for mutual European cooperation, the pamphlet called for Christians to "accept certain specific limitations on their own economic desires" "willingly." Moral suasion here reinforced the CMP pamphlet's patriotic arguments for Americans to restrain their consumerist wants.[58]

Conclusion

The Committee for the Marshall Plan to Aid European Recovery played a key role in fashioning a public image of the Marshall Plan as an essential, but essentially benign, rational, common sense, straightforward economic assistance program to help the United States' friends in Europe rebuild their war-shattered economies. Not only would Americans be "neighborly" towards Europe by helping friends in need, but the $13 billion Marshall Plan would also benefit the U.S. economy and ensure a prosperous, peaceful world. By explaining the Marshall Plan to the public in plain language, the CMP played an important role in mobilizing support for the Marshall Plan legislation, which ultimately passed with wide margins in both the House and the Senate.[59]

The broad coalition that the CMP built among established interest groups, including organized labor, big business, religious groups, farmer organizations, women's groups, internationalists, and others, is in itself highly impressive, as was the CMP's fundraising skills and ability to churn out publicity materials. In simple, familiar language, the CMP articulated a sweeping change in U.S. foreign policy bankrolled by the American taxpayer towards a new internationalist direction. U.S. dollars would reshape the structures of the Western European economic system in order to ensure American prosperity at home and world stability. A combination of U.S. economic interventions (through the Marshall Plan, World Bank, and other activities) and support for the Cold War abroad along with liberal economic and social policies at home would come to characterize Cold War consensus liberalism. Postwar liberalism, however, rested on an implicitly anticommunist foundation that acknowledged the existence of a division between the "free world" of the United States and its allies, and the competing, totalitarian Soviet bloc.

Although the impetus for the Marshall Plan, unlike the earlier Truman Doctrine, was not to combat communism overtly through military aid, the ERP still carried the implicit assumption that communism would flourish wherever people lived in misery and economic difficulty. In bringing liberals skeptical of the harsh rhetoric of the Truman Doctrine back into the Truman-led Democratic Party and helping to marginalize the Wallace movement, the CMP and the Marshall Plan played an important role in shaping the direction of U.S. liberalism during the Cold War. Therefore, the Committee for the Marshall Plan and other supporting organizations played a pivotal role in the passage of the Marshall Plan legislation and contributed greatly to the creation of the powerful Marshall Plan mythos that remains potent even now.

Notes

1 Earlier versions of this essay were presented by the author at the 2004 Society for Historians of American Foreign Relations (SHAFR) conference held in Austin, Texas, and at the 2004 George Washington University-University of California, Santa Barbara Graduate Student Conference on the Cold War held in Washington, D.C. The author thanks Mary Furner, David Schuster, Francis Gavin, Arne Westad, and LSE Cold War Studies Centre members for their invaluable comments on earlier versions of this work.

2 This $125 billion figure, and all subsequent references to 2009 figures, was calculated using the inflation calculator on the Federal Reserve Bank of Minneapolis website, http://www.minneapolisfed.org, accessed 1 June 2009. The $500 billion figure comes from Greg Behrman, *The Most Noble Adventure: The Marshall Plan and the Time When America Helped Save Europe* (New York: Free, 2007), 4.

3 U.S. Senate Committee on Appropriations, Foreign Operations Subcommittee, "Hearing on the FY05 Budget Request for HIV/AIDS: Testimony of Bono, Founding Member, DATA," 18 May 2004. Bono stated, "Today we need the same audacity, imagination, and all-out commitment of a modern Marshall Plan. The Marshall Plan built a bulwark against Communism; today, for half the cost, we can build a bulwark against the extremism of our age." Moises Naim, "Demise of a Metaphor, Review of *The Most Noble Adventure* by Greg Behrman," *Washington Post,* Sunday, 4 November 2007, p. BW06.

4 Clarence E. Wunderlin, *Robert A. Taft: Ideas, Tradition, and Party in U.S. Foreign Policy* (Lanham, MD: SR Books/Rowman & Littlefield, 2005), 123.

5 Robert A. Taft to Herbert C. Hoover, 11 July 1947. Clarence E. Wunderlin, ed. *The Papers of Robert A. Taft*, Vol. 3 1945–1948 (Kent, OH: Kent State UP, 2003), 301–02.

6 "Nonpartisan Unit Headed By Stimson To Back European Aid," *New York Times*, 16 November 1947, p. 1–2.

7 "Friendship Train Nears City," *New York Times*, 17 November 1947, front page.

8 "Our Responsibility," *The CIO News*, Monday, 17 November 1947, cover page.

9 "Report on the Activities of the Committee for the Marshall Plan to Aid European Recovery," by the Executive Director, 5 April 1948, Committee for the Marshall Plan papers, Box 3, Memoranda & Correspondence, 1947–1948 file, Harry S Truman Library (HSTL), Independence, MO.

10 *Foreign Relations of the United States*: Diplomatic Papers, 1947, Vol. 3 (Washington, DC: Government Printing Office, 1972), 234–36.

11 On the CMP's views, see "Committee for the Marshall Plan to Aid European Recovery, A Statement of Purpose," 2. Committee for the Marshall Plan papers, Box 3, CMP: Memoranda & Reports, 1947–1948 file, HSTL. For more on "Cold War consensus liberalism," see the description of the non-Communist Left in Arthur M. Schlesinger, *The Vital Center: The Politics of Freedom* (Boston: Houghton Mifflin, 1949), 145–46, 153–54, 167–69, and Kevin Mattson, *Intellectuals in Action: The Origins of the New Left and Radical Liberalism, 1945–1970* (University Park, PA: Pennsylvania State UP, 2002), 16. For the Marshall Plan's reincorporation of dissident liberals, see Howard Brick, *Daniel Bell and the Decline of Intellectual Radicalism: Social Theory and Political Reconciliation in the 1940s* (Madison, WI: U of Wisconsin P, 1986), 144; George Charney, *A Long Journey* (Chicago: Quadrangle Books, 1968), 178; Richard H. Pells, *The Liberal Mind in a Conservative Age: American Intellectuals in the 1940s and 1950s*, 2nd ed. (Middletown, CT: Wesleyan UP, 1989), 110; Nelson Lichtenstein, "Labor in the Truman Era: Origins of the 'Private Welfare State,'" in *The Truman Presidency*, ed. Michael J. Lacey (New York: Woodrow Wilson Center, 1989), 147, and Mattson, *Intellectuals in Action*, 221.

12 Pells, *The Liberal Mind*, 63, 66–67, 69–70. Details on the "Wallace Plan" can be found in Henry Agard Wallace, *Toward World Peace* (New York: Reynal & Hitchcock, 1948), 37–46, and in Henry A. Wallace, *The Wallace Plan Vs. The (Hoover) (Dulles) Marshall Plan: Testimony by Henry A. Wallace before the House Committee on Foreign Affairs, Tuesday, February 24, 1948* (New York: National Wallace for President Committee, 1948). Clayton's quote is from a Memorandum by Undersecretary of State for Economic Affairs Will Clayton, "The European Crisis," 27 May 1947, *Foreign Relations of the United States* 3 (1947): 230–32. Italics are in the original.

13 Chapter 7 of Michael Wala, *The Council on Foreign Relations and American Foreign Policy in the Early Cold War* (Providence, RI: Beghahn, 1994), is the best starting point in the CMP literature. See also Michael Wala, "Selling the Marshall Plan at Home: The Committee for the Marshall Plan to Aid European Recovery," *Diplomatic History* 10 (1986): 247–65 and "Selling War and Selling Peace: The Non-Partisan Committee for Peace, the Committee to Defend America, and the Committee for the Marshall Plan," *Amerikastudien (American Studies)* 30 (1985): 91–105. Other works include Bernard Lemelin, "The Committee for the Marshall Plan: Activities and Impact, 1947–1948," *Society for Historians of Foreign Relations Newsletter* 25.4 (December 1994): 1–15; Scott Lucas, *Freedom's War: The American Crusade against the Soviet Union* (New York: New York UP, 1999); Richard E. Neustadt, *Presidential Power: The Politics of Leadership* (New York: Wiley, 1960); John Bledsoe Bonds, *Bipartisan Strategy: Selling the Marshall Plan* (Westport, CT: Praeger, 2002), and Behrman, *The Most Noble Adventure*. Some contemporary observers called the CMP the "Citizen's Committee for the Marshall Plan" or "Stimson Committee." For the sake of consistency and accuracy, this paper uses CMP and the Committee for the Marshall Plan throughout.

14 "Hugh Moore to Fred C. McKee, Dr. James T. Shotwell, Dr. William Emerson, Mr. Clark M. Eichelberger, Dr. Henry A. Atkinson, Miss Margaret Olson, Mr. Harold L. Oram," 8 September 1947, Hugh Moore's New York File, CMP Box 3, CMP Correspondence, 1947–1952 file, HSTL. For more detail on the AAUN connection, see Wala, "Selling," 250–52. Wala also finds parallels with the prewar Committee to Defend America because Eichelberger served in both groups. See Wala, "Selling," 252, n. 16.

15 On CMP structure, see "Minutes of Organizing Meeting of Committee For the Marshall Plan To Aid Europe," 30 October 1947, CMP papers, box 1, CMP Executive Committee—Minutes & Agenda 1947, and "Report on the Activities of The Committee For the Marshall Plan To Aid European Recovery," submitted by the Executive Director, 5 April 1948, CMP papers, box 3, Memoranda & Correspondence, 1947–1948 file, HSTL.

16 For lists of Executive Council members, see the CMP Executive Committee minutes, or the CMP's 17 November 1947 ads in the *New York Times, New York Herald-Tribune*, and *Washington Post*. The ad lists seventeen Executive Committee members; adding Mrs. Willkie would make eighteen. Over 150 National Council members are listed in the advertisements. For Edith Wilk as Mrs. Wendell Willkie, see "Indiana Advocate," *Time Magazine*, 31 July 1939 http://www.time.com/time/magazine/article/0,9171,761803-2,00.html, accessed 26 Dec. 2008.

17 Rauh to Acheson, 24 October 1947, Dean Acheson papers, Marshall Plan talks—California, Washington, Minnesota trip 1947 file, folder 1, HSTL.

18 Political Action Policy, ADA in New York State, 3 April 1948, Lehman Papers, Americans for Democratic Action, 1948–1951, Lehman Suite, Columbia University, New York.

19 CMP Executive Committee Minutes, New York Yacht Club, 13 November 1947. CMP Executive Committee Minutes and Agenda 1947, CMP (Box 1 of 3), Herbert H. Lehman Papers, General Correspondence, Lehman Suite, Columbia University, New York. Acheson, *Present at the Creation: My Years in the State Department* (New York: Norton, 1969), 240.

20 See Wala, *Council on Foreign Relations*, Chapter 7.

21 See Robert P. Patterson to Henry L. Stimson, 14 October 1947, Robert P. Patterson papers, Box 41 (General Correspondence, 1947–1952, Marshall Plan, October-November 1947), Library of Congress, Washington, D.C.

22 Dean Acheson to Harold L. Oram (Western Union telegram), 3 November 1947, Dean Acheson Papers, Box 4, Committee for the Marshall Plan: Correspondence [1 of 3], HSTL. Acheson suggested several individuals be invited to join CMP, including Adlai Stevenson, Hubert Humphrey, and James Carey. John Ferguson ("Ferg") to Acheson, 23 November 1947, Acheson Papers, Box 4, CMP: Correspondence [1 of 3], HSTL. Ferguson wrote, in perhaps unsurprisingly glowing terms, "Thanks again for your help yesterday. You and Harold are certainly the mainstays of our operation."

23 The Executive Director's report lists regional committees for the New York area, New England (with subcommittees in Vermont, New Hampshire, Maine, and Rhode Island), Philadelphia, Baltimore, New Jersey, and a women's division. The Executive Committee minutes for 11 December 1947 mention the formation of a Des Moines chapter and the 18 December 1947 minutes mention the start of a Hollywood chapter. See also John H. Ferguson to Dean G. Acheson, 9 December 1947, Dean Acheson Papers, Box 4, Committee for the Marshall Plan: Correspondence, 1947–1948 [1 of 3], HSTL, in which Ferguson states "I think you might like to know that we are already sparking the organization of a regional committee of farm groups from Des Moines." The Robert P. Patterson papers at the Library of Congress contain correspondence to some of these regional committees. Regional Committee Chairmen included William Marston Seabury for New York, Dr. Philip Lohman for Vermont, John A. Sinclair for New Hampshire, Guy Gannett for Maine, Rupert Thompson for Rhode Island, William L. Batt for Philadelphia, former Senator George L. Radcliffe for Baltimore, and Percy S. Young for New Jersey.

24 Paul Hines, Executive Director, New England Committee for the Marshall Plan to Aid European Recovery, 25 Faneuil Hall Square, Boston, MA, to John H. Ferguson, Executive Director, Marshall Plan Committee, 31 March 1948. Henry Parkman, Jr., was a Boston lawyer with an extensive record of public service including military service during World War II, joining in 1943 as a lieutenant colonel in the office of the Under-Secretary of War and rising to brigadier general by January 1946, when he left the army. He later served from 1950–1951 as chief of the Economic Cooperation

Administration (ECA) in France, the Marshall Plan administering agency and from 1954–1955 as Assistant U.S. High Commissioner for Germany, assistant to James B. Conant. "Henry Parkman Jr. Dead at 64; Former U.S. Official in Germany," *The New York Times*, 28 May 1958, p. 31. Parkman organized the New England Committee at the request of CMP (National) Chairman Patterson. Minutes of Executive Committee Meeting, Committee for the Marshall Plan, 26 November 1947. Executive Committee Minutes & Agenda 1947, CMP Papers, Box 1, HSTL.

25 See William L. Clayton to Hugh Moore, 11 May 1948; Hugh Moore to Karl Hoblitzelle, 24 May 1948; and Hugh Moore to William L. Clayton, 24 May 1948. William L. Clayton Papers, Box 78, HSTL. Will Clayton, a noted Texas cotton broker, was a key architect of the Marshall Plan, serving in the federal government from 1940–1947. For a rather favorable assessment of his role with the Marshall Plan, see Gregory A. Fossedal, *Our Finest Hour: Will Clayton, the Marshall Plan, and the Triumph of Democracy* (Stanford, CA: Hoover Institution, 1993).

26 Minutes of the CMP Executive Committee, 11 December 1947. Lehman Papers, General Correspondence, CMP.

27 Laird Bell to John H. Ferguson, 14 January 1948. Acheson Papers, Box 4, CMP: Correspondence, 1947–1948 [1 of 3], HSTL.

28 "Committee for the Marshall Plan—list of members by states," Dean Acheson papers, Box 3, Political and Governmental File (National Defense, Senator Langer Correspondence, Atomic Energy, Public Administration Clearing House, Committee for the Marshall Plan, Marshall Plan talks), HSTL. "Contributions ($500 and over)," attached to Form A, 8 January 1948 and 6 April 1948, CMP papers, Box 1, CMP—Lobbying Act forms file, HSTL. The 1940 census data is from Frank Hobbs and Nicole Stoops, Appendix A—Detailed Tables, Table 1—Total Population for the United States, Regions, and States: 1900 to 2000, *Demographic Trends in the 20th Century: Census 2000 Special Reports* (Washington, D.C.: U.S. Census Bureau, November 2002), A1.

29 CMP "National Council Members," Papers of Dean Acheson, Box 3, Politics and Governmental File (National Defense, Senator Langer Correspondence, Atomic Energy, Public Administration Clearing House, Committee for the Marshall Plan, Marshall Plan talks), CMP-list of members by states, Acheson (file), HSTL. Charles Taft was the brother of Senator Robert A. Taft (R-Ohio).

30 Eric Johnston, "Partnership Capitalism," *The Atlantic Monthly*, July 1947: 25–28.

31 See the featured clients page on The Oram Group's website, at http://www.oramgroup.com/03clients.html, accessed 1 June 2009. For the Oram Group and the AFV, see Joseph G. Morgan, *The Vietnam Lobby: The American Friends of Vietnam, 1955–1975* (Chapel Hill, NC: U of North Carolina P, 1997).

32 1947 CMP "Quarterly Payroll Report," "New York State Department of Labor," CMP Box 1, CMP-Income Tax Forms file, HSTL. "Executive Committee Meeting Minutes," 8 January 1948, CMP Box 1, CMP Executive Committee Minutes & Agenda, 1947 file. CMP Receipts for Contributions file, CMP Box 1, HSTL. "Contributions ($500 and Over)," attached to Form A dated 8 January 1948, CMP Box 1, CMP Lobbying Act forms (file), HSTL.

33 CMP Donation Receipt #7559, made out to Miss Lila J. Hood, County Extension Home Economist, Agriculture & Home Economics, Waterloo, Iowa, acknowledging a contribution of $1.40, 21 May 1948. CMP papers, CMP Receipts for Contributions file, CMP Box 1, HSTL.

34 Haskins & Sells CPA, "Accountant's Report," 30 August 1948, CMP Box 1, CMP Accountant's Report file, HST. Executive Director's Report on CMP Activities, HSTL.

35 Interview with Harold Stein, 7 August 1952. Oral History Interviews on the Marshall Plan, conducted by Harry B. Price, Folder: August-October, 1952, Papers of Harry B. Price, Box 1, HSTL.

36 Wala, *Council on Foreign Relations*, 263.

37 Ibid., 247.

38 "Munro Leaf, Author, Dead at 71; Creator of Ferdinand the Bull" (obituary), *New York Times*, 22 December 1976, 32. Samuel F. Wells, Jr., "Sounding the Tocsin: NSC 68 and the Soviet Threat," *International Security* 4.2 (1979): 146. "Times of their Lives: Nine Authors and Illustrators Look Back on Significant Chapters from their Illustrious Lives," *Publishers Weekly*, 20 February 1995, 132. "Ferdinand Makes His Screen Debut," *New York Times*, 23 October 1938, 165.

39 "Stop Hitler Now!" advertisement, *The New York Times*, 10 June 1946, 36. For details on Roosevelt's reaction, see Wala, *Council on Foreign Relation*, 176–77.

40 *Stop Stalin Now!*, Dean Acheson papers, Box 2, CMP correspondence 1947–1948 (folder 2) file,

HSTL. Michael H. Hunt, *Ideology and U.S. Foreign Policy* (New Haven, CT: Yale UP, 1987), 124, 154.

41 Hartley sketched out many of these themes in a letter to the editor in *The New York Times*, 25 November 1947, 28.

42 Livingston Hartley, *The Marshall Plan or Else* (Washington, D.C.: Public Affairs Press, 1948). Melvyn P. Leffler, *The Specter of Communism: The United States and the Origins of the Cold War, 1917–1953*, 1st ed. (New York: Hill and Wang, 1994), 62–63.

43 Americans for Democratic Action, *Toward Total Peace: A Liberal Foreign Policy for the United States* (Washington, D.C.: n.p., 1947), 34–35, 42–43.

44 Ibid., 42–43. N. Gordon Levin, *Woodrow Wilson and World Politics: America's Response to War and Revolution* (New York: Oxford UP, 1968), 4, 260.

45 *The Marshall Plan Is Up To You!* (New York: Committee for the Marshall Plan To Aid European Recovery), 4. Hartley, *Marshall Plan*, 1.

46 *The Marshall Plan Is Up To You!*, 5–7. Notably the definition of a "sucker" as "a greenhorn, simpleton," originated in North America, according to *Oxford English Dictionary (OED)* "sucker," definition 1b.

47 George C. Peden, "Economic Aspects of British Perceptions of Power on the Eve of the Cold War," in *Power in Europe? Great Britain, France, Italy, and Germany in a Postwar World, 1945–1950*, ed. Josef Becker and Franz Knipping (Berlin: Walter de Gruyter, 1986), 241.

48 Holland, "Beginning to Get Suspicious," *Chicago Tribune*, 1948, in Dean Acheson, Box 3, CMP correspondence, 1947–1948 (folder 2), Acheson file, HSTL.

49 *The Marshall Plan Is Up To You!*, 9, 15, 16, 18, 21.

50 Ibid., 21, 6. Lizabeth Cohen, *A Consumer's Republic: The Politics of Mass Consumption in Postwar America*, 1st Vintage Books ed. (New York: Vintage Books, 2004), 109.

51 *The Marshall Plan Is Up To You!*, 7. Cohen, *A Consumer's Republic*, 70, 109.

52 *The Marshall Plan Is Up To You!*, 20.

53 Munro Leaf, *Who is the Man Against the Marshall Plan?* (New York: Committee for the Marshall Plan), in CMP Box 3, Memoranda & Correspondence file, HSTL.

54 Ibid.

55 Ibid. Henry Agard Wallace, *Let's Come out Fighting* (New York: United Electrical Radio and Machine Workers of America, 1947), 14–15. Forrestal joined William A. Read and Company of New York (later Dillon, Read, and Company) in 1916 and remained with the firm (except during World War I), rising to become president in 1938, before leaving the firm in 1940 to become a special assistant to FDR. Harriman, son of railroad baron E.H. Harriman, in 1919 formed W.A. Harriman & Company, an investment house, and then co-founded Harriman Brothers & Company, a private bank, the next year. Both later joined with Brown Brothers to become Brown Brothers Harriman & Company.

56 Ibid.

57 Wunderlin, ed., *Papers of Robert A. Taft*, 375.

58 *The Churches and the European Recovery Plan* (New York: The Federal Council of the Churches of Christ in America, 1948), in the papers of J. Howard McGrath, Legislative File, Marshall Plan, HSTL.

59 Lucas, *Freedom's War*, 40. Lucas considers the CMP as "influential with key centers of opinion," although he is less sure about general public approval for the Marshall Plan. Bonds (*Bipartisan Strategy*, 190, 191) details the final vote tallies for Marshall Plan legislation. Bonds argues that "to the last, the issue had been in doubt," suggesting that approval of the Marshall Plan was a long, involved process (*Bipartisan Strategy*, 192). Wala argues that although "less successful with regard to the general public," the CMP "induced Congress to believe that the American people overwhelmingly supported Marshall's initiative" (*Council on Foreign Relations*, 214).

Section II:

Media Representations of the Marshall Plan in a Comparative European Context

David W. Ellwood

Film and the Marshall Plan

The Picture Today

Marshall Plan films are fashionable. Marshall Plan propaganda is fashionable. The recent surge of interest in it is remarkable, especially in the last three or four years. For three years, a special section of the Berlin Film Festival covered it,[1] and in 2006 the New York Film Festival had special section on it. Two new documentaries were aired on the Arte television channel in 2007—from Belgium and Greece—for the sixtieth anniversary. Two BBC radio programs in three years covered it; the latest was broadcast in spring 2008. The one-woman campaign by Sandra Schulberg, daughter of a Marshall Plan filmmaker, brought the films to light again, especially in Berlin and various parts of the United States. Recently, the Central State Archive of Rome put out the official catalogue of the remarkable collection of over 500 items of film material deposited in the Prefettura of Trieste between 1947 and 1959, now available to researchers in Rome, and containing much European Recovery Program (ERP) material.[2]

Books? Victoria de Grazia's classic, of course, discusses it. Greg Behrman's colorful celebration briefly pays tribute to it. Brian McKenzie's volume on France is the most substantial yet on the fate of the propaganda campaign as a whole in a single nation, while Barry Machado's new volume, sponsored by the George Marshall Foundation, includes a whole chapter on the theme.[3] Meanwhile, conferences of young researchers, such as the one in Dublin in January 2008, give it special space, and there are big doctoral theses, such as David Snyder's on The Netherlands, and the one Regina Longo is preparing at the University of California (Los Angeles), specially dedicated to the films.[4] Linda and Eric Christenson, those indefatigable film gatherers, surely know of more, especially in the United States. Today, no serious discussion of the Marshall Plan, unless it's focused on hardcore economics, would dream of overlooking the propaganda/information/education/ psychological warfare dimension of the effort. This emphasis is new.

Observers might speculate for some time as to why the new wave of interest should have built up over the last few years. As the Behrman and Machado volumes of celebration show, some of the reasons are pretty obvious and hardly need emphasizing. Beyond them, it's obvious that the myth of the Marshall Plan lives, and many can make lists of worldwide appeals to its magic inspiration.

I have long believed that the myth of the Marshall Plan was born under the Plan itself and represents the greatest, most enduring triumph of the European Recovery Program information/propaganda effort. I am convinced that the film program was at the heart of that effort. But the films functioned integrally and achieved their greatest effects in the presence of all the many other forms of Marshall Plan communication, as well as the U.S. mass-media wave in general, brought over by a variety of public and private agencies, including Hollywood.

Was this the greatest international propaganda/information program ever seen in peace-time, as I have long believed? I have been openly attacked by Barry Machado, the Marshall Foundation man, in his new book, for saying so. "Hasn't this guy ever heard of the Cominform?" asks Machado. Perhaps he doesn't like my use of the word "propaganda" in this context. I insist that the Marshall Plan's use of it was the result of a much greater and more conscious effort than Machado would acknowledge. It enjoyed the support of sixteen national governments, their broadcasting systems, and their newspaper allies; it functioned everywhere in these nations at all levels of society, not just among the working masses of two or three key countries; it was flanked by the ongoing efforts of the U.S. Information Service (USIS); it spoke the language of concrete results and physical goods on a scale which was—for a short while—unmatched; finally, it used an infinite number of media, including—indirectly—Hollywood, in a crescendo of inventiveness. The crucial elections of April 1948 in Italy show the difference such efforts made. Financed in part by the Soviets, the Left bloc mobilized through mass rallies and demonstrations, speeches, poster campaigns, magazines, and newspapers. The conservative bloc, aided in secret by the United States, could count on the government and its media, the Vatican, a great private mobilization by Italo-Americans, and allies in the conservative media. While the Left relied on the spoken and printed word, the Right mobilized *film*—newsreels, documentaries, and ideological propaganda—and showed that it understood the vastly superior charisma and penetrating and persuasive power of the moving image. It was a lesson the Marshall Plan information officers in Italy, a key country, never forgot.

In 1990, a post-Cold War conference in Bologna compared the fate of the U.S. and Soviet myths in Italy over the previous forty-five years. A leading left-wing intellectual of the time, Enzo Forcella, exclaimed at one point: "The myths of America kept their promises and won through!"[5] It turned out he was referring to images he had seen in films in 1949 of American workers driving to work at the wheel of their own cars, an unimaginable notion in the poverty-stricken, divided Italy of that epoch. We always worry about "reception" when we talk of Marshall Plan films; well, there's an example, spanning forty-one years. But the point here is another: we have no way of knowing whether Forcella saw those images in a Hollywood film, a USIS documentary, an ERP product, in some combination of them, or somewhere else. Historically, then, the ERP material should not be separated from the circumstances of its immediate production in all their dimensions at home and abroad. More emphatically of course, it must never be considered in isolation from the full, multi-layered context of its consumption.

So why should we concentrate our attention especially on the Marshall Plan film material? Hollywood's features were and are made to supply entertainment, though, of course, they have always done much more than that, and the Marshall Planners knew it. USIS documentaries were made very explicitly to advertise a foreign policy, a set of Cold War values and norms, and a vision of the U.S. way of life. Marshall Plan films were made to sell one extraordinary, unprecedented, temporary, highly technical, ever-evolving *project*. They had to help convince Americans, especially those in power who came over to check the results, who were a very important audience. More directly, the films were made to change the minds of *all* the peoples of sixteen quite disparate nations, peoples with vastly different levels of education, income, political awareness, power, and heritages of attitudes towards the United States. Not only were they supposed to persuade, the films were also called upon to inform, to educate, and—in the end—to convert. They were an integral part of the ERP as a Cold War weapon, and at the same time, they aimed to get as close as possible to those the Program was supposed to be benefiting in order to channel attitudes, mentalities, and expectations in the direction of progress as Americans understood it, the direction of the mass production for mass consumption modernization explained so well by Victoria de Grazia.

"You, too, can be like us"; that was the (implied) message of Marshall Plan information, an invitation to emulation which tended to disguise the fact that the effort was about enablement, not empowerment, and was deeply conditional in its method and timing.[6] In other words, *if* the Europeans followed the U.S. prescriptions in the right way and quickly, they could reasonably expect to see a transformation of their living standards.

The ERP Choice of Cinema as the Key Means of Persuasion[7]

There is no mystery about the operating principles which the information staff (mainly journalists and broadcasters, *not* advertisers or public relations people), applied in their campaign. They were arrived at fairly quickly and changed little up to the outbreak of the Korean War. A January 1950 report by the information director in Rome explained, "Carry the message of the Marshall Plan to the people. Carry it to them directly—it won't permeate down. And give it to them so that they can understand it."

The basic thrust, then, was for a truly mass program using "every method possible [...] to reach Giuseppe in the factory or Giovanni in the fields," or as the Paris office put it, "slugging it out way down among the masses." More specifically, ERP information divisions were expected to increase the sense of national identification and participation in the Plan and to direct special attention to key target groups, particularly trade unionists, agricultural workers, housewives (as managers of the "economics of the household"), and executives in business, industry, and the government. They were also enjoined to avoid direct confrontation with the massive waves of Communist propaganda directed against the Plan. Above all, they were requested to be respectful of every form of local sovereignty and avoid accusations of "interference."

When applied on the ground, these methods proved extremely flexible, and no idea seemed too large or daring for the Information program in its heyday. As long as they were directed at workers, managers, or employers, the keywords were always mass production, scientific management, and, above all, productivity. In each country, there were specialized reviews on the subject, joint committees, trips to inspect U.S. factories, conferences, and eventually, in some places, even "productivity villages" where model factories and workers' communities could be seen in action. For other groups in society—government employees, teachers, families, even school children—the promises were more jobs, higher living standards, peace in Europe through cooperation, and trade. With special treatments of these questions for each different communications medium, the Information Program came to express its ideas in terms of tens of documentary films, hundreds of radio programs, thousands of mobile film shows, millions of copies of its pamphlets, and tens of millions of spectators for its exhibitions and movie events.

On the U.S. Senate floor in July 1950, in words reminiscent of Vladimir Lenin and Benito Mussolini as well as Woodrow Wilson, the cinema was lauded as "the most powerful means we have" for communicating "this American story" to the world. Senator Alexander Wiley of Wisconsin paid tribute to the Hollywood industry, the United States' film culture, and the role of the government in using cinema abroad in the Cold War struggle. As for the Marshall Plan, Congress was told that in the whole of Western Europe fifty ERP documentaries and newsreels were circulating, seen every week by upwards of 40 million people, divided between 30 million for the newsreels and 10 million for the documentaries. They would cover subjects as diverse as tourism in New York, new methods for breeding livestock, a sample of U.S. newsreels, and the latest techniques in plastic surgery. There was a significant number of titles dedicated to showing progress in U.S. agriculture and industry. "Our enquiries in various countries," commented the ERP Information Division, "have shown to us the great potential of the cinema in transmitting information in ways that spectators can understand, believe and remember."

Intense discussion developed among the information experts regarding how to translate into film language the two abstract concepts which were the most difficult to treat, yet the most important for the entire ERP project: productivity and European integration. Two classic documentaries were the outcome of this debate: *Productivity—Key to Plenty* and the animated cartoon *The Shoemaker and the Hatter,* a remarkable explanation of the principles of markets and the division of labor. Films such as these were seen in all the participating countries and accompanied specially-made newsreels which showed the Marshall Plan at work in a variety of them.

The first documentaries, in 16mm black and white film, were distributed as trailers to accompany the main features in first-run and second-run cinemas in towns throughout the participating nations. In poorer countries, the films were also transported by van into the remotest villages. No medium worked better in lands where illiteracy was high and cinemas were found only in the larger towns. Audience estimates talked of "four, five or six million spectators" for each product in Italy. The Rome mission told Congress in January 1950: "The Italian people like color and life, hence the Mission decided that they must be informed through color and life [...] The Italians like entertainment, and this fact has been remembered too. In the movie projections put on by the sound trucks of the Mission, it is not unusual—and it is very gratifying to the crowd—to see a Mickey Mouse animated cartoon." As was the case so often in the United States' modernizing efforts in the world, the medium was the message, or at least one of them.

The Phase of Disappointment

But the Americans were never to be satisfied with the progress achieved by their early efforts at connecting up entertainment, persuasion, and education. Just explaining what the Marshall Plan was turned out to be far harder than expected. The first head of the information effort was Al Friendly, a very prominent journalist in his time, well presented in Barry Machado's book. He commented later: "The idea that one nation would transfer part of its current output to a group of other nations, with very few strings attached and for the benefit of all, was too paradoxical for easy acceptance." There were other difficulties. The campaign had been set up in part because, as Friendly put it, not only did the Europeans not know about U.S. aid, "they don't even know their own countries are cooperating with each other." Yet the ERP was intended especially to promote European self-help, stimulating cooperation and coordination without outside interference. Thus a basic tension emerged in the campaign which sometimes worked creatively, often not, especially as this weakness was exploited ceaselessly by the Communist movement's aggressive campaign of opposition. The director of the Industrial Division in Holland said pithily: "[T]he United States was paying the piper and it was always a great problem how loudly we could call the tune."

The self-evident rightness of the Plan's goals and methods turned out to be harder to project than expected, and gradually awareness spread of the difficulties of applying abstract principles and concepts to complex and often chaotic local situations with the communications techniques of the day. The outcome was frustration with the short-term results, especially when measured in terms of the rise and fall of support for Leftist parties and unions. "[T]he European workman listens listlessly while we tell him we are saving Europe, unconvinced that it *his* Europe we are saving," complained a senior staff member in Paris in September 1949.

In the early days, it had not been difficult for the Information Officers to perceive that the working people of Europe were not particularly interested in the Marshall Plan battle against Communism. Even less did they show any faith in the Plan's hope of continent-wide financial stability by 1952 because this, in the popular view, meant stability for the traditional ruling groups, not for them. Instead, said an expert in the Paris headquarters, "what the European workman mainly wants, I believe, is a promise of a larger stake in his country's economy—enough income to enjoy better food, a new suit, a picnic or the movies, less cramped quarters, a chance to retire when he is old."

By the end of 1949, experience and extensive opinion polling had brought a significant shift in outlook, to the point where the strategists felt obliged to realize that "the majority of Europeans today" had one over-riding concern of their own: *security*. What did they mean by security? It was easy to state: "employment, health and old-age benefits. It means further that a man's life, when begun, contains the reasonable assurance and expectation of a rational progress towards a reasonable conclusion." But the basic ERP objectives of higher productivity and European "economic unification" would not be affected in any way, felt the writer, since only by these means could the Europeans, in fact, achieve the social security they so anxiously sought.

From the summer of 1950 onward, the organization of the information campaign changed in response to the recognized need for more effective contact with local reality. The new urgency induced by the outbreak of the Korean War was also much in evidence. In a country like Italy, a system of subcontracts began to delegate to local scriptwriters and directors the fabrication of film propaganda material, using schemes furnished by the sponsor, but translated into the visual and spoken language of the Italian context. In the films of the Organizzazione Epoca, the United States was, as such, nowhere to be seen. Instead, they displayed the Italian achievements of the Plan: new housing projects, efforts to boost agriculture, irrigation schemes, and make-work projects of every kind, always collective efforts which would provide employment, security, and implicitly hope of a better life to come for the mass of the population.[8]

In 1952, devolution persuaded the Irish mission to sponsor a docudrama entitled *The Promise of Barty O'Brien,* written by the prominent writer Sean O'Faolain and acted by professionals from the Abbey Theatre in Dublin. This striking film makes no effort to hide the conflicts which arise when the propositions of U.S.-style modernity, represented in this case by the electrification of a poor Irish farm, meet the resistance of traditional ways. The farmer's son becomes a technician, thanks to ERP help, but the old man resists until the final proof of the benefits of electric current are—with the turn of a switch—lit up for all to see. Respect is paid to the centrality of agriculture in Ireland's life and prospects, and the difficulties of the country's struggle to reconcile traditional identities with the call of modernity are faced directly.[9]

In contrast, the mission in France never learned how to build up the local production of means of persuasion, much less a demand for them. In 1952, *Jour de Peine* was released, in principle a film homage to the struggle of French factory workers trying to organize a strike for better wages. But in a situation of intense political and social tension, its pro-consensus ending angered everyone, and there were calls for it to be changed or not shown at all. Whether fighting communism or boosting their vision of democratic progress, commented government officials, the Americans had failed to "'understand and love' the country in which they were called to operate [...] It is indispensable to know its history, traditions, and principles, but even more important and difficult is to sense the beat of its heart." The benevolent audacity of the Plan had backfired, said these views, because "the French refuse to admit that without America France would not exist." One estimate suggested that three-quarters of the films produced by the ERP were such an insult to French national pride that they could not be shown in France.[10]

A Longer View

But detailed analysis of European attitudes about the United States supplied to U.S. intelligence services by an anonymous Italian observer in 1953 suggested not only the limits, but also something of the successes of the United States' efforts at changing attitudes and mentalities. "Ninety-five percent of all Europeans—friends and enemies of America—judge American society by what they see at the cinema," said the report. It went on to declare that from Hollywood's products many had taken away a dreadful impression of the country, of its crime and corruption, and of the venality and brutality of its ruling groups in particular. But the medium

> [...] was useful above all in reinforcing the European admiration for the American standard of living, for American technique. A Plymouth or a Chevrolet is considered a great luxury even in countries, such as Italy, which have important car industries of their own. The possession of a refrigerator is sufficient on its own to identify a family as belonging to the richest levels of the bourgeoisie. Undoubtedly film has given the US a propaganda triumph, to the extent that it has reminded Europeans of their traditionally optimistic vision of the "American paradise."[11]

The propaganda effort of the Marshall Plan turned American myth into American model, and together with Hollywood cinema, fed what a senior ERP man called the "revolution of rising expectations," that grand twentieth-century democratic transformation which led "the ordinary citizen (to demand) that he share in the benefits of industrialism," as another American thinker put it.[12] The technocrats' attempt to modernize institutions and attitudes on what they believed was the United States' own pattern represented the highest point, the most explicit one, in that twentieth-century trend which super-imposed the U.S. model of modernization on whatever efforts European societies were making to meet the great contemporary challenges of mass democracy, mass production, and mass communications. As one of the ERP's most influential brains, Richard M. Bissell, explained in 1951, the United States could lead most effectively by the force of its example and its powerful appeal across all sections of European society:

> Coca-Cola and Hollywood movies may be regarded as two products of a shallow and crude civilization. But American machinery, American labor relations, and American management and engineering are everywhere respected [...]. What is needed is a peaceful revolution which can incorporate into the European economic system certain established and attractive features of our own, ranging from high volumes to collective bargaining [... this] will require a profound shift in social attitudes, attuning them to the mid-twentieth century.[13]

Every participating nation in the Marshall Plan showed examples of how this reformism was blunted, how difficult it was to manage interdependence when the U.S.

and Western European sides believed in such different ideas of what the road to the future should be.[14] But on one point all the players were united: if Europe could grow economically using the U.S. model or some local variation of it, everything might be possible. Moreover, when the Old World's "economic miracle" did, indeed, finally arrive after 1954, "catch-up growth" on the Marshall Plan model would turn out to be one of the greatest forces driving it onwards and upwards.

Notes

1 This produced a DVD containing samples of ERP films and, in 2006, the book *Selling Democracy: Friendly Persuasion*, edited Rainer Rother, both published by the Deutschen Historiches Museum, Berlin.

2 Giulia Barrera and Giovanna Tosatti, eds., *United States Information Service di Trieste: Catalogo del fondo cinematografico, 1941-1966* (Rome: Ministero per I Beni e le Attività Culturali, 2007).

3 Victoria de Grazia, *Irresistible Empire: America's Advance through Twentieth-Century Europe* (Cambridge, MA: Harvard UP, 2005), 345–50; Greg Behrman, *The Most Noble Adventure: The Marshall Plan and the Time when America Helped Save Europe* (New York: Free, 2007), 292–93; Brian Angus McKenzie, *Remaking France: Americanization, Public Diplomacy, and the Marshall Plan* (New York: Berghahn Books, 2005); Barry Machado, *In Search of a Usable Past: The Marshall Plan and Postwar Reconstruction Today* (Lexington, VA: George C. Marshall Foundation, 2007), Chapter 2.

4 "Propaganda and the Mass Media in the Making of Cold War Europe," 11–13 January 2007, University College Dublin; David J. Snyder, "U.S. Public Diplomacy in the New Netherlands, 1945–1958: Policy, Ideology, and the Instrumentality of American Power," PhD. diss., Southern Illinois University, Carbondale, Dec. 2006.

5 Conference proceedings in P.P. D'Attorre ed., *Nemici per la pelle: Sogno americano e mito sovietico nell'Italia contemporanea* (Milan: Angeli, 1991); Forcella's intervention is conserved on audiotape at the Istituto Gramsci, Bologna.

6 Victoria de Grazia points out elsewhere in this collection that the ERP did not promise high mass consumption as a direct result of its efforts. But the word "prosperity" often appeared, and in such a fashion as to suggest that prosperity need not be stable, but could be expanded infinitely.

7 These pages are based on Ellwood, "The Propaganda of the Marshall Plan in Italy in a Cold War Context," in *The Cultural Cold War in Western Europe 1945–1960*, ed. Giles Scott-Smith and Hans Krabbendam (London: Frank Cass, 2003), and Ellwood, "Italian Modernization and the Propaganda of the Marshall Plan," in *The Art of Persuasion: Political Communication in Italy from 1945 to the 1990s*, ed. L. Cheles and L. Sponza (Manchester: Manchester UP, 2001).

8 In the Rome/Trieste catalogue (see note 2) which includes forty-nine ERP titles, over half present results, as compared to twelve to fourteen on economic education in general, ten technical training films, and two docudramas.

9 Bernadette Whelan, *Ireland and the Marshall Plan, 1947–1957* (Dublin: Four Courts, 2000), 379–81.

10 McKenzie, *Remaking France*, 235.

11 Original citation in Ellwood, "Italian Modernization," 44; the Dutch reception of the full spectrum of U.S. film products was much more ambiguous and skeptical; see Snyder, "U.S. Public," 497–98.

12 Harlan A. Cleveland, "Reflections on the "Revolution of Rising Expectations," Address at Colgate University, 9 July 1950, in National Archives, Record Group 469, Assistant Administrator for Program, Deputy Assistant Administrator, Subject Files of Harlan Cleveland; Perry Miller, "The Reimportation of Ideas," in *The Impact of America on European Culture*, ed. Bertrand Russell et. al. (Boston: Beacon, 1951), 85; Miller's article was the response of a distinguished American literary critic to a series of essays by English and an Irish writer on the subject of the title.

13 Richard M. Bissell, Jr., "The Impact of Rearmament on the Free World Economy," *Foreign Affairs* (April 1951): 385–405, here 404–05.

14 The Dutch example of this truth is illustrated in Snyder, "U.S. Public," Chapter 5, on technical assistance.

Hans-Jürgen Schröder

Visualizing the Marshall Plan in Western Germany:

Films, Exhibits, Posters

When Secretary of State George C. Marshall announced a European Recovery Program (ERP) in his famous speech of 5 June 1947 at Harvard University, one could not have predicted that this Marshall Plan would be the most successful foreign aid program ever.[1] In part, this success was due to a massive propaganda campaign unprecedented in times of peace. A huge propaganda machine was set in motion by both the United States and the European countries that received Marshall Plan aid. In the respective bilateral treaties with the U.S. government, the recipient countries agreed to "recognize that it is in their mutual interest that full publicity be given to the objectives and progress of the joint program for European recovery." It was also "recognized that wide dissemination of information on the progress of the program is desirable in order to develop the sense of common effort and mutual aid" which "are essential to the accomplishment of the objectives of the program."[2] In the following, the term "propaganda" that has been discredited by totalitarian regimes is used in the sense of the general definition of the *Oxford English Dictionary* as the "systematic propagation of information or ideas by an interested party."[3]

Given this definition, Marshall Plan propaganda had four major goals:

1. to convince the population in the recipient countries by explaining the economic and political goals of ERP: economic recovery and political stability;
2. to win support at home (Congress and the public at large);
3. to contain Soviet influence and to "counteract" Communist propaganda efforts, primarily in Europe: liberal capitalism and democracy vs. state socialism and tyranny; and
4. to neutralize ambitions of the European non-communist left (NCL) to establish Europe as a so-called "third force."

In their propaganda efforts, the U.S. government and European Marshall Plan officials took full advantage of a broad spectrum of traditional and modern mass media such as newspapers, postcards, photos, posters, brochures, stickers, radio, and film. Until a few years ago, many of these sources had largely been neglected by historians who traditionally have concentrated their research on textual sources. This neglect of audio and visual sources is particularly true for moving images. In the 1990s, one of the former members of the Marshall Plan administration, Albert Hemsing, drew attention to the significance of the Marshall Plan film program for historical research.[4] Under the auspices of the Economic Cooperation Administration (ECA), more than 250 films had been produced primarily in Europe, the bulk of which are accessible at the National Archives of the United States at College Park, Maryland, and various film archives in Europe.[5] Thanks to the research undertaken by Linda Christenson and her excellent filmography, we are now well-informed about the scope of the ECA film program.[6] During the past few years, a selection of Marshall Plan films has repeatedly been presented to the public both in the United States and in Europe under the slogan "Selling Democracy."[7] The Berlin film festival's Berlinale of the years 2004, 2005, and 2006 might be cited as widely publicized examples.[8] On the occasion of the 2006 Berlin film festival, a selection of films was published on DVD by the German Federal Agency for Civic Education under the title *Selling Democracy: Die Filme des Marshallplans/The Films of the Marshall Plan*.[9] However, most historians of the twentieth century have not yet "discovered" the Marshall Plan films as source material. This is amazing because these moving images offer important insight into U.S. diplomatic strategies toward Europe after World War II, the Cold War propaganda battle, the economic reconstruction of Western Europe, and the origins of the European integration process.

In this context, Austria and Germany were of particular importance. Both countries and their capitals were divided into four occupational zones, and both countries had common borders with the emerging Eastern bloc. Given their geopolitical situations, both countries seemed particularly exposed to Communist propaganda. But the countries' proximity to the Soviet bloc opened opportunities also for U.S. propaganda inroads into the East. Therefore, it is no surprise that Austria and Germany were of key importance for U.S. Marshall Plan propaganda. In the following, Germany serves as a case study to present some major elements of the Marshall Plan film program. These are supplemented by remarks on Marshall Plan exhibits and posters in Western Germany.

Film

In the context of the Marshall Plan film program, Germany had two vital functions. First of all, West Germany was an integral part of and a typical example for the application of the film program in all recipient countries. Many Marshall Plan films were voiced in German to better reach the West German audience. In addition, some moving images addressed specific German problems. The broad spectrum of Marshall Plan films is reflected in six major categories: newsreels, documentaries, feature films, cartoons, productivity films, and—in the case of Germany—(re-)orientation films. Characterizations of these categories will be presented in the following. The enclosed DVD and accompanying website contains typical examples for each of these categories.

Newsreels

Since the 1930s, newsreels had become an important instrument of information and propaganda.[10] Thus it is no surprise that the Economic Cooperation Administration had included this medium in their film activities. Two series were produced in the early 1950s: ERP in Action[11] and 1-2-3: A Monthly Review from Europe.[12] These newsreels which were "dedicated to stories of social progress, international cooperation, productivity, and strength through security" presented documentary evidence on the progress of the European Recovery Program. Each issue dealt with at least three Marshall Plan recipient countries in order to stress the broad approach of the ERP and the cooperative European character of the whole undertaking. The two examples on the attached DVD include features on France, Greece, the BENELUX states, and West Germany. The section on Germany focuses on the dynamic preparations for the 1950 Berlin Industrial Exhibition. The monthly report 1-2-3 was also voiced in German and shown as *Europa im Bild*.[13]

More important for West Germany, however, was the newsreel *Welt im Film*.[14] This joint U.S.-British venture was an excellent instrument to enlist the Germans' support for U.S. policy in West Germany and to counteract the East German newsreel *Der Augenzeuge*.[15] After George Marshall's Harvard speech, *Welt im Film* was used regularly by the Office of Military Government (OMGUS) and (after the founding of the Federal Republic) by the High Commission for Germany (HICOG) to explain the Marshall Plan's goals and to document its progress in West Germany and Europe.[16] Parts of ERP in Action, the 1-2-3, and the *Welt im Film* footage were later used for the compilation of Marshall Plan documentaries in West Germany.

Documentaries

Most Marshall Plan films were documentaries. Their main purpose was to represent visually the goals and achievements of the European Recovery Program. Among the numerous productions are three series that merit special mention: The Marshall Plan at Work, Strength for the Free World, and The Changing Face of Europe. The Marshall Plan at Work dealt with specific aspects of twelve individual ERP recipient countries. However, they were not primarily produced to inform the audiences in the respective countries. Their main purpose was to visualize how specific country approaches fit into the overall efforts for European recovery. The series' documentary *The Marshall Plan at Work in Western Germany*[17]with its focus on one country is a typical example. However, it also represents a special case, since it had to deal with Germany's dual role as a former enemy and as a participant in the ERP.

The film's creators put the reconstruction of West Germany in a larger European framework by emphasizing the indisputable interdependence of the German and the European economies; Germany was presented as both a market and a producer for most European countries: "Today, industrial Germany is still the factory of Europe." The filmmakers leave no doubt that the nations of Europe "need her goods as they never did before. The wheels of Europe are still closely geared to the wheels of German industry." This interdependence is convincingly represented by interlocking cogwheels, while the spoken text draws attention to the grim alternative: "The recovery of Europe must surely lag and falter until these German factories are in full production once again." But West German recovery is not seen as an end in itself; West Germany's reconstruction is presented as a necessary step towards overall European reconstruction. Both the West German economic structure and the close interdependence of Germany's economy with that of other European nations left no alternative. Some argue that this seemed to be the only way to justify economic support for a country that was responsible for war and economic chaos. The concentration on strictly economic problems obviously was a strategy to avoid political criticism from countries that had been victims of Nazi aggression or from the American taxpayer who only a few years earlier had bought saving bonds to contribute to Germany's defeat. However, students of history should not lose sight of the political dimension. By stressing West Germany's economic contribution to European recovery, one could also argue that Germany belonged to the European family and, therefore, should no longer be regarded as an outcast. Economic necessities made it imperative to overcome political antagonisms that had shaped Europe's past. As to the other films of the series, such political arguments were unnecessary, since all other recipient countries had been victims of Nazi aggression. This also applies to Austria as can be seen in *The Marshall Plan at Work in Austria.*[18]

The series Strength for the Free World was started in 1952 after the European Recovery Program had shifted its priorities from economic recovery to Western defense. The militarization of the Marshall Plan is already reflected in the subtitle and the opening statement:

> A weekly program presenting documentary evidence of the progress the free world is making for its strength through mutual security. On this foundation of greater economic and social strength the rearmament of the allied nations is being built. All around the world the free people are uniting to resist war and to withstand aggression. These films produced abroad by the people of the free nations present new evidence of their will and strength for a lasting peace.

The most important production of the series is *Your Eighty Dollars.*[19]

The film *Your Eighty Dollars* is a report to the American taxpayers who had spent roughly eighty dollars per capita to rescue Europe from economic misery and the threat of Communism. After all, these eighty dollars were a sound investment not only in European reconstruction after the war, but also in the security of the United States and the free world at large. In a year-by-year chronology, the economic and political achievements are presented visually. By dramatizing ideological challenges from Communism and military threats from alleged Soviet expansion, the filmmakers created the impression that the military build-up of the West was an urgent necessity. After 1948 and 1949—the years of peril and decision—the economic turnaround in Europe had become visible in 1950—"the year of expansion." But in an increasingly hostile international environment and especially after the Communist aggression in Korea, military preparedness in the West had become a priority. Therefore, 1951 had become "the year of defense," and in this context, Europe was of vital importance: "Europe is still the decision area in any world conflict of any kind. Her wealth can make its controller ruler of most if not all of the earth."

Developments in Europe are the central theme of the series The Changing Face of Europe. The series' six films are progress reports about what had already been achieved in Western Europe by 1950 in such important fields as agriculture and industry (*Three Hundred Million Mouths* and *Men and Machines*), housing (*Somewhere to Live*), transport (*Clearing the Lines*), health (*The Good Life*), and energy (*Power for All*). Despite the overall positive balance sheet, the films leave no doubt that much more needed to be done. There still are too many man-made barriers in Europe which have to be overcome. Through the free movement of people, ideas, goods, and capital, the European nations must intensify their cooperation and ultimately become one greater unit. "We must declare our desire for a single Europe," is the message of the series' film *Clearing the Line*.[20]

The bulk of the Marshall Plan documentaries were not part of specific series. They were either so-called "one-country" productions or devoted to topics of interest for all recipient countries. A broad spectrum of themes was covered.

Again and again, the United States' desire for Europe to unite was visualized and sometimes dramatized against the background of the Cold War. Europeans had to make a choice. It was *The Hour of Choice*[21]as a 1951 production suggests, that was also voiced in the German version, *Die Stunde der Entscheidung*."[22] The film begins with a look back at this "complex continent" called Europe. Despite a common cultural legacy, Europe had always been divided by frontiers: "Down the centuries the frontiers have stood marking the differences of geography and race," and "we cannot remember a time when Europe did not know these symbols of our separation." The peoples of Europe seemed to be "content to enjoy each behind the separate barrier." Europeans were "partners, yet rivals—friends, yet strangers—allies, yet antagonists." When talking about unity, "unity in difference" was the answer: "Unity in difference, that was the formula to cover the conflicts in our lives. Unity in difference, it seemed to be the doctrine that was sensible, mature; a triumph of high civilization."

The film notes, however, that the Second World War had brought about fundamental change in Europe: "Unity in difference—in the shock and ruin of two fearful wars that dream has vanished." The filmmakers' lesson for the future is clear: "In difference there can be no unity. At last we have awakened to stern and stubborn facts," the narrator explains. Winston Churchill is presented as witness to the necessity of European cooperation. In his famous Zurich speech of 1946, the former Prime Minister had called for European unity: "We must build a kind of United States of Europe. If Europe were once united [...] there would be no limit to the happiness, to the prosperity and the glory which its three or four hundred million people would enjoy. [...] Let Europe arise!"[23]

On the long road towards European unity, some important steps had already been realized. In particular, the film draws attention to the Schuman Plan and the Council of Europe. But even more important seemed to be the first signs of economic recovery. These "miracles of reconstruction" had only been possible because

Europeans had "set aside the difference for a common good." These common efforts "from the North of Norway to the toe of Italy" had produced "astonishing success." But this progress was primarily due to help from the United States: "Across the Atlantic stands a mighty nation born of our own diversity, made one for many by the voluntary will of forty-eight United States in difference." Marshall's Harvard message is referred to as "a soldier's voice but speaking now in terms of selfless statesmanship." The announcement of the Marshall Plan is described as the catalyst for European recovery: "European ideas and work, American materials and machines, these together have transformed Europe in the last few years, raised from ruins to new life and hope."

European unity was vital for the continent's survival, but this unity alone would not be sufficient, would not yet guarantee the survival of Europe. Allegedly, European recovery could only be achieved in a transatlantic framework. In blunt terms, the Europeans were informed that they "have been awakened to the harsh reality that Western Europe is no longer the undisputed center of the world." This transatlantic context is particularly important when it comes to "the crucial question of our own defense." While Western Europe is dependent on the United States to resist potential attacks from the East, Europe's economic contribution to Western defense is regarded as vital for the security of the Free World. "In the North Atlantic Treaty organization we have made still another act of faith, made a start towards pooling men and materials and resources for the common security of the Western world." Moreover, as "we in Europe show in growing strength our confidence to resist attack, so we may expect the nations of North America to join with us in all their might." The "pledge of their support" is presented in a statement by General Dwight D. Eisenhower. Finally, the narrator concludes: "At last we have realized that the only guarantee of safety that we have lies in the united forces of our united peoples. [...] Let the barriers banish, for today we need every ounce of strength that our united effort can put forward."

Despite their obvious dependence on the United States, Europeans were told that they have any number of reasons to be proud:

> Look at us Europeans: 200 million men and women, able, versatile, intelligent, look at our power to produce. Without the barriers between us our productivity could fulfil far more than peacetime needs; combined with that of friends across the ocean it could be overwhelming if war should thrust upon us. [...] Let the barriers banish. For all that we possess of energy and skill can only yield its full reward if we are united in aim, in mind, in heart, in action. Let those who follow say of us that in the hour of choice we chose the cause of duty to each other, that through the unity of Europe we brought the world closer to the unity of all mankind.

There is no doubt that *The Hour of Choice* is also a reminder that even the one-country films must always be seen in the European and the transatlantic framework of the Marshall Plan.

Re-Orientation/Orientation Films

Some of the one-country films about Germany were produced by U.S. film units in that country. From the very beginning, the documentary film medium was a vital part of U.S. occupational policy. The OMGUS Documentary Film Unit had produced a number of films that specifically addressed the Germans with the primary goal of fostering the process of democratization.[24] The initial work had been prepared by the so-called "German Committee" with the goal "to create a program of re-information and indoctrination, following German defeat, for occupied Austria and Germany." This information program "was to assist future occupational authorities in trying to make the Germans and the Austrians people with whom the rest of us might live in peace."[25] What was first called re-education was later called re-orientation or just orientation films. After the founding of the Federal Republic of Germany and the dissolution of OMGUS, the film activities were taken care of by the Office of the High Commissioner for Germany (HICOG). The primary purpose of both OMGUS and HICOG's film production was to enlist West German support for U.S reconstruction policy in Germany. With West Germany's inclusion into the European Recovery Program, these productions became an integral part of Marshall Plan propaganda in Germany. Typical examples are *Me and Mr. Marshall*[26] and *Made in Germany*.[27]

Me and Mr. Marshall was produced "under the auspices of Information Control Division, Office of Military Government for Germany (U.S.), as part of the reorientation program for the German people. It is now being shown, both commercially and non-commercially, throughout the U.S. zone of Germany."[28] The narrator is Hans Fischer, a young German who had decided to work in the Ruhr coal mines. He presents his experience as a newcomer in the coal mining business and shares with the audience his reflections on his job in the pit and the importance of coal for both German and European economic developments: "Coal is the crux of the whole thing." Hans describes conditions in Germany and Europe after the war and explains why something had to be done to reverse the "vicious circle" that hampered economic recovery: "[...] there is not enough coal because there is not enough machinery—there is not enough machinery because there is not enough steel—and there is not enough steel because there is not enough coal." He also draws attention to the agricultural sector: "No farm equipment—no food; no food—no production; no production—no exports; no exports—no imports; no imports—no farm equipment; no farm equipment—no food; and you are back were you started, with nothing." But thanks to George Marshall's initiative, these downward trends could be stopped and ultimately reversed. The film draws attention to the mechanisms of the European Recovery Program. These are explained by George Marshall himself, and efforts by the United States to revive production through a kind of "pump priming" by infusing U.S. dollars are presented visually by animated graphics. While George Marshall provides the grand design and U.S. dollars, Hans Fischer's hard work in the German Ruhr mines is visible evidence of individual contributions to make the Marshall Plan a success. At the end of the film, Fischer expresses confidence in the European Recovery Program when he identifies himself as "an employee of Mister Marshall."

While *Me and Mr. Marshall* concentrates on the problem of coal supplies, the focus of *Made in Germany* is on German industrial exports. The film stresses the importance of German exports for West Germany's economic recovery and asserts that Germany has to be made "self-supporting again through normal export-import trade." The Germans are assured that, in cooperation with the British, the United States had undertaken numerous efforts such as currency reform and the activities of the Joint Export/Import Agency (JEIA) to stimulate West German export trade. But since the German economy is "dependent on certain raw materials that Germany couldn't produce," the question was "how to finance the needed imports." The answer is the Marshall Plan. "Now there was money to buy certain raw materials," and these "cheap raw materials were turned into expensive finished products and shipped abroad to buy more raw materials." Thus the West Germans are told they have good reason to be self-confident. This is already reflected in the film's title. *Made in Germany* is again a stamp of quality for a number of German products which traditionally had been in demand on the world markets: "The world-famous cameras and the celebrated machines, cars for children, cars for grown-ups, typewriters, bicycles, radio tools, gloves, stockings, furs, yes, and whole fleets of ships; [...] everything from tailor-made wallpaper designs to porcelain chinaware; everything from dolls to thorough bred dogs, Kuckuck-clocks, pencils and women's fashion." German ingenuity and American generosity would bring about the revival of German exports as a precondition for economic recovery. To emphasize the spirit of cooperation, the narrator switches to using "we": "This is the story of the great combined effort which, like the goods we produce, is made in Germany."[29]

While *Me and Mr. Marshall* and *Made in Germany* focus on the economic dimensions of postwar West Germany, various other one-country films on Germany reflect the direct Cold War confrontation. *Zwei Städte* is an impressive example.[30] The opening credits inform viewers that the film was "shot partly on the west side of the Iron Curtain and partly to the east."[31] The film compares the economic situation in Dresden with that of Stuttgart. Both cities had been heavily damaged during the war. While Dresden—referred to as "a city of communist posters"—still lies in ruins, Stuttgart is already on the road to recovery. The story of both cities is presented as visible proof that the planned economy of the East has not achieved any economic progress at all. Stuttgart, on the other hand, has already become a symbol of economic recovery in the West. Here, the principles of a free market economy, such as economic freedom which allows individuals to take the initiative, a sound currency, and Marshall Plan aid brought about visible results. *Zwei Städte* is part of the Cold War ideological battle. It presents visual evidence that the Communist ideology (*Weltanschauung*) is a dead-end road. In contrast, the improved living standard in Stuttgart is due to the consequent implementation of private capitalism and U.S. support through the Marshall Plan. *Zwei Städte* is an important counterattack against Communist propaganda. The progress in Stuttgart's reconstruction is presented as a visible proof of Western superiority.

Germany's most important battlefield was Berlin. Here, an immediate comparison between West and East was part of everyday life. Therefore, it is no surprise that Berlin was the subject of numerous OMGUS and HICOG films. *Air of Freedom*[32] (*Das ist die Berliner Luft*[33]) is a good example.

Feature Films

Although most moving images on the Marshall Plan took a primarily documentary approach, some productions can be characterized as feature films. One excellent example is *The Story of Koula*. Obviously, the main task of this 1951 production was to promote ERP agricultural activities in Greece. In order to assist small farmers, the ECA shipped American mules to Greece to compensate for the war losses of donkeys. One of the numerous mules sent to Greece from the United States is named Koula. But neither the mule nor the farmers seem to get along well with each other. Eventually, the only person who knows how to handle the stubborn animal is the young boy Kiriakos. With great patience and the assistance of the family's donkey, he teaches the new arrival from the United States how to plough the fields. In the end, the mule's integration into everyday farming turns out to be a success story.

Although *The Story of Koula* is a so-called one-country film, it was voiced in eleven languages including German, where it was titled *Koula*, and became popular in most of the other ERP countries. Of course, the story was perfect for winning the hearts of any audience.[34] The young boy and the animal are the movie's "heroes." They act in an agricultural environment which, especially after the war, appears to be vital for survival and also the foundation for a better future. The story includes important messages which transcended a specific Greek perspective: the American mule was much bigger than the Greek donkey, thus symbolizing U.S. superiority. Of course, the movie is a reminder that help came from the United States. In addition, the friendship between the mule and the donkey seem to symbolize cooperation between the New World and "old" Europe with its best traditions as represented by Greek history. Finally, the young boy's work is a reminder that shaping the future of a new Europe would lie in the hands of the young generation. It was necessary to leave the past behind and look forward.

Such a positive outlook is presented in another one-country film: *Ferienfahrt mit Barbara*.[35] The film starts with a reminder that a vital raw material, oil, is shipped from the United States to Western Europe. This brings an improved supply of gas for West German cars and motorbikes. An expanded bus service by the Deutsche Post is shown as a convincing example. It means higher mobility for business and leisure travelers. On his bus ride to the Black Forest, Fritz, a young employee, meets a traveling salesman, who proudly presents his new merchandise. Due to the Marshall Plan, he is able to offer high quality textile products. Later on, Fritz's friend Barbara boards the bus. For the next five minutes, the focus is on the young couple. When they approach the village of Himmelreich (Kingdom of Heaven), Barbara expresses her happiness: "I want to embrace the whole world." Her wish to dance with Fritz is fulfilled in a small beer garden. During the dance, Barbara joins into the music and sings: "[...] *du bist mein großes Glück* [...] *du und ich, du und ich, ich und du.*" Later on, Barbara and Fritz meet the salesman again. He reports about the new spirit in the West German business community. Thanks to the Marshall Plan, there is now enough supply product to satisfy customers' demand. What follows is a brief down to earth description of Marshall Plan counterpart funds and how these accounts are used to stimulate production.

On the bus ride home, Barbara expresses her feeling that life in Germany had somewhat improved compared to what had happened in the past. But Fritz wants Barbara to forget about the past: "Now we must look forward, work, and regain confidence. I am not afraid anymore. If we can work again, we will get back to our feet again: You and me, Europe and the world." The young man's positive outlook is visually reinforced by a crowd of happy children waving to the passengers on the bus. The melody of the song "You and I, and Me and You" is resumed, underscoring the overall optimistic mood on West Germany's road to recovery. Feature films like *Ferienfahrt mit Barbara* and *The Story of Koula* clearly demonstrate the advantage that films had because they could be more entertaining than a sometimes "dry" documentary could.

Cartoons

Cartoons are probably the best example of how entertainment and propaganda could be successfully combined. European audiences were particularly attracted by cartoons produced in color such as *The Shoemaker and the Hatter.*[36] This very popular film was shown throughout Europe in eleven versions due to its being dubbed in different languages.[37] It was made in 1950 by John Halas and Joy Batchelor, the same team that later in 1954 produced the famous animated cartoon *Animal Farm.* In the cartoon, two neighbors—a shoemaker and a hatter—represent divergent philosophies of how best to organize their businesses after the war. The hatter believes in producing few hats at high prices, protected by a tariff wall. The shoemaker, on the other hand, believes in low cost mass production and profit through exports in a free trade environment. By demonstrating that free trade means prosperity, the shoemaker's "modern" approach turns out to be successful, and the hatter is proven wrong. But in the end, free trade brings prosperity to both of them. The shoemaker's business prospers, and the hatter finds a new job in the transportation business which is booming due to the growing flow of free trade.

To further emphasize arguments in favor of European cooperation, U.S. propaganda also drew attention to the history of the United States. A typical example is the animated cartoon *Tom Schuler—Cobbler Statesman.*[38] During the formative phase of the United States, the fictional Tom Schuler had come to America. The young man settles in an American colony as a shoemaker. As a businessman, he is confronted with various difficulties of trade between the colonies. A trip to Philadelphia to buy leather proves particularly frustrating. At the same time, however, Tom's visit to Philadelphia is an important political experience. Tom Schuler learns about the Constitutional Convention, and he realizes that the Constitution could only be formulated by compromise and negotiation. After returning to his home colony, Tom Schuler is elected a member of the convention to ratify the Constitution. After ratification, Tom becomes a witness to economic and political progress. Old enmities, suspicions, and borders that had separated the colonies disappear. As a result, commerce increases in the new United States. The road to prosperity is open. This American success story as visualized in the cartoon is not only presented as a lesson about U.S. history, but as a model for postwar Europe, by saying, essentially: Look at our history. Free trade and political compromise resulted in an unprecedented prosperity. This can also be achieved by Europeans!

Productivity Films

One of the Marshall Plan's central goals was the promotion of productivity in agriculture and industry. Here, the most immediate task was of a short-range nature. In order to satisfy even the most urgent demands of the European population, the agricultural output had to be raised drastically, especially in West Germany, and the influx of millions of refugees meant increased demand for food. In addition, the loss of Germany's eastern territories with their predominantly agricultural industry had to be compensated for. Beyond their humanitarian aspects, efforts to overcome food shortages were vital for industrial recovery. It was obvious that hungry workers needed more calories to improve industrial output. This close interdependence of food supply and productivity and its importance for West German recovery was repeatedly emphasized for the coal mining industry. *Me and Mr. Marshall* is a striking example of this.

In addition to these immediate challenges, Washington's quest for higher productivity had a long-range perspective: a higher standard of living. Here again, the United States served as a model. The permanent advance of productivity in agriculture and in industry, it was argued, had brought about an ever increasing standard of living for the average American, a development unparalleled in the world. References to the history of the United States as a model for Europe were repeatedly underscored by praising the blessings of the American way of life with the world's highest standard of living. How was it possible for the United States to be that successful? The answer was productivity. Therefore, intensive productivity drives were launched by the Marshall Plan administration to convince Europeans of the advantages of the U.S. mass production model; "the practicability of productivity has been preached by hosts of Americans," a member of HICOG summarized in 1954.[39] *Productivity—Key to Plenty*[40] and *Productivity—Key to Progress*[41] are the titles of films which place U.S. economic progress in a historical perspective. The superiority of U.S. economic development to that of other countries is aggressively visualized. The United States is presented as a model without any realistic alternative. The message, again, is "You, too, can be like us!"[42]

While some productivity films addressed the general public in Europe, the bulk of this genre was produced for the specialists in agriculture and, above all, in industry. Most of these films were voiced in German, since Austria and Germany were at the center of U.S. productivity drives. The "greatest opportunity to succeed" seemed to lie "in promoting our ideas through the workers and in using trade unions as the medium of promotion." In this context of "preaching the gospel of productivity," the film program was judged to "play an important role through collecting or producing films depicting technological advance in America and how it has benefited workers and industry."[43] A broad spectrum of topics was covered as is already visible from the titles like *Build with Steel* (*Stahlbauweise*), *Lubrication* (*Glatter Lauf durch Schmierung*), and *Springs and Automation* (*Räder und Federn*).[44]

The productivity drives were not limited to technical assistance or the improvement of the production process in agriculture and industry. Higher productivity was also to be achieved by the adaptation of American management models. The quest for higher productivity must, therefore, be seen in a broader context of the "Americanisation of European business."[45]

By and large, the more or less informal U.S. productivity drives seemed to have been successful. As Director-General of the Federation of British Industries Sir Norman Kipping put it, "The method of the oppressive conqueror is to force upon others the acceptance of his own philosophies. At the very least he says 'Copy us; do as we do' and uses his economic power to secure compliance. But the model of America is to show by example, to give others an opportunity see and adapt American methods to their own very differing conditions."[46]

Exhibits

Marshall Plan exhibits were another instrument to represent visually the major elements of the European Recovery Program. One of these undertakings deserves special mentioning: the Deutsche Industrieausstellung Berlin 1950. This German Industry Exhibition, which took place from 1 through 15 October 1950, was much more than a presentation of goods made in Germany. In the divided city, it was also a political demonstration. It is an "admirable documentation" of West Berlin's "will to live," as the weekly *Die Zeit* commented.[47] The newspaper also reflected on the exhibition's international implications when it mentioned that "languages of all peoples" could be heard in the exhibition halls. These political and international dimensions were emphasized by Berlin's director of fairs and exhibits: "We have not only given the world an overwhelming demonstration of true democratic ideas, we have also demonstrated that the nations of the free world are working side by side for the mutual welfare of all through practical cooperation."[48]

Above all, the industrial exhibition was an excellent opportunity to demonstrate achievements of ERP programs for Berlin and to advertise the mechanisms of the Marshall Plan and its benefits to the public. A special building on Berlin's exhibition grounds, the Marshall House, served this purpose. The genesis of the building, which was erected under the auspices of the High Commissioner for Germany, John McCloy, was in itself a symbol of the Marshall Plan's dynamism. Planning started on 18 June 1950, and the laying of the cornerstone took place only six weeks later. Major General Maxwell Taylor, the U.S. commander of Berlin, spoke at the ceremony when a copy of the charter of the Foreign Assistance Act of 1948 was inserted in the cornerstone. Construction was completed within two months on 30 September 1950, one day prior to the opening of the industrial fair.

At the opening of the Marshall House, huge crowds "stormed" the building to see the exhibit on life in the United States and the Marshall Plan. Charts, posters, models, and mechanical devices were presented in the ERP exhibit to illustrate the functioning European Recovery Program and the manner in which West Berlin fitted into it. Special emphasis was placed on the economic progress already made and the cooperation achieved by the nations of Western Europe, including West Germany. The displays were not limited to explaining the European Recovery Program. The Marshall House also showed snapshots from the United States, such as a diorama of transportation in a typical U.S. port, including trains, wharves, airport, and municipal installations.

A widely used facility was the 235-seat movie theater. It "was always filled for its continuous hour-long showing of documentary films on American life and scenes," the HICOG Information Bulletin reported.[49] In addition to the onsite information, the visitors were offered a broad variety of printed material on the Marshall Plan and the American way of life: "Distributed were 2,000,000 pieces of literature, including copies of the U.S.-published *Die Neue Zeitung*, publications of Amerika Dienst (U.S. Feature Service), and ERP pamphlets."[50]

The Marshall House ERP exhibition was supplemented by the presentation of a six-room prefabricated tract home replete with furnishings, which had been assembled beside the Marshall House. *America at Home*[51] (*Amerika zu Hause*) was a model U.S. home with modern appliances. This presentation of the American way of life attracted such a huge number of visitors that police had to be posted at the entrances.[52]

Both the industrial exhibition and the Marshall House exhibits attracted more visitors than had been anticipated. During the two weeks from 1 to 15 October, more than 750,000 visitors showed interest in the Marshall House displays. More than 50 percent were residents of Soviet-controlled East Berlin and East Germany who wanted "to get a truthful picture of American life and the benefits of the Marshall Plan to participating countries."

These informational elements are also reflected in the already mentioned film *Air of Freedom* which is a good example of U.S. propaganda behind the Iron Curtain and a demonstration of progress in West Berlin. First the focus is on Radio in the American Sector (RIAS), the U.S. broadcaster with its programs of entertainment and news for the people of West Berlin and Communist East Berlin. The central theme is progress of economic reconstruction in Berlin's western sectors on the occasion of Berlin's first industrial fair after the war and the dedication of the Marshall House on the fair grounds, which is opened by ECA Administrator Paul Hoffman. The film's entertainment section is devoted to a concert with musicians from various European countries. The broadcast is aired all over Western Europe as an "audible" proof that West Berlin's *Air of Freedom* cannot be suppressed although the Western sectors are surrounded by Communists. The various messages are clear. Having survived the Berlin blockade of 1948/1949, the people of Berlin, who can rely on Marshall Plan funds, are resolved to continue the reconstruction of their city, and West Berlin's geographical position behind the Iron Curtain does not mean isolation from the West. The U.S. presence and cultural exchange with Western Europe are guaranties for an ongoing "air of freedom," the new Marshall House being a symbol of progress and U.S. presence. Its significance is visually well documented in the still picture branches of the National Archives at College Park, Maryland, and the Landesarchiv Berlin.[53]

From the very beginning, the Marshall House was planned as a permanent building on Berlin's exhibition grounds to serve as a meeting place and exhibition hall. During the 1950s, the Marshall House hosted many important exhibits such as *We Build a Better Life* (*Wir Bauen ein Besseres Leben*). It was shown during the 1952 Berlin industrial fair and then sent to Stuttgart and other German towns.[54] The exhibit's main purpose was "to demonstrate that a higher standard of living can be attained by the peoples of the Atlantic community through increased productivity."[55] The American High Commission for Germany was convinced "that the exhibition proved to be an enormously effective educational force" which had made "a large number of people think more concretely about the better life that could be achieved for Germany and Europe through progress and cooperation."[56] Interviews had shown that most visitors had left the exhibition with an overall positive impression.[57] A year later, during the 1953 industrial fair, the successful work of the Marshall House was resumed with a similar exhibit titled *Community Life* (*Zusammenleben*).[58] Through these and other exhibits or conferences, the Marshall House became an important institution in Berlin's postwar public life. Therefore, it was classified as a historical monument in 1988. Fifteen years later, it was described by the Berlin monument commission not only as an "outstanding monument" of Germany's postwar history, but also as "indispensable evidence" of German-U.S. political relations.[59] In 2008, the Marshall House was refurbished and remodeled and celebrated a "shining comeback."[60] The Marshall House undoubtedly has been an important cornerstone of German-U.S. relations and still is an architectural reminder of the Marshall Plan's success.

Posters

The most important message of all Marshall Plan propaganda media was to inform the European public that help came from the United States. The Marshall Plan logo "For European Recovery—Supplied by the United States of America" was attached to all goods that were shipped from the New World to the European continent. Photos of the goods delivered at European ports were sent to the press. However, one didn't have to read a newspaper to be informed about the positive effects of the Marshall Plan. The traditional medium of posters spread the necessary information in the public sphere. Unfortunately, these posters were not collected systematically. Those posters that had not been discarded are spread over numerous archives or held by private collectors on both sides of the Atlantic. In addition, various Marshall Plan posters have been offered on Internet auction cites.

Conclusion

Films and exhibits were instrumental in making the Marshall Plan a success story because these media were able to win the hearts and minds of the population. The combination of information and entertainment was a sometimes very subtle approach for presenting the Marshall Plan's essentials to a broad audience. The messages that were visualized to propagandize the European Recovery Program can be summarized as follows.

1. There is no alternative to the Marshall Plan.
2. Progress can only be achieved by intra-European cooperation.
3. Economic progress can be seen by everybody.
4. The economic recovery proves the vitality of private capitalism.
5. Productivity is a key to Europe's prosperity.
6. Economic progress is the foundation of democracy and individual liberty.
7. Communism is a threat to economic progress and political stability.
8. The Marshall Plan is essential for Western defense.
9. West Germany's economic potential is essential for European recovery.
10. West Germany's cooperation with other Marshall Plan countries is the best way to integrate the new Germany into the West as a safeguard against potential German ambitions to dominate Europe again.
11. Berlin is a vital outpost for the Free World.
12. The United States is the only power that can provide leadership for the West.

All these messages are parts of one central leitmotiv: *Alle sollen besser leben* (all should live better).[61] This postulate of the Marshall Plan philosophy converged with the essence of West Germany's social market policy. Its ultimate goal—as its "father," Ludwig Erhard, had claimed—was *Wohlstand für alle*[62] (wealth for all).[63] These slogans were given credibility by the so-called *Wirtschaftswunder* (economic miracle) of the ERP. Even the less privileged could cherish the illusion that they, too, would ultimately benefit from the overall economic recovery. Within less than a decade after Germany's unconditional surrender, West Germany had been reestablished as a leading industrial power. This road from total destruction is well documented in the DVD's selection of posters. In the misery of the postwar years, the overriding task was to overcome scarcity (*Mangel*). Shoes, leather, and textiles were supplied by the Marshall Plan. Contrary to allegations from the Communist East, the European Recovery Program's activities meant employment opportunities, and the ERP also helped build housing facilities. In this propaganda battle, Berlin is of special importance. But a better life for all could only be achieved through intra-European cooperation, so the barriers to free trade had to be opened. In this context, Germany again became a member of the Western world, a partner of the common ship sailing towards a recovery in full swing: *All Our Colours to the Mast*. This West German membership in international cooperation offered the new German republic an excellent chance to make its voice heard again in the international arena: "*Deutschland spricht mit*!" The Marshall Plan's pump priming set in motion a chain reaction which led from a fight against misery to the economic and political reconstruction of West Germany. The various steps forward are documented in the posters of the 1940s and the 1950s promoting the Marshall Plan. For their intended audience, these posters were also a constant visual reminder that help came from America: "For European Recovery—Supplied by the United States of America." In Germany's collective memory, this is the Marshall Plan's most important legacy.

Notes

1 An excellent overview of the literature can be found in Organisation for Economic Co-operation and Development, ed., *The European Reconstruction, 1948–1961: Bibliography on the Organisation for European Economic Co-operation* (Paris: Organisation for European Economic Co-operation, 1996); the most recent publication on the European Recovery Program is Greg Behrman's *The Most Noble Adventure: The Marshall Plan and the Reconstruction of Post-War Europe* (London: Aurum, 2008).

2 "Economic Cooperation Agreement between the United States of America and Austria," *United States Statutes at Large* 62, part 2 (1948): 2143f.

3 *The Oxford English Dictionary*, 2nd ed. (Oxford: Oxford UP, 1989), 632.

4 Albert Hemsing, "The Marshall Plan's European Film Unit, 1948–1955: A Memoir and Filmography," *Historical Journal of Film, Radio and Television* 14 (1994): 269–97; compare also Sandra Schulberg, "'Selling Democracy': Films Delivered Marshall Plan's Message to Post-World War II Europe," *Prologue: Quarterly of the National Archives and Records Administration* 38.3 (Fall 2006): 3–11.

5 National Archives (NA), College Park, Maryland, Motion Picture, Sound, and Video Branch.

6 Linda R. Christenson, "Marshall Plan Filmography Listing," George C. Marshall Motion Pictures, http://www.marshallfilms.org/mpf.asp, accessed 18 June 2009.

7 Compare Selling Democracy: Films of the Marshall Plan 1948–1953, http://www.sellingdemocracy.org, accessed 20 June 2009.

8 *Selling Democracy. Welcome Mr. Marshall: Films of the Marshall Plan: 1947–1955. A Program of Internationale Filmfestspiele Berlin in Association with the Museum of German History and the Bundesarchiv/Filmarchiv* (Berlin: Internationale Filmfestspiele, 2004); Rainer Rother, ed., *Selling Democracy: Winning the Peace. Eine Broschüre zur Filmreihe der Internationalen Filmfestspiele Berlin, des Deutschen Historischen Museums und des Bundesarchiv-Filmarchivs* (Berlin: Internationale Filmfestspiele, 2006); Rainer Rother, ed., *Selling Democracy: Friendly Persuasion. Eine Broschüre zur Filmreihe der internationalen Filmfestspiele Berlin, de Bundesarchiv-Filmarchivs und des Deutschen Historischen Museums in Zusammenarbeit mit der Bundeszentrale für politische Bildung* (Berlin: Internationale Filmfestspiele, 2006).

9 Bundeszentrale für politische Bildung (German Federal Agency for Civic Education), *Selling Democracy: Die Filme des Marshallplans/The Films of the Marshall Plan*, 2006, Bonn, DVD (hereafter cited as the DVD *Selling Democracy*).

10 Compare Raymond Fielding, *The American Newsreel: A Complete History, 1911–1967* (Jefferson, NC: McFarland 2006); Annamaria Benckert, ed., *"Wir hatten einen Lacher": Die Geschichte der deutschen Wochenschauen* (Hamburg: Universität Hamburg, 2002).

11 Produced by the ECA Film Unit in cooperation with Fox-Movietone News; for individual titles, see Christenson, Marshall Plan Filmography.

12 Compare with ibid.

13 Bundesarchiv-Filmarchiv Berlin. There are currently no reference copies for research available.

14 Compare Bundesarchiv-Filmarchiv Berlin, *Welt im Film* (*WiF*) 2/1945—*WiF* 291/1950; Peter Bucher, ed., *Wochenschauen und Dokumentarfilme 1895–1950 im Bundesarchiv-Filmarchiv* (Koblenz: Bundesarchiv, 1984), 153–226, and Archives of the Deutsch Wochenschau GmbH in Hamburg with their excellent search engine at http://www.deutsche-wochenschau.de/, accessed 18 June 2009.

15 A selection is published on video: *Der Augenzeuge*, Die DEFA-Wochenschau, 2001, Berlin, DVD, Icestorm Entertainment.

16 See especially the extensive coverage of the Marshall Plan in *Welt im Film* (*WiF*) no. 246, 14 February 1950; *WIF* no. 254, 13 April 1950; *WiF* no. 291, 29 December 1950; cf. Jutta Gröschl, *Die Deutschlandpolitik der vier Grossmächte in der Berichterstattung der deutschen Wochenschauen, 1945–1949: Ein Beitrag zur Diskussion um den Film als historische Quelle* (Berlin: De Gruyter, 1997).

17 NA, Record Group (RG) 111.MSA/1060.

18 NA, RG 306/306.03337.

19 The film's significance is underlined by the fact that it inspired the organizers of the international conference which was held on the sixtieth anniversary of the Marshall Plan in New Orleans to the title of their publication of the conference papers.

20 NA, RG 111.MSA/1135.

21 NA, RG, 306.05661.

22 Bundesarchiv-Filmarchiv; currently, no reference copy for research is available.

23 Statement made on 19 September 1946; see The Churchill Society, http://www.churchill-society-london.org.uk, accesssed 18 June 2009.

24 Cf. Brigitte J. Hahn, *Umerziehung durch Dokumentarfilm? Ein Instrument amerikanischer Kulturpolitik im Nachkriegsdeutschland* (Munich: Lit Verlag, 1997); Melanie Nolte, "Die US-amerikanische Demokratisierungspolitik in Westdeutschland: Propagandafilme 1948–1951," M.A. thesis, University of Giessen, 2006.

25 Robert Joseph, "Our Film Program in Germany: How Far Was It a Success?," *Hollywood Quarterly* 2.2 (January 1947): 123.

26 NA, RG 111-MSA/1064.

27 Bundesarchiv-Filmarchiv, no. 152; German version in: NA, RG 306/1211.

28 Opening credits.

29 A detailed interpretation by Hahn, *Umerziehung*, 325–35.

30 Bundesarchiv-Filmarchiv, no. 2076, published on the DVD *Selling Democracy*.

31 Cf. the opening credits: "*Ein Filmstreifen, teils westlich, teils östlich des Eisernen Vorhanges aufgenommen.*"

32 Published with German subtitles on the DVD *Selling Democracy*.

33 Bundesarchiv-Filmarchiv, no. 851.

34 This seems to bet true even sixty years later. At the Vienna conference, *Koula* was extensively referred to in three different presentations.

35 Bundesarchiv-Filmarchiv, no. 2092.

36 NA, RG 306/06353.

37 The German version, *Der Schuhmacher und der Hutmacher*, is on the DVD *Selling Democracy*.

38 NA, RG 306/08989.

39 Memorandum McKelvey, 12 November 1954, NA, RG 469, Mission to Germany, Audio-Visual Aids Section, Records Relating to the Film Program, 1950–1956, Technical Work, Box 10.

40 NA, RG 286/301.

41 NA, RG 306/00918.

42 D.W. Ellwood, "Die Botschaft des Marshallplans" ("The Message of the Marshall Plan"), in *Selling Democracy: Friendly Persuasion*, ed. Rother, 7.

43 Memorandum McKelvey, 12 November 1954, NA, RG 469, Mission to Germany, Audio-Visual Aids Section, Records Relating to the Film Program, 1950–1956, Technical Work, Box 10.

44 Archives of Kinemathek, Hamburg.

45 Matthias Kipping and Ove Bjanar, eds., *The Americanisation of European Business: The Marshall Plan and the Transfer of U.S. Management Models* (London: Routledge, 1998); cf. especially Bent Boel, "The European Productivity Agency: A Faithful Prophet of the American Model?," ibid., 37–54, and Christian Kleinschmidt, "An Americanised Company in Germany: Die Vereinigte Glanzstoff-Fabriken AG," in ibid., 171–89.

46 Quoted by Matthias Kipping, "'Operation Impact': Converting European Employers to the American Creed," in *Americanisation of European Business*, ed. Kipping and Bjanar, 55–73, here 55.

47 "Berlin wirbt für seinen Export," *Die Zeit*, 12 October 1950.

48 HICOG Information Bulletin, November 1950, 13.

49 HICOG Information Bulletin, November 1950, 12.

50 HICOG Information Bulletin, November 1950, 12.
51 *Amerika zu Hause: Deutsche Industrie-Ausstellung, Berlin, 1.-15. Oktober 1950* (Berlin: n.p., 1950).
52 Greg Castillo, "Domesticating the Cold War: Household Consumption as Propaganda in Marshall Plan Germany," *Journal of Contemporary History* 40.2 (2005): 261–88.
53 See examples on enclosed DVD.
54 Cf. Frank Schumacher, *Kalter Krieg und Propaganda: Die USA, der Kampf um die Weltmeinung und die ideelle Westbindung der Bundesrepublik Deutschland, 1945–1955* (Trier: Wissenschaftlicher Verlag, 2000), 243ff.
55 HICOG Information Bulletin, February 1953, 2.
56 HICOG to State Department, 9 February 1953, NA, RG 59, Central Files 511.62a, 1950–1954, box 2446.
57 Cf. HICOG report no. 166, 23 December 1952: An Evaluation of the Effectiveness of the Marshallhaus Exhibit, NA, RG 306, U.S. Information Agency, Office of Research, Special Reports, 1951–1963.
58 Cf. HICOG report no. 190, 16 November 1953: The Marshall House Exhibit at the 1953 Industrial Fair. An Evaluation of West Berlin and East German Reactions, NA, RG 306, U.S. Information Agency, Office of Research, Special Reports, 1951–1963.
59 Beschlüsse des Landesdenkmalrats Berlin aus seiner 18. Sitzung vom 10.02.2003, www.stadtentwicklung.berlin.de/denkmal/landesdenkmalrat/de/, accessed 16 June 2009.
60 "Neue Event-Location erstrahlt im alten Glanz," *Messe Berlin Magazin* 1 (2009): 4f.
61 The title of the productivity exhibition at Düsseldorf is the title of the exhibition guide: *Alle sollen besser leben!: Grosse Rationalisierungs-Ausstellung 1953. Düsseldorf vom 18. Juli bis 16. August 1953* (Düsseldorf: Rationalisierungs-Ausstellung, 1953 (exhibition guide).
62 Ludwig Erhard, *Wohlstand für alle*, Düsseldorf 1957 (Cologne: Anaconda, 2009).
63 The English translation of Erhard was published as *Prosperity through Competition* (London: Thames and Hudson, 1958).

Helge Danielsen and Helge Pharo

Reception and Representations of the Marshall Plan in Norway

Introduction

The Marshall Plan struck at the roots of crucial economic and political controversies in post-World War II Norway. Some were already fully out in the open when George C. Marshall gave his Harvard speech in early June of 1947. Others gained prominence as first the proposal and then subsequent U.S. demands for European cooperation, planning, and liberalization forced the postwar Norwegian Labor government to make painful politico-economic choices, while at the same time being dependent on Marshall Plan aid. The U.S. demands for reciprocal European efforts caused problems, but also provided opportunities for the Norwegian government as it tried to achieve its ambitious reconstruction and development goals.

Media responses reflect the wide-ranging political and economic ramifications of the plan for Norway.[1] The relative lack of interest in the specifics of aid transfers in the most important national papers probably also reflects the importance of the overarching political implications of the plan. It's tempting to conclude that the one consumer-oriented response to the plan that we have identified in the national papers is also linked to the domestic dilemmas and strains caused by both Labor's economic policies and the division of Europe.

The following essay first deals briefly with the initial responses to the plan by the Labor government, the opposition, and national newspapers, paying particular attention to the cleavages in the Norwegian body politic that the wartime consensus had partly papered over. Next, how the papers discussed the Marshall Plan until the early 1950s is covered. Finally, an exhibition of consumer goods in 1950 is considered due to its being well-suited for drawing several of the major issues together.

Before exploring the government and newspaper responses, a brief look at the postwar political scene in Norway is warranted. In the fall election of 1945, Labor won an absolute majority of the seats in the *Storting*, Norway's parliament. The Party gained seventy-six out of 150 seats, with just over 41 percent of the vote. The Communist Party gained eleven seats with just less than 12 percent of the vote. Labor maintained its absolute majority until the election of 1961, while the communists declined precipitously after the full onset of the Cold War and for all practical purposes disappeared as a parliamentary power after 1949. The Conservative Party was always the largest of the center-right opposition parties, yet never surpassed 20 percent of the vote during the first postwar elections. Its relationship with the other non-socialist opposition parties was always somewhat uneasy and rarely close. Only in 1963 did these parties manage to put together a formal coalition; then in the 1965 election, they gained an absolute parliamentary majority. The coalition disintegrated over the European issue in 1971, as it was rent by the same sort of disagreements encountered when dealing with the Marshall Plan.[2]

Early Reactions and Changing Policies

Official Norwegian reactions to Marshall's speech were remarkably reticent and slow in coming. The Cabinet was clearly at a loss regarding what to do and found it had no choice but to procrastinate while trying to find out how potential foes and allies as well as the Scandinavian neighbors and neutral Switzerland were going to respond. Almost ten days after the speech, Foreign Minister Halvard M. Lange told a Reuter's correspondent that there would be no answer as yet, but that he could speculate that Norway would welcome any reconstruction initiative that reduced rather than heightened tensions in Europe. A further ten days later, Lange was quoted in *Arbeiderbladet*, the governing Labor Party mouthpiece, as saying that Norway would not commit herself until the Soviet Union had responded.[3] In a cabinet conference discussing economic policy issues on 17 June 1947, Lange considered it preferable for Norway not to participate in the Marshall Plan if economically feasible.[4]

Whether the Labor government would have seriously considered not joining the Marshall Plan as we now know it, cannot be firmly established, yet it is highly unlikely. In mid-June of 1947, even the key members of the Cabinet did not know what it was that they were considering not joining, or who the other participants would be. The point is that any sort of real or apparent Western alignment would pose problems for both foreign policy and domestic politics and might have wide-ranging ramifications in both fields. The consequences for foreign policy can be considered first.

Norway's foreign policy from 1944 to early 1948 has been dubbed "bridge-building." Because of its exposed geopolitical position between the Western powers and the Soviet Union, the wartime coalition and the postwar Labor governments saw this policy as being in Norway's own best interests as well as in the interest of preserving peace in Europe. Thus Norway would try to maintain or build bridges between the wartime allies; in practice, however, bridge-building boiled down to keeping as low a profile as possible over issues where East and West strongly disagreed. This policy was predicated on the assumption that the former allies would, in fact, be able to maintain a minimally amicable relationship after the war. Were antagonisms to grow to the point where war might threaten, the key foreign policymakers agreed that the fallback option of joining the West must be taken.[5]

As the Labor government saw it in June 1947, the international situation did not yet warrant moving to the reserve position. Not joining could, however, only be seen as an option until all of Europe west of the Iron Curtain except for Finland and Spain opted to participate. The Cabinet was quick to grasp the point that near universal participation from Western Europe made joining virtually inevitable, for the corollary was that not joining would be a much greater departure from bridge-building.[6]

Norway for some time continued its bridge-building policies within the Marshall Plan organization almost until the Prague coup in February of 1948. The subsequent Soviet Pact proposal to Finland and the rumors about a similar proposal to Norway made the Cabinet turn to the West. However, initially the estimates for dollar needs were set artificially low, and the Norwegians argued for aid to be distributed through the United Nations Economic Commission for Europe, contrary to the wishes not only of the Americans, but of the French and the British as well. The Cabinet, as well as the Norwegian delegation to the Paris negotiations, kept dragging its feet in terms of the organizational set-up for the distribution of aid, and Norway as opposed to all the other participants was represented only by technical experts at the opening meeting.[7]

Bridge-building was also tailored to maintain a national foreign policy consensus and to avoid domestic strife, for the Labor Party left and the resurgent Communist Party were skeptical of the Western capitalist and imperialist powers and quite admiring of the Soviet Union. By the spring of 1947, however, the domestic consensus was starting to unravel. The powerful secretary of the Labor Party, Haakon Lie, as well as Secretary of Defense Jens Christian Hauge, who very much had the ear of Prime Minister Einar Gerhardsen, were by this time increasingly in favor of strengthening ties with the West; so was the majority of the center-right parliamentarians.[8] Skepticism of the capitalist and industrialized West was not confined to the far- and center-left political forces, however. Parliamentary debates in 1946 and 1947 over a loan through the U.S. Export-Import Bank, which required that 50 percent of the goods be carried on U.S. ships, caused strong opposition across the political spectrum due to its great disregard for the interests of small states. Shipping, of course, was by far Norway's most important earner of foreign exchange.[9]

Finally, in order to place the Norwegian press reactions to the Marshall Plan offer and its further development in its fuller context, one must keep in mind that there were serious disagreements over economic policies and goals both between and within the two major political blocs in Norway, the Labor Party on the one hand and the center-right parties on the other.[10] The Farmers' Party in particular decried industrialization and, as one of their most prominent parliamentarians, Gabriel Moseid, put it, embraced the foundation for "our existence as a free, independent, culturally and morally advanced people, is above all our wealth derived from agriculture, forestry and fisheries." He feared that any intentional or unintentional degradation of the basic industries would make Norwegians "[...] a poor people at the mercy [...] of the powerful states of the world." The communists were quite pleased to support the strongly nationalist and distinctly nostalgic rhetoric of the Farmers' Party.[11]

The Labor Party certainly did not harbor any enthusiastic supporters of U.S. capitalism. The party's leading politicians, planners, and pundits were with some exceptions fairly ignorant of the U.S. economy and political system, and genuinely skeptical of the U.S. ability to avoid a repetition of the post-World War I depression. Norway was, on the one hand, highly dependent on the United States for reconstruction purposes while on the other both fearing and looking forward to profiting from a U.S. depression. This ambivalence contributed to rapid changes of mind and strategy through 1946 to 1948. In 1946 and early 1947, the need for dollars was highlighted. Still the situation was not seen to be critical until the late summer of 1947, yet serious enough for the Ministry of Finance to doctor the books somewhat for the situation to appear less grim to the *Storting* and the opposition, as well as the Americans. The cool public response to the Marshall Plan was in part built on a presentation of the foreign exchange situation that was clearly at variance with the actual state of affairs. Norwegian dollar needs were seriously underestimated for political reasons. Though actual requirements were gradually adjusted upwards throughout the fall of 1947, the initial estimates came back to haunt the Norwegian Cabinet in the late winter of 1948. Even if Norway by then had turned to the West, grants and loans were much below what was considered vital. [12]

Furthermore, Labor representatives from rural and peripheral areas tended to be both strongly nationalist, frequently with a neutralist bent, and to a degree skeptical of modernization in the guise of large-scale industrialization as pursued by its own government. Labor harbored the same internal tensions as the center-right groups, though in a somewhat different mix because support for modernization policies was much stronger than in the other bloc, while opposition against possible Western alignment was also more pronounced.[13] There was in the *Storting* and in the parties across the political spectrum considerable opposition to the austerity policy of the Labor government that accompanied the government's reconstruction and subsequent industrialization drive. Labor's chief planner, Minister of Finance and later of Trade Erik Brofoss, was constantly worried and worked up over the demand for investments in non-essential industries and activities. As he put it in a letter to one of his close collaborators in early 1949: "I am in the absurd situation that in the *Storting* anyone can stand up and speak in favor of a new stretch of road, for new railroad facilities, for new schools, for new prisons, for new—I don't know what, but for nothing that will contribute to solving our foreign exchange problems."[14] Thus the issue of how to respond to the Marshall Plan and later of how to act within the framework of the Organization for European Economic Cooperation (OEEC) posed a number of challenges to both the Labor Party and the opposition within the fields of both foreign and economic policy. These challenges were partly a consequence of quite basic cleavages between Labor and the center-right, but just as frequently were the result of criss-crossing cleavages within and between the camps. These criss-crossing cleavages of support for and opposition against the government's policies are reflected in the major newspapers discussed herein.

As mentioned above, the fact that the Marshall Plan touched upon so many different and key foreign and economic policy issues is a major reason why the main Norwegian papers were primarily concerned with the political and economic implications of the plan, internationally and nationally. The goods entering Norway under the aegis of the Plan—be they consumer goods, investment goods, fuel, or raw materials—are mentioned only briefly in the major papers consulted for this study.

The Press and Political Parties

It is somewhat unclear how well parliamentary debates and media coverage reflect broadly shared or sharply opposed views of the United States and the Marshall Plan and Norway's participation in it. Parliamentary debates were above all concerned with the broader ramifications of the Plan in the context of postwar Norwegian foreign and domestic policies and so was the press from the moment the Plan was launched. Thus the written record may not adequately reflect the views and concerns of all those who did not belong to the elected or opinion-shaping elite.

The newspapers at the time were, with only a few exceptions, mouthpieces of the respective political parties. The papers of the left were under more direct party control than were those of the center-right, but they were almost all warriors of the different worthy causes. Papers and politicians analyzed the plan through the lenses of party programs and established policies and preferences. It may be argued, though the evidence is inconclusive, that many Norwegians initially were more enthusiastic about the plan than the response of the press, parliamentarians, and the Cabinet conveys. However, public opinion surveys are of very limited use, so no fully reliable way of knowing to what extent official and press reactions were representative exists. Frode Liland in his 1992 thesis finds quite broadly shared pro-American sentiments in the immediate postwar years. He also somewhat tentatively points to a divergence between elite and popular responses to American culture, graphically portrayed by a quote from the prominent Labor novelist Nils Johan Rud who decried "the thick box of synthetic USA": "We need to maintain the sovereignty of our souls, our cultural independence. A people losing that, loses its independence for ever."[15] Furthermore, a literal reading of the Norwegian press could easily lead to the conclusion that skepticism of the United States was widespread.

When considering the issue, one must first keep in mind that in 1947 Norwegians had lived through decades of depression and wartime and postwar scarcity and rationing. To further build a case for a more welcoming attitude in the population at large than can be found at the top political level and in the press, one may have recourse to what is vaguely known as widely diffused pro-American sentiments in Norway. There were quite close contacts between the (relatively speaking) huge Norwegian emigrant population in the United States and the home country. By 1900, more than 700,000 Norwegians had emigrated to the United States. At that time, the home population numbered about 2 million. Even before the many exchanges that followed upon the Marshall Plan, the United States was a beacon of modernization, and U.S. popular culture—movies and music in particular—enjoyed a major following. Sports contacts were many and varied in winter as well as summer sports. American track and field stars had on a regular basis competed in a major meet in Oslo in the interwar period, and the meet was resurrected after the war. The U.S. Embassy in 1950 praised the organizers for their efforts as a means to promoting better understanding between the two countries. Another avenue to better understanding was probably the many skilled Norwegian workers in frequent transit between the two countries.[16] From 1949 onwards, exchanges through the Fulbright and other programs were of high importance in the mainly successful efforts of the United States to establish and maintain good relations with, among other groups, Norwegian scholars, politicians, media representatives, and trade union leaders.[17]

This essay results from reading five major papers, four of them based in Oslo and one in Bergen, for the period from late September 1947 into the first half of 1952. Discussion herein about the period from June to the end of September relies on the 1969 thesis by Svein Andreassen on the initial Norwegian press reactions to the Marshall Plan.[18]

Of the five papers analyzed for the whole five-year period, *Bergens Tidende* was probably the most regionally oriented. However, as a paper aligned with the more internationalist wing of the Liberal Party and located in an extremely outward looking trading and shipping city, it probably had the best foreign affairs coverage of all Norwegian newspapers at the time.[19] The other papers were all located in Oslo and had explicitly national ambitions. *Friheten* was the national mouthpiece of the Communist Party. *Arbeiderbladet* was the official organ of the governing Labor Party. *Aftenposten* was the main conservative paper with quite intimate links to both the Conservative Party and to shipping, finance, and trade milieus, as well as to the manufacturing industry. *Dagbladet* was probably less of a party newspaper than the other Oslo papers, but was affiliated with the Liberal Party. It was an intellectually freewheeling paper, in some respects explicitly anti-authoritarian and, thus, frequently critical of Labor's quite strict party discipline. Its image was that of internationalism and radical nationalism at the same time. With the exception of *Friheten*, the papers did not always parrot the party line, but *Arbeiderbladet* generally did not move far from it. The other three largely conformed to the positions of the parties they were seen to represent. In the case of the first year of the Marshall Plan, especially the first half, press reactions in particular reflected the respective papers' and parties' concern for the consequences of the Plan on Norway's bridge-building policy.[20] The diverging views of *Dagbladet* and *Bergens Tidende* reflect the fact that the Liberal Party since its founding in 1884 had always been one of conflicting opinions and interests.

The initial Norwegian press reactions were quicker in coming than those of the government, but generally speaking, they were no more positive. Just like the government's opinions, the papers' positions were informed by fear that the Marshall Plan would cause great power confrontations in Europe and undermine bridge-building.[21] Reports from the U.S. Embassy and the United States Information Service (USIS) confirm that once the Americans were back in Norway after the war they made serious efforts to influence the Norwegian media and that the media were generally—*Friheten* and the other Communist papers excepted—positive to the materials they received.[22] However, media coverage of the Marshall Plan appears by and large to have been based on reports by the foreign correspondents of the main papers and on reports by the international press agencies as well as by a reading of the major international newspapers. Up to a point, the papers covered the Marshall Plan and the evolution of the OEEC in much the same way. Articles were strongly concerned with the politics of the plan and the politics of Western

European cooperation, as well as with developments within the different participating states and the United States.

The views of *Arbeiderbladet* and the three center-right papers were in most respects quite close to those of the Labor government as far as its perceptions of developments abroad were concerned. *Friheten*, as mentioned, parroted Moscow, but quite moderately during the first half year and to a degree also until early 1949 when Norway joined the North Atlantic Treaty Organization (NATO). Also, a reader of *Friheten* would have had a fairly well informed view of what the schisms, preferences, and problems of the participating countries were. Domestic U.S. policies inside and outside of the Congress and the White House were quite accurately reported, for they were based on stories by the better informed press in the United States and the major European states. The vagaries of the U.S. economy and those of the Western European states were less closely followed and certainly must have appeared less comprehensible to the average reader, but were still reported in a mostly sober manner. In retrospect one can see, which is hardly surprising, that the press tended to dramatize relatively minor crises and make ill-founded forecasts. But so did the Norwegian diplomatic service as well as the main U.S. papers. The reports that made it to the pages of the main Norwegian papers were mainly quite judicious and accurate as far as their portrayal of the international scene was concerned.[23]

The split between *Friheten* and the other four papers persisted and became increasingly pronounced after the founding of the Cominform in the fall of 1947. Up to that point, all but *Bergens Tidende* had a partly shared understanding of the motives and driving forces of the Marshall Plan proposal. They tended to see the proposal as a means to avoid a crisis of overproduction. The Americans needed to expand in foreign markets to maintain their economic system. To the communists, the U.S. system was brutally exploitative; to the Labor Party, it was merely in crisis. *Dagbladet* and *Aftenposten*, to a degree, shared the perception of overproduction as the primary cause, but painted it in less dramatic terms. *Bergens Tidende* was alone in rejecting the standard Norwegian newspaper interpretation, which was also to a degree shared by key Cabinet members and economic planners, as discussed above.[24]

The respective views of American motives for Marshall Aid largely reflected the different papers' commitment to bridge-building. *Bergens Tidende*, to a degree joined by *Aftenposten*, by the early summer of 1947 had given up on bridge-building and tended to see the impending great power conflict as one between democracy and totalitarian communism. The paper was in no doubt as to where Norway belonged in such a struggle and said that Norway needed to align with the Anglo-American powers. The paper's foreign policy analysts found that the overproduction theory did not fit the facts of the situation. The United States was motivated by ideology and balance of power considerations. Western Europe would not survive without U.S. support. It does not appear that *Bergens Tidende* rejected the overproduction thesis because it had found that bridge-building was no longer viable, but it is possible that the two positions were interlinked in the sense that skepticism of bridge-building made the paper less susceptible to the overproduction thesis. On the other hand, *Aftenposten* subscribed somewhat to the overproduction thesis, while at the same time concluding that bridge-building had outlived itself. In its analysis as well, the implication was that Norway had to look to the West for closer cooperation, if not yet for protection. Defense cooperation was still not an option, even if the conflict was seen to be one between democracy and totalitarian rule.[25]

Arbeiderbladet, to a degree accompanied by *Dagbladet*, promoted the overproduction thesis and stayed with bridge-building. In the worldview of *Arbeiderbladet*, the Marshall Plan was not a move to protect democracy in Western Europe, but an expression of the rivalry of two great powers. Soviet policies in Eastern Europe were seen as defensive rather than aiming at European supremacy. As for the United States, the Marshall Plan and the Truman Doctrine were seen as two halves of the same whole. Thus bridge-building could still be justified. By the end of September, *Arbeiderbladet* and *Dagbladet* were moving closer to the views expressed by the other two papers, and by early 1948, the Labor press had largely moved to the position of the papers of the center-right. The struggle was no longer between two more or less indistinguishable great powers, but one between light and darkness. From late 1947 onward, then, the debates and disagreements over the Marshall Plan—barring the communist press—did not turn on the causes of the plan and overarching U.S. intentions, but on the implications of the plan for Norwegian planning and economic policies.[26]

On one major issue that specifically concerned Norway all the parties and papers agreed: the U.S. shipping clause was an unacceptable part of the Marshall Plan. The motivations probably differed between the communists and the rest, but all agreed that the 50 percent clause was unacceptable. Because of a shortage rather than a surplus of ships, the question never became a serious bone of contention between the Norwegians and the Americans. Yet it is striking that, as in the debates on the Exim Bank loans earlier (see above), the center-right opposition and the communists were more concerned with the shipping clause than was the Labor government and its press.[27]

As mentioned above, the Cabinet's decision to downplay Norwegian financial needs as part of its continued bridge-building within the Marshall Plan organization backfired when both the Europeans in Paris and the Americans in Washington, D.C. took the Norwegian estimates at face value. When the division of loans and grants was announced in the spring of 1948, Norwegian press reactions were indignant, and the center-right papers were critical of both the Americans and the Labor government. Labor spokesmen somewhat lamely defended the Cabinet by explaining that the situation had looked different a year earlier.[28] This sort of criticism was a one-time affair, for the Labor government subsequently proved to be quite adept at persuading both the Economic Cooperation Administration (ECA) and the Office of the Special Representative of its financial needs.[29]

Two key issues of Norwegian economic and foreign economic policy were very much affected by the Marshall Plan. One was that of long-term planning as demanded by the Americans and the OEEC in 1948, and the other was that of liberalization as demanded by the Americans the subsequent year. The U.S. demand for a four-year plan suited the Labor Party perfectly. Conversely, it provoked the center-right both because long-term planning was anathema to many of their parliamentarians and because Labor's proposed plan involved significant structural changes of the Norwegian economy and a fundamental restructuring of the agricultural sector, which was also required to provide labor for industrial expansion.[30]

From 1948 to 1949, the ECA moved from seeing planning as the solution to Western Europe's ills to prescribing liberalization instead. As the Americans changed strategy, so too, did the Norwegian political parties reverse positions.[31] The center-right parties were largely in favor of liberalization and also supported it for tactical reasons because the extensive system of quantitative regulations also was seen to be part and parcel of the Norwegian planned economy. Thus the U.S. demand for trade liberalization was hailed as a major step forward for supporters of a more open and competitive and less regulated economy. *Aftenposten* and *Bergens Tidende*, the latter in particular, were strong proponents of liberalization. *Dagbladet* to a degree followed suit, yet was more concerned with national control of the economy.[32]

The question of whether Labor's postwar system of economic controls was merely transitional in order to steer Norway through the problems of postwar scarcities and imbalances or was intended as permanent features of an intrusive regulatory state has long been a matter of contention among Norwegian historians. This essay subscribes to the view that Labor viewed controls and regulations as a necessary, but temporary, means of getting Norway through a period of postwar turbulence. The Norwegian government was certainly not in the forefront of the liberalizers and frequently argued that Norway, as a rather less developed state, needed a relatively long period to dismantle controls. Furthermore, the Norwegian planners were concerned that the Americans, supported not the least by the Germans, were concerned with liberalization as a goal in and of itself rather than as a means of growth, prosperity, and full employment.[33] Full employment was an article of faith within the Labor Party. *Arbeiderbladet*, while in favor of liberalization, also reflected the party caveats about not moving so fast and creating other imbalances and risking unemployment.[34]

In the papers, both planning and liberalization were tied to the more overarching issue of how to mete out the credit for Norway's economic development in the postwar period. *Aftenposten* and *Bergens Tidende* tended to give credit to the Marshall Plan, while *Arbeiderbladet*, as the 1949 election approached, increasingly claimed that Labor's planning policies must be given pride of place and that the Marshall Plan was secondary. *Arbeiderbladet*, in fact, tended to wax increasingly less lyrical about the Plan as the election came closer.[35]

At the tail end of the Marshall Plan period and as Norway was getting ever more tightly woven into the emerging networks of NATO, Labor launched its North Norway Plan to accelerate the development of the northernmost regions of the country that were less developed than the rest and had been the hardest hit by the war. At much the same time, work was started on a major aluminum plant at Sunndalsøra, on the northwestern coast of the southern half of Norway. Both of these major initiatives needed U.S. aid, and Prime Minister Gerhardsen traveled to the United States in 1951 to solicit funding. Both the center-right papers and prominent politicians reacted quite strongly, not against the North Norway Plan, nor largely against the building of the aluminum works as such, but against the way the government had allegedly handled the planning process. Their arguments were of a constitutional nature. The government was accused of having discussed the issues with the Americans first and secured financing without having informed the *Storting*. *Arbeiderbladet* did not really join the fray, but largely left the center-right critics to themselves.[36] To the center-right press and politicians, of course, these were not isolated instances, but part of a pattern of Labor disdain for the *Storting*. A prominent Norwegian historian in 1963 dubbed the governing system after the war to be that of a one party state.[37] As far as Norway's foreign relations are concerned, the theory has not weathered the test of time very well, but it clearly pointed to a well-founded frustration among the center-right parties about their and the *Storting*'s limited influence under Labor's period of absolute majority rule.

Media Representations—Main Trends

As suggested above, it is striking that the interest in what the Marshall Plan actually brought to Norway was relatively limited. This may be a consequence of the fact that much of what arrived was fuel, grain, and what to the general reader must have been fairly non-descript capital goods inputs. It may also be a consequence of the papers reviewed for this essay. Occasionally, lists of goods coming in under the Marshall Plan were published and occasionally highlighted were tractors and bulldozers. However, the newspapers included in this analysis apparently had more of a focus on the planning, design, and implementation of the Marshall Plan and on its political meaning, rather than on its practical outcome and consequences in Norway. In this respect, the papers surveyed are probably not entirely representative for the Norwegian media at large (the media situation in Norway being characterized by a high number of small, local publications) because local or regional newspapers would probably have been more preoccupied by achievements taking place in their respective districts. As mentioned, the newspapers dealt with here were published either in Oslo or in Bergen, and three of them can be considered to varying degrees to be official representatives of the Conservative, the Social Democratic, and the Communist Parties, respectively. Some instances of how the results of the European Recovery Program (ERP) in Norway were communicated do, however, exist. An interesting case was in itself a representation, namely an exhibition of consumer goods produced in Norway with support from Marshall Aid funds, on display in Oslo's main department store in November 1950, and broadly covered in the city's newspapers. Before analyzing this display—both as a case in itself and as a media event—exploring some aspects of the official ERP propaganda of the United States in Norway, in particular through the use of film, is enlightening.

"Plugging the Marshall Plan Story"

As mentioned above, attempts were made by the information branch of the ECA Mission, in cooperation with both the U.S. Embassy and the USIS in Norway, both to secure media coverage of the ERP and to supply the media with stories that put the program in a positive light. The full story of the propaganda and information activities of the United States concerning the Marshall Plan in Norway remains to be written. Nevertheless, the existing research on the subject suggests that in addition to cooperating with and influencing newspaper editors and journalists, the use of exchanges (such as in technical study groups) and the use of films were central elements in this program. Reports from the U.S. Embassy and the USIS in Norway from the ERP period not only confirm that to "plug the Marshall Plan story" was an important task, but also suggest that the output was fairly large and that the attitudes of the Norwegian media were generally positive to the material provided by official U.S. sources, with the exception that the communist newspapers were highly critical and state radio was somewhat less receptive to this kind of output than the larger newspapers.[38]

The subject of the ERP stories promoted through such Foreign Service channels included facts and figures on shipments under the Marshall Plan, decisions on support for and the development of various investment projects, and coverage of developments in other countries participating in the program. Marshall Plan anniversaries and other events—like the return of Norwegians who had participated in technical study group visits to the United States—were also the subjects of media exploitation. The technical study groups were important both for spreading knowledge of the Marshall Plan, and as a possible source of inspiration for increased productivity in Norway, in showing how different trades and industries were functioning in the United States. In February 1950, a group of thirteen mechanical engineers and machinists went to study U.S. shop practices, and two engineers left to study the U.S. pulp and paper industry. Later the same year, a group of industrialists and technical scholars were sent to the United States. Other subjects covered in this program were the organization of Hotels and Youth Hostels and the production of watches, to mention only a few examples from the reports referred to above.[39]

The USIS and the ECA information branch also cooperated directly with the Norwegian government, organizations, and individuals in their approach to the media. The Ministry of Foreign Affairs was, for example, supportive in publishing media stories on the second anniversary of the ERP, and people from within the labor movement were instrumental in attempts to reach organized labor, an important target group for a variety of reasons. For instance, in the early spring of 1950, many social democratic newspapers published an article written by the editor of the Labor Press Agency, Inge Scheflo, in which he countered so-called misrepresentations of the Marshall Plan by arguing that the United States had given "[...] just as much in gifts and loans to countries with democratically socialist governments as to countries with bourgeois governments."[40] In 1948, the same press agency on several occasions supplied its network of subscribing social democratic newspapers with statements from ERP officials on the importance of the trade unions for European recovery and with promises that ECA administrations throughout Europe would listen to and cooperate with local unions. These statements were translated and adapted by Anders Buraas, foreign correspondent to London and Washington for *Arbeiderbladet*.[41]

In order to reach the labor unions and local branches of the governing Labor Party, the use of films was highly important. Documentaries and newsreels were produced by both the ECA and other U.S. agencies and distributed to local audiences in Norway through a variety of channels. Such films were shown in ordinary movie houses as a result of cooperation with both the state-run and the municipal film agencies. Non-governmental organizations were also instrumental in presenting films to a large audience, and one of the main outlets was the Labor Educational Foundation (*Arbeidernes Opplysningsforbund*, or AOF), that supplied adult education classes and groups and societies within the labor movement with films and other materials. The use of films to create positive images of the Marshall Plan (and of the United States, for that matter) was, however, not reserved to this movement. On an institutional level, the ECA and the USIS cooperated with a string of governmental and civic organizations, including, for example, the welfare office of the merchant navy, farmer's organizations, and the temperance movement. The number of clients such as teams, organizations, groups, and individuals reportedly increased from 500 to 750 during the second half of 1951. Among these clients were seventy-five so-called traveling secretaries, employed by one of the teams or organizations, who borrowed a number of films at a time and toured smaller villages in the remote parts of the country for a couple of months, showing U.S. produced films to the local population. During the above mentioned period, approximately 140,000 people saw one or more films produced and/or distributed by the ECA or the USIS in Norway, according to reports from the Norwegian organizations involved in their distribution. In addition, approximately three film showings per week were organized in or near Oslo, and some estimates claim that at times the film program reached as many as 80,000 viewers per month.[42] The film collection at this time consisted of 311 different films; most of them existed in six copies (five with Norwegian soundtracks, and one in English). It is not surprising that the reporting information officer in Oslo in January 1952 concluded, "Virtually all strata of Norwegian society were included among audiences seeing USIE and ECA films, ranking from the rank-and-file of the trade union movement, merchant seamen and farm workers to youth, women's and businessman's groups, armed forces organizations, public schools and scientific societies."[43]

The role of films concerning Norway and the Marshall Plan was, as in most other cases, dual. On the one hand, there were the films about the ERP and related issues, intended for propaganda use in Norway. On the other hand, there were films produced and recorded in Norway, intended for use both locally and in other countries participating in the reconstruction program; these films had at least two missions: to illustrate how the ERP could work in practice and to improve knowledge of another participating country. Both categories are of interest in this context.[44] The subjects of these films tended to be variations of a set of main themes, including what Norway had to offer in a wider cooperation with other European countries (for example, hydroelectric power, fisheries, a merchant marine), often in combination with examples of how these resources were utilized for the benefit of postwar recovery as a result of financial, practical, or technical aid provided through the Marshall Plan. A classic example of the integration of these narratives is the film *Breakthrough* (or *Aura* in Norwegian, named after the location of a hydroelectric plant) from 1950, which shows the final construction of this plant and the beginning of the production of electrical power there as a result of unified efforts. The import of equipment and construction materials from different European countries was described as a prerequisite for completing the construction; however, it would have been of no use had it not been combined with local know-how represented both by engineers and construction workers.[45] The main theme of (inter-European) cooperation is also reflected in the film through scenes showing large teams of workers (literally) pulling in the same direction. The general benefit of the interaction between local natural resources and aid from abroad is also the main subject in films like *Every Hour Counts* (*Hver time teller*), produced in Norway in 1951 and intended for use in Norwegian schools, dealing with the reconstruction of the fishing fleet, and the film on Norway in the series *The Marshall Plan at Work* (1950), dealing with a wide range of Norwegian industries that benefited from the ERP, including power plants, shipyards, steel mills, paper mills, and sardine factories. The message of these films, for both Norwegians and other Europeans, was obviously that to fulfill the potential of a nation, cooperation with others was—if not a necessity—highly preferable. A few films stretched this point even further, hinting at the possible benefits of tearing down national borders and, as such, arguing for a transnational integration that went beyond mere cooperation. Examples of this are *The Living Stream* from 1951, produced in Sweden for the ECA in Sweden, Denmark and Norway, highlighting the interdependence of these nations and at the same time depicting them as part of a larger whole, and the British production *Power for All* from 1951, on power production in different parts of Europe and the potential benefits of a transnational power grid.[46]

These films, like most of the other output from the ECA and USIS in this period, were fairly well received both by general audiences and in the press. Examples of the opposite may also be found. Several factors could hamper the potential impact of the materials used; exposing a lack of knowledge of Norwegian culture and society was definitely one of them. An illustrative example is the feedback from Oslo on a radio program on Norway in the *This Is Europe* series, produced by the ECA in 1950. This presentation was mainly intended for use in the United States, but would possibly also have been aired for Norwegian audiences. In the opinion of the information officers in Oslo, this was not advisable. In fact, they felt that it would be "[...] unfortunate if it reached Norwegian ears." There were several reasons why, including a script described as amateurish and written by a person with only superficial knowledge of Norway. In addition, neither the announcer nor the American actors contributing to the show were able to pronounce "[...] even the commonest Norwegian names."[47] Not only was it preferable that this broadcast was never used in Norway, neither the USIS nor ECA officials in Oslo saw it as particularly useful as a communication of the results of the ERP for even an American audience.

The Marshall Plan on Display

From the 7 to 18 November 1950, an exhibition of consumer goods produced in Norway with support from Marshall Aid funds was on display at Steen & Strøm, one of the leading department stores in Oslo. This spectacle in itself contributed to creating and promoting images of the Marshall Plan in Norway; in addition, the media coverage of the exhibition both supplemented and increased its effect. The initiative came from the management of Steen & Strøm that was inspired by a similar exhibition in Copenhagen. In cooperation with the ECA Mission, the Norwegian Ministry of Foreign Affairs, and thirty Norwegian enterprises who had received Marshall Aid, the store organized an exhibition called *Norske varer gjennom Marshall-hjelpen* (*Norwegian Consumer Goods through Marshall Aid*). The participating companies mainly represented the textile industry, producers of work and oilfield clothing, shoe factories, the rubber industry, and producers of porcelain, steel, and aluminum goods and knives. The companies all had window exhibits as well as small presentations of their products at different locations throughout the department store. To a certain extent, the goods on display were for sale, even if the main objective was to *present* the results of the aid received, not to sell them. In the course of the eleven days the goods were on display, a total of 149,905 individuals visited. On the second day of the show alone, 21,291 people visited; this represented an all time high in the history of Steen & Strøm—the last record being a total of 21,077 on the last Saturday before Christmas in 1946. The population of Oslo in 1950 was approximately 430,000.

Among the participants at the opening were the Norwegian prime minister and two other cabinet members, representatives from the ECA Mission, USIS, and the U.S. Embassy in Norway, and representatives from the ECA Missions to the other Scandinavian countries as well as Leland Barrows, executive assistant at the ECA Paris. Each part of the exhibition was accompanied by a short text explaining how the company in question had received ERP aid (be it through technical assistance, foreign currency funding, or access to new machinery or raw materials). According to a magazine published by Steen & Strøm and intended for staff and business partners, these texts were "more informative than column-long articles on the Marshall Plan being published in the newspapers from time to time, articles being read mainly by those who have a special interest in the subject." The magazine also claimed that for the first time since the start of the ERP, ordinary people were presented with a comprehensive image of the Marshall Plan and its results.[48] Despite this implicit criticism of the press coverage of the Marshall Plan in general, the same magazine expressed satisfaction with how the media had covered Steen & Strøm's own exhibition, noting that the newspapers mainly had gotten their stories straight as a result of an instructive press conference prior to the opening. Other coverage included a film recorded during the opening of the exhibition to be broadcast in the United States and in the other ERP countries and to be shown like a newsreel before the featured film in Norwegian cinemas; a ten-minute conversation between John E. Gross, leader of the ECA Mission in Norway, and Steen & Strøm chairman Erling Steen[49] to be broadcast on the foreign program service of Norwegian national radio; and mentions during the main radio news show a couple of times.

The media representation of the exhibit was not only a result of the editorial coverage of the event, but also of the advertisements for the exhibition and the companies participating in it. On opening day, ads ran in nine of the newspapers in the capital, presenting the exhibition and its objectives and mentioning the companies represented. In the course of the exhibition, three half-page ads appeared in different newspapers each day, so that all of the companies involved were presented to a larger audience at least once. The ads were meant to address those who did not have the opportunity to visit the exhibition and to see what use the factory in question had made of the aid received.

The general advertisement stated that the aim of the exhibition was to show the significance of the ERP for the production of Norwegian consumer goods. The tone of the text was rather sober and factual, highlighting that during the two years of the ERP, Norwegian companies had been given the opportunity to increase and expand their production and, thus, contribute to reducing the effects of war and occupation. Import of machinery and raw materials had made it possible both to maintain the level of employment, and to "[...] bring the country a giant step forward." The ads for the various enterprises were a mixture of factual information on the form of aid received and straightforward marketing. For instance, Brødrene Øyo (producers of tools and knives) explained that through the ERP it had been able to import both necessary machines and raw materials from the United Kingdom and the United States and as a result of this was able to produce stainless steel table-knives with white handles—hitherto only seen in Norway as imported goods. Focusing on the Norwegian origin of the consumer goods highlighted the effect of the foreign aid: it made possible the production of elegant knives, nylon stockings, and household goods in aluminum or porcelain and upheld and expanded production within the textile industry. According to John E. Gross, the display of goods was all the more remarkable since the "[...] emphasis on recovery in Norway has been in fields other than the production of goods for consumption."[50] The availability of consumer goods in 1950 was still limited; thus the advertisements in the newspapers probably made a substantial impact on the general public. The layout of the ads left no doubt as to the importance of the U.S. aid program for this development in consumer goods production. How did the editorial coverage of the exhibition relate to this? Most of the articles on the opening day reproduced the information that was to be found in the exhibition and in the organizer's information on it—supplemented in some cases with statements on the importance of sound and well-functioning economic and political systems for national security.[51] *Aftenposten* stated that the exhibition was instructive for "those of us who have no personal need for locomotives or large power plants, but who are content with a little linen sheeting every now and then, a few nylon stockings two or three times a year, and an aluminum kettle for every birthday."[52] This newspaper, along with several others, thus used the occasion to illustrate that the ERP in Norway would also result in increased access to goods of which there had been a shortage, but in line with the information and sales policy communicated by the organizers also noted that there would be more to come, that despite the possibility of buying some of the displayed goods, the exhibition was mainly a show for informational purposes, not a sales fair.

Final Comments

Also on this issue, the communist *Friheten* differed from the majority of newspapers. Its coverage took place under the headline "The Marshall Plan Provides Record-Breaking Profits for American and Norwegian Trusts," arguing that the "aid" led to rearmament, a period of high prices, and a low standard of living for the Norwegian population and that the participating countries were made dependant upon the United States, both financially and politically. According to the paper, imported goods under the ERP had to be purchased at black-market prices. The praise for the recovery plan from the participating enterprises was explained by claims that they had gotten their share of the surplus created through a rise in prices and devaluation of the local currency. All other newspapers took a different and more positive approach. Conservative, liberal, and social democratic newspapers were all preoccupied with how this was an example of what consequences the ERP—and its long-term effects—would have for everyday life and for consumer opportunities in the years to come. The effects of the plan would not only be increased production of consumer goods, but increased production of high-quality goods *in Norway*.[53] *Arbeiderbladet* made the words of Minister of Trade and Commerce Erik Brofoss its own, stating that since the ERP would not go on for ever, it had been the right thing to do to use the accessible funding to invest in national production and in increased activity locally to make the country less dependant on the import of consumer goods. The newspaper also quoted Gross, who had described this policy as an expression of how Norway had received and used the foreign aid in the "same spirit as it had been given."[54] Even in their coverage of a case that had an explicit focus on the consequences of the ERP for ordinary people, the Norwegian media were eager to see the potential social benefits of the program in relation to the political implications of it. Several papers, but especially the largest ones, made the point that the aim of the ERP was both economic well-being and a lasting peace and that both ambitions could best be reached through the kind of transatlantic cooperation that both the program and, eventually, the military alliance represented. An important nuance in this representation of the Marshall Plan was, however, that when it came to economic well-being and access to consumer goods, the plan represented a promise for the future.

As a means to increase and bolster the Atlantic orientation of the main Norwegian media, as well as their support for financial, military, and political cooperation, the ERP apparently fulfilled its objective well before it was finished. As for the Steen & Strøm exhibition, it represented an image of Marshall aid and its consequences that was similar to the one in the main media. At the same time, the exhibition reflected various, partly conflicting, aspects of the postwar reconstruction strategies in Norway: Labor's planned economy, with its austerity policies and high investment rate, both met with approval and encountered strong criticism. By 1950, the clamor for more and a wider range of consumer goods was clearly becoming a challenge in Norway because rationing was still extensive. The Steen & Strøm exhibition catered to both those in favor of the government's policies and its critics. It demonstrated that the investments made possible by the Marshall Plan were already making possible a wider variety of domestically produced consumer goods than had been available in the interwar period, and once controls, rationing, and regulations were dismantled, these would be available to everyone. In addition, the exhibition reached out to those who argued for buying Norwegian. In a short-term perspective, it was, thus, successful on a number of levels. In the longer run, of course, liberalization would finish off quite a number of the new consumer goods manufacturers that were founded and expanded during this period.

Notes

1 We want to thank Martine Svanevik for her thorough analysis of five of Norway's most important newspapers in the 1947–1952 period. She sums up her main findings in the unpublished paper "Marshallplanen og Norge—Avisdekning og småtrykk 1947–1952," dated 18 March 2008.

2 For an excellent English language analysis of Norway's foreign relations since the Middle Ages, see Olav Riste, *Norway's Foreign Relations—A History*, 2nd ed. (Oslo: Universitetsforlaget, 2005); for the still most recent introductory text to Norwegian history in English, see R. Danielsen et al., *Norway: A History from the Vikings to Our Own Times* (Oslo: Universitetsforlaget, 1995). Both of these works are too brief to deal with the intricacies of Norwegian Marshall Plan policies; for a discussion in Norwegian, see Helge Ø. Pharo, "Gjenreisning og utenrikspolitikk" ("Reconstruction and Foreign Policy"), in *Historiker og veileder: Festskrift til Jakob Sverdrup*, ed. Trond Bergh and Helge Ø. Pharo (Oslo: Tiden, 1989), 163–202; see also Even Lange, *Samling om felles mål: 1935–1970*, vol. 11, Aschehougs Norgeshistorie (Oslo: Aschehoug, 2005), 152–237; and Trond Bergh, *Storhetstid*, vol. 5, Arbeiderbevegelsens historie i Norge (Oslo: Tiden, 1987), 160–88 and 224–71; for a detailed analysis of Norway's response to the Marshall Plan during 1947, see Helge Ø. Pharo, "Bridgebuilding and Reconstruction: Norway Faces the Marshall Plan," *Scandinavian Journal of History* 1.1/2 (1976): 125–53. Another contribution in English is Kai Roger Pedersen's, "The United States and Norwegian Reconstruction, 1945–1953," Ph.D. diss., University of Rochester, 1989.

3 Archives of the Norwegian Foreign Ministry, Norwegian National Archives, henceforth ANFM, 25.4/47, 14 June 1947. Norwegian language historical studies are usually referred to as UD with the archival code added; *Arbeiderbladet*, 26 June 1947.

4 Nils Langhelle Papers. Archives and Library of the Labor Movement, ALLM (in Norwegian, Arbeiderbevegelsens arkiv og bibliotek), Notebook 1945–47, 17 June 1947. Langhelle very much went along with Lange as a center-right member of the Cabinet; he was a fellow historian and in many instances acted as substitute for Lange in NATO and at UN meetings during the 1950s in particular.

5 Pharo, "Bridgebuilding and Reconstruction"; Riste, *Norway's Foreign Relations*, 183–205.

6 Magne Skodvin's *Norden eller Nato: Utenriksdepartementet og alliansespørsmålet 1947–1949* (Oslo: Universitetsforlaget, 1971), though in many respects dated and at times rather too close to the official version of the road to NATO, is a very perceptive introduction to Foreign Minister Lange's thinking; see also Jakob Sverdrup, *Inn i storpolitikken 1940–1949*, vol. 4, Norsk utenrikspolitikks historie (Oslo: Universitetsforlaget, 1996), 277–301; Knut E. Eriksen, *DNA og NATO: en redegjørelse for debatten og vedtakene i Det norske arbeiderparti 1948–49* (Oslo: Gyldendal, 1971), 19–71.

7 Pharo, "Bridgebuilding and Reconstruction"; Riste, *Norway's Foreign Relations*, 195–205.

8 Pharo, "Bridgebuilding and Reconstruction," 129–30; Olav Njølstad, *Jens Christian Hauge—Fullt og Helt* (Oslo: Aschehoug, 2008), 310–23; Eriksen, *DNA og NATO*, 19–71.

9 Pharo, "Gjenreisning og utenrikspolitikk," 172–74, 177, 179. For the debate, and in particular conservative spokesman Rolf Strangers' critique of the loan agreement, see *Stortingstidende* (St.t., parliamentary proceedings) 7 (1947): 1022.

10 The Labor Party was constituted by several key voter groups: industrial workers, small-scale farmers and forestry workers, and small-scale fishermen and fishing hands. In the postwar period, a significant influx of intellectuals and recent university graduates occurred. Labor enjoyed its greatest support in the east, center, and north of Norway. The Party's modernization and industrialization drive was met with considerable skepticism if not outright opposition from its primary sector voters and their parliamentary representatives. As for the center-right parties, the Conservative, the Liberal, the Farmers' and the Christian People's, all of them had strong primary sector representation. The Farmers' Party almost exclusively, but the Liberals and Conservatives too, were more inclined towards modernization and industrialization, but skeptical of Labor's planning efforts and preference for relatively large-scale manufacturing industries.

11 St.t. 7 (1946): 345, 1506, 1873. The Farmers' Party above all represented the dominant social strata in rural areas.

12 Pharo, "Bridge-building and Reconstruction," 130–33; Pharo, "Gjenreisning og utenrikspolitikk," 172–80.

13 Einar Lie, *Ambisjon og tradisjon: Finansdepartementet, 1945–1965* (Oslo: Universitetsforlaget, 1995), 115–26; Bergh, *Storhetstid,* 160–177; Eriksen, *DNA og NATO,* 19–71.

14 Quoted from Lie, *Ambisjon og tradisjon,* 118. The recipient was Petter Jakob Bjerve, at the time on leave to study in the United States. Bjerve was soon to become director of the Norwegian Bureau of Statistics; just over a decade later, he would serve as Minister of Finance.

15 See Frode Liland, "De som elsket Amerika: Kollektive forestillinger om Amerika i Norge, 1945–1949" ("Those Who Loved America: Collective Perceptions of America in Norway, 1945–1949"), M.A. thesis, University of Oslo, 1992, quote on page 83 from *Dagbladet,* 26 March 1949, for general conclusions, see 136.

16 Helge Ø. Pharo, *Tjalve: 100 år* (Oslo: Schibsted, 1990), 119. Even in small-town Norway, American athletes competed in track meets into the early 1970s. The 1964 Olympic champion in the 400 meters, Mike Larrabee, set a track record in the southeastern town of Sarpsborg in 1956; see also Liland, "De som elsket Amerika," 33; Even Lange, "Norske ingeniører i Amerika 1900–1950. En moderne svennevandring," in *Historiker og veileder,* ed. Bergh and Pharo, 252–68; Liland, 58, also points to the fact that a women's journal, *Alle Kvinners Blad,* in 1948 advertised a NOK 10,000 scholarship open to housewives and students of home economics to go to the United States to study rationalization of housework (58). The United States was the model of what was modern to the Labor movement, as well. After the 1949 devaluation, the Norwegian crown was pegged to the dollar at 7.14.

17 Norwegian participation in the various exchange programs organized by the U.S. State Department or affiliated agencies was high, both in proportion to the Norwegian population and in absolute figures. See "United States Grantee Directory Fiscal Year 1965," Bureau of Educational and Cultural Affairs, U.S. Department of State, Mar. 1966. See also Helge Danielsen, "Making Friends at Court: Slow and Indirect Media in U.S. Public Diplomacy in Norway, 1950–1965," *Contemporary European History* 18.2 (May 2009): 179–98.

18 For specific issues and articles, we refer to the newspapers themselves; for more general impressions, we rely on Martine Svanevik's paper and Svein Andreassen, "Norge og Marshallplanen: Pressereaksjoner og norsk holdning i tiden 5. juni-22. september 1947," M.A. thesis, University of Oslo, 1969. Andreassen included twenty papers and two periodicals in his survey, which includes virtually all the main national papers and a number of the most important regional ones.

19 On the excellence of the *Bergens Tidende*'s coverage of foreign affairs, see Andreassen, "Norge og Marshallplanen," 10–11; Svanevik makes the same observation; see also Eriksen, *DNA og NATO.*

20 A more broadly based survey should include all the main regional papers, both the normally dominant center-right ones and the smaller Labor papers. The main regional papers number about twenty. The most important national paper missing from our survey, but included in Andreassen's, is *Verdens Gang,* a paper that was resurrected in 1945 to serve as a non-party mouthpiece of core elements of the wartime resistance. A key foreign affairs analyst was Hans Engen, who was very close to Foreign Minister Lange and later became the press officer of Norway's UN embassy and then UN ambassador. Engen's views of international affairs are known to have been very close to Lange's own. In the late 1950s, he was appointed Undersecretary of State, and at the time of his early death in 1966, he was ambassador to the United States, the key post of the Norwegian diplomatic service.

21 Andreassen, "Norge og Marshallplanen," 4–14.

22 See Helge Danielsen, "Mediating Public Diplomacy: Local Conditions and U.S. Public Diplomacy in Norway in the 1950s," forthcoming in *Washington and Beyond: Public Diplomacy and U.S. Foreign Relations, Toward an International History*, ed. Brian Etheridge and Kenneth Osgood (Leiden: Brill Academic); see also Danielsen, "Making Friends at Court."

23 Svanevik, "Marshallplanen og Norge"; Andreassen, "Norge og Marshallplanen," 85–88.

24 Andreassen, "Norge og Marshallplanen," 15–19. It is worth noticing, however, that the very prominent government economist Eivind Erichsen in an article in the current affairs journal *Internasjonal Politikk* 4 (1947) in the summer of 1947 was quite critical of the overproduction theory.

25 Andreassen, "Norge og Marshallplanen," 4–14

26 Ibid., 7, 87–88; Svanevik, "Marshallplanen og Norge"; *Arbeiderbladet*, 17 November 1947; also *Dagbladet*, 3 October 1947, though it still highlights the necessity for bridge-building.

27 *Aftenposten*, 10 January, 31 March, 28 August, 14 December 1948; *Arbeiderbladet*, 1 October 1947, 12 May 1951; *Bergens Tidende*, 12 June 1948, 31 March 1950. The comments were, however, matter-of-fact rather than outspokenly critical.

28 *Aftenposten*, 22 April, 26 April, 11 June 1948; *Arbeiderbladet*, 21 April, 27 April, 7 June 1948; *Bergens Tidende*, 26 April 1948; *Dagbladet*, 21 May, 26 May, 7 June 1948.

29 ECA/Oslo was always a staunch supporter of Norwegian estimates of its own needs. ECA/W and the Office of the Special Representative in Paris were frequently more critical, but mostly went along with Oslo. See Helge Ø. Pharo, "Marshallplanen sett fra amerikansk side. Norge i komparativt perspektiv," *Historisk tidsskrift* 68.2 (1989): 184–209.

30 Pharo, "Gjenreisning og utenrikspolitikk," 190–96.

31 Such reorientations were facilitated by the fact that the communists lost their representation in the *Storting* in the fall 1949 elections.

32 *Aftenposten*, 27 September and 21 October 1949, 30 December 1950; *Arbeiderbladet*, 8 February and 21 February 1950; *Bergens Tidende*, 3 November 1949; *Dagbladet*, 20 October 1949; the Farmers' Party was essentially protectionist as it was in the aftermath of World War I. Since we have not checked any of their papers, we do not know whether or to what extent they distinguished between protection of the agricultural sector and liberalization in other fields.

33 See, for example, Even Lange and Helge Ø. Pharo, "Have Your Cake and Eat It, Too, National Policy and Private Interest in a Small Open Economy: The Case of Norway," in *Pathbreakers: Small European Countries Responding to Globalisation and Deglobalisation*, ed. Margrit Müller and Timo Myllyntaus (Bern: P. Lang, 2008), 152–74; Helge Ø. Pharo, "Ingen vei utenom? Norge i integrasjonsprosessene i Europa 1946–1994," in *Utenfor, annerledes og suveren: Norge under EØS-avtalen*, ed. Dag H. Claes and Bent S. Tranøy (Bergen: Fagbokforlaget, 1999), 15–38; T. Grønlie, *Forvaltning og fullmaktslovgivning som etterkrigshistorisk forskningsfelt* (Bergen: LOS-senteret, 1993); Helge Ø. Pharo, "Post-Cold War Historiography in Norway," in *The Cold War and the Nordic Countries: Historiography at a Crossroads*, ed. Thorsten B. Olesen (Odense: UP of Southern Denmark, 2004), 97–142.

34 *Arbeiderbladet* 19 August and 27 August 1949, 1 April 1950; even *Aftenposten* made a point of full employment in addition to liberalization and competition, 30 December 1950.

35 *Aftenposten*, 2 December 1948, 19 September 1949, 14 October 1947, 19 November 1948, 27 July and 5 September 1949, 8 February and 21 February 1950; *Bergens Tidende*, 2 December 1948, 31 December 1949; *Dagbladet* joined in the praise for planning and the Marshall Plan, 2 September 1949, also 15 January 1949.

36 *Aftenposten*, 19 June, 21 June, 26 July, 27 July 1951; *Arbeiderbladet*, 8 June and 19 June 1951; *Bergens Tidende*, 14 June, 21 July, 8 August 1951; *Dagbladet*, 18 June, 19 June, 20 June, 21 June, 27 July, 31 July, 9 August, 18 August 1951; Knut E. Eriksen and Helge Ø. Pharo, *Kald krig og internasjonalisering*, vol. 5, Norsk utenrikspolitikks historie (Oslo: Universitetsforlaget, 1997), 18.

37 Jens Arup Seip, *Fra embedsmannsstat til ettpartistat og andre essays* (Oslo: Universitetsforlaget, 1963).

38 See, for instance, monthly reports from USIS-Oslo (Oslo) to the Department of State (State), 10 February 1950, 9 March 1950, 3 April 1950, 5 May 1950, and 12 June 1950, as well as a semi-annual report dated 11 April 1951, covering the period from 31 May to 30 November 1950, all in Record Group (RG) 59, Central Files, Decimal File 1950–1954, 511.57–511.576, Box 2415, National Archives, College Park, Maryland (hereafter NA) and USIE-Oslo to the Department of State, 1

September 1950, Semi-annual Evaluation Report for USIE, covering the period from 1 January to 31 May, 1950, in RG 59, Department of State, Central Files, 1950–54, 511.57–511.576, Box 2414, NA. See also Danielsen, "Making Friends at Court" and Danielsen, "Mediating."

39 In addition to being effective events securing media coverage of the Marshall Plan, these technical study groups had a large impact as a source of inspiration and learning in different contexts. No comprehensive analyses exist of this and other efforts by the United States to promote increased productivity and other ERP objectives in Norway, but a fairly recent study on the Norwegian Consumer Cooperatives highlights how these cooperatives, in part on the basis of knowledge acquired from studying U.S. practices, had a large impact on the development of everyday retail business in Norway in the first decades after World War II. See Even Lange, ed., *Organisert kjøpekraft: Forbrukersamvirkets historie i Norge* (Oslo: Pax, 2006). It is also highly likely that individuals participating in such group trips to the United States under the sponsorship of ECA Norway developed a fairly positive attitude toward the United States in general and later functioned as local experts on the United States both in private and professional contexts. The potential value of having such experts was of high importance in the use of exchange programs as a form of public diplomacy in Norway throughout the 1950s and in the early 1960s; Danielsen, "Making Friends at Court."

40 Oslo to State, 9 March 1950, in RG 59, Central Files, Decimal File 1950–1954, 511.57–511.576, Box 2415, NA.

41 Oddbjørn Melle: *Supermakter og kaldkrig-arenaer* (Oslo: Abstrakt forlag, 2008), 175.

42 See Country Paper for Norway, July 1950, RG 59, Records Relating to International Information Activities 1938–53, Box 41. According to a calculation made by the historian Stian Bones, throughout the 1950s between 1 and 1.25 million people *annually* watched a film distributed by USIS. Stian Bones, "I oppdemmingspolitikkens grenseland. Nord-Norge i den kalde krigen 1947–70," Ph.D. diss., University of Tromsø, 2007.

43 Oslo to State, 11 January 1952, Six Sections of the USIE/Oslo Semi-annual Evaluation Report, RG 59, Central Files, 1950–1954, 511.57–511.576, Box 2415, NA.

44 This section is mainly based on the viewing of selected Marshall Plan films and on descriptions/abstracts of films as provided in the filmography compiled by Linda R. Christenson, "Marshall Plan Filmography Listing," George C. Marshall Motion Pictures, http://www.marshallfilms.org/mpf.asp, accessed several times in the summer and fall of 2008.

45 The construction of the plant had started in the interwar period and was delayed by financial depression in the 1930s. German efforts at finishing the plant during the occupation of Norway faltered as a result of sabotage actions by the Norwegian resistance movement.

46 In addition to the symbolic and European aspects of such films, the choice of subjects could be seen in relation to ongoing debates and negotiations on Scandinavian cooperation, such as on the export of power from Norway to the other Nordic countries and on a Scandinavian customs union; Eriksen and Pharo, *Kald krig og internasjonalisering*, 156ff and 162ff.

47 Oslo to State 16 March 1950, RG 59, Central Files, 1950–1954, 511.57–511.576, Box 2416, NA.

48 See *Steen & Strøms Magasin* 7.39 (Christmas/December 1950): 5.

49 Erling Steen (1891–1961), was co-owner and chairman of the Steen & Strøm department store. He received his education in Germany, France, and the United States and had spent one year at a department store in Boston just after World War I. He held a number of positions in trade organizations and was a member of the Oslo Chamber of Commerce and the Economic Coordination Council after the Second World War. He also had links to prominent members of the Norwegian Labor movement through his participation in the Norwegian resistance movement and after being incarcerated at Grini, a prison camp outside Oslo, during the German occupation. Steen was president of the Norwegian Red Cross from 1947 to 1957 and chairman of the Norwegian Refugee Council from 1953 to 1958. He was of a liberal political persuasion and, thus, critical of the quantitative regulations in Norway after 1945. *Norsk biografisk leksikon*, vol. 14 (Oslo: Aschehoug, 1962); "Erling Steen," *Store Norske Leksikon*, http://snl.no/Erling_Steen, accessed 10 March 2009.

50 From Gross's speech at the opening of the exhibit in *Steen & Strøms Magasin*.

51 See, for instance, the dailies *Morgenposten* and *Verdens Gang*, 7 January 1950.

52 *Aftenposten*, 7 December 1950.

53 See *Aftenposten*, morning ed., 8 November 1950.

54 *Arbeiderbladet*, 8 November 1950.

Stelios Zachariou

The Dichotomy of Projecting the Marshall Plan in Greece:

The Ideological Battle vs. the Rehabilitation Effort

The legacy of the Marshall Plan as panacea from the postwar devastation remains, to this day, a landmark in modern European history. The diachronic importance of the European Recovery Program (ERP) stems from its irrefutable success as a coagulator for transatlantic socioeconomic and military relations while acting at the same time as a catalyst for European rehabilitation. Throughout the Marshall Plan years, American administrators on both sides of the Atlantic worked tirelessly to revive the industrial infrastructure of European countries, along with the spirit of their exhausted inhabitants.[1]

In order to effectively achieve this goal, however, the Marshall Plan had to be successfully promoted both at home and among the citizens of the sixteen recipient nations. The burden of this task in Europe was left mostly to the ERP missions whose guidelines in this undertaking were summarized by the Office of Information of the Economic Cooperation Administration (OIECA) in four general functions:

- To make available to both the U.S. and the international press material that could be used in reporting about the various activities of the Marshall Plan.
- To promote understanding among the European People of the motives of the United States in extending recovery aid, to explain the objectives and methods of the program, to tell the amount of help which America is extending, and to create an awareness in Europe about the ERP, its progress and operations.
- To explain the close relationship of the ERP to U.S. foreign policy in Europe and to counteract Communist propaganda against the Marshall Plan.
- To inform the recipient countries about the steps which were necessary if economic stability was to be attained by the end of the Marshall Plan in 1952.[2]

Applying these principles while implementing the Marshall Plan in Greece, however, would prove economically challenging and politically risky, considering that the otherwise mutually reinforcing priorities of reconstruction and geopolitical security would clash. Given the unique circumstances in Greece, promoting the Marshall Plan would prove even more challenging.

Unlike the fifteen other recipient nations of Marshall Plan aid, Greece would have to juxtapose reconstruction with a civil war which lasted until October 1949, in essence the two most critical years of the implementation of the Plan, when Congress appropriated over $5 billion for the period 1948–1949 and $3.5 billion for 194–950.[3] The civil war in Greece would force government officials to redirect attention from reconstruction efforts to an emphasis on defeating the communist-led Democratic Army which inaugurated the third and final phase of its armed struggle following the attack on a police station in the village of Litohoro, located on the base of Mount Olympus. This attack would mark the last effort of the Democratic Army of Greece to attempt a take over of government.[4] When the Marshall Plan was set in motion, counterpart funds, which in accordance to ECA rules had to be invested in economic rehabilitation projects and reconstruction, were instead absorbed by the national budget in order to accommodate the requirements of the armed forces in the fight to thwart the communists and to accommodate the influx into the urban centers of refugees fleeing the embattled zones of the civil war. Today, it is almost impossible to verify the exact appropriation of counterpart funds because the archival holdings of the Bank of Greece, which managed the counterpart funds account, have been destroyed or lost.

The distinctness which defined post World War II Greece and the anxiety which gripped both Greek and American officials was heavily stressed in the plethora of articles in the U.S. press which projected the crisis in Greece as a definitive struggle between the forces of democracy and communism. It should thus come as no surprise that media representations of U.S. aid to Greece had strong political undertones of anti-communism, while press reporting on Greek developments stressed rehabilitation efforts for the refugees created by the Civil War, amounting to over half a million, and reconstruction projects that were of primary importance to the operations against the defeat of the Democratic Army.[5] Inevitably, the situation that the Civil War created forced the deferment of reconstruction plans that would bolster the agrarian and industrial sector, for the period after the end of hostilities. At the same time, funds that were directed into non-military infrastructure projects aimed at assisting the war effort directly.[6] Such projects included the construction of roads, harbors, and airfields and the rebuilding of the railway system that had been heavily damaged from the war, which linked the capital to the embattled zones, especially in the north.[7] When the Civil War ended in October 1949, it was estimated that of the $648 million which Greece had received in U.S. aid by the middle of 1949, $529 million (81.6 percent) was spent on the military requirements of the civil war.[8] Around the same time, a State Department Aide Memoir would note that "only by eliminating a substantial portion of the drain upon the Greek economy imposed by the maintenance of forces of the present magnitude can an effective economic rehabilitation program be implemented on a scale necessary for Greece to reap substantial long range benefits."[9] Considering the reconstruction that was unrelated to the military campaign efforts and begun after the end of the Civil War, it becomes apparent that the information program and media representation in Greece stressing development related projects began at a much later date than was the case in other European countries.

Given the uniqueness of the post-World War II developments in Greece, projection and presentation of the Marshall Plan program in this particular country must be seen not in a continuum, but rather in two separate sections. First, the period from the inauguration of the Marshall Plan until October 1949, and second, the period from October 1949 until December 1952, when the Marshall Plan officially ended in Greece. Thus, Greece, along with Austria, a country occupied in part by Soviet forces until the signing of the Austrian State Treaty in May 1955, was hampered from fully utilizing the funds provided by the Marshall Plan. Consequently, leaders of both countries were unable to focus on the requirements that would allow them to rebuild their respective nations, while creating an industrial foundation. Such a prospect was especially difficult for Greece, marred by the first armed struggle of the Cold War which added to the destructive process of the World War.

October Summer 1948 through September 1949

In a discussion of the first period, it is important to keep in mind that when Marshall Plan Aid began to flow into Greece in the summer of 1948, the country was in the midst of a civil war, with government forces planning their final operations against the communists. In the United States, press reports about Greece stressed the struggle against the communist-led Democratic Army, the inability of the American Mission of Aid to Greece (AMAG) to act effectively, and, subsequently, the inability of the Athens contingency of the Economic Cooperation Administration (ECA) to implement a reconstruction program that would revive the Greek economy and industry before the defeat of the Communists. Even before the implementation of the Marshall Plan, the *Christian Science Monitor* would note in February 1948 that "[...] reconstruction obviously is a cart-before-the-horse approach to Greek problems [...] having recognized that the United States must first of all help the Greeks to win an armed struggle against the guerrillas [...]."[10] Less than a month later, the *New York Times* would publish an article stressing the urgency of the situation by indicating that in Greece "the cold war is no longer cold but hot, and that, as stressed by President Truman [...] the situation [...] is not primarily economic but military, and must be met by military means."[11] The preeminent fear of the Truman Administration that the Mediterranean would be transformed into a Soviet lake, severing passage through the Dardanelles and barring access to the Middle East, was accentuated with the prospect of a communist electoral victory in the 18 April 1948 elections in Italy.[12] Such prospects would set the geopolitical considerations above the planning prospects of reconstruction and development. Concern about geopolitical dominance was, thus, the defining consideration that initially guided U.S. strategy in Greece and would guide U.S. foreign policy throughout the world after the outbreak of the Korean War.

Affected by the ongoing developments, media coverage of the Marshall Plan in Greece was overshadowed by (A) developments in the Civil War), (B) the lack of political stability due to the frequent and erratic reshuffling of governmental posts, and (C) the inflationary pressures that made the currency unstable and, subsequently, untrustworthy. Despite these hurdles, the new Ministry of Coordination, under the leadership of Stephanos Stephanopoulos, was tasked with the responsibility of coordinating the implementation efforts of the ERP. In order to promote this undertaking and create a momentum of home like other Marshall Plan recipients, the Ministry of Coordination published a weekly pamphlet titled *Battle for Survival* (*Αγών Επιβίωσης*), in order to inform Greek citizens of the works and projects funded under the Marshall Plan program. The name of the publication alone is indicative of the gravity of the situation in Greece and of the prism through which the Marshall Plan was perceived. The weekly publication, created by the division of the Ministry of Coordination for the Implementation of Reconstruction, began its circulation in September of 1948 and provided statistical information regarding the allocation of funds, as well as the projects which were being funded by Marshall Plan Aid and supervised by the ECA mission in Greece.[13] It is important to note that Greece had the largest Mission of all ERP recipient countries, which is representative of the shortage of manpower in the civil government, to undertake the responsibilities of a coordinating effort to implement an effective reconstruction program. Indicative of the weak structure of the Greek civil government was the fact that the ECA Mission in Athens was the only one that had a "Civil Government" branch, a division that focused on ways to create a more efficient form of governance for Greece.[14] Complementing the ECA mission was also a large number of U.S. volunteer organizations which played an active role in the Greek recovery process.[15]

Despite the numerical advantages, during the first two years all efforts to revamp the Greek economy were overshadowed by the threat of communist victory and the need to defeat the Democratic Army and secure Greece in the Western camp. Press reports and images emanating from Greece would stress the importance of the Marshall Plan as a conduit for the success of the government forces against the communist-led Democratic Army and also as a provider of basic necessities such as food, clothing, and housing for the refugees of the civil war. Thus, ERP efforts were implemented through a strict politico-military prism of preponderance of power for fear of a communist takeover postponing the macroeconomic resurrection of a nation caught between an ideological Scylla and Charybdis.

October 1949 to December 1962

Once the Civil War ended, the ECA Mission shifted its focus to the reconstruction efforts, inaugurating the second period of the Marshall Plan effort in Greece. The United States Information Service (USIS) played a pivotal role in this task by educating Greek civilians about the initiatives undertaken through the Marshall Plan to rebuild Greece.[16] There were seven USIS offices throughout Greece that functioned as reading and cultural centers for the local Greek communities.[17] These centers acted as a viaduct of information where leaflets were distributed about the local, regional, and national development projects. It was also in these centers that the USIS publication *Free World* was distributed providing information about life in the United States and accentuating the benefits of a free and democratically elected government. Furthermore, the vessel Samuel Gridley Howe toured the Greek islands in an effort to inform the isolated islanders of the implementation of the Marshall Plan in Greece, while at the same time acting as a "cultural propagandist" of U.S. democratic principles, for it carried a permanent exhibit on board touting the contributions and achievements that Marshall Plan aid offered. Additionally, the ECA Mission in Athens circulated regular press releases about the activities and the achievements of U.S. aid at work.

At the same time, the Greek government was less effective in promoting the Marshall Plan, in part due to the emphasis on the requirements of the Civil War, but also because from liberation in 1944 to the end of 1951, there were over twenty-six different governments in office, an indicator of the highly volatile political situation in Greece.[18] Due to the frequent parliamentary transitions, which resulted in changes of government officials in key ministerial posts, a decision was made to establish a ministry that would coordinate intra-ministerial efforts for the applications of the Marshall Plan. The daily newspapers of the period projected the Marshall Plan through their ideological prisms, that is, either as an important economic aid effort that saved Greece from communism, or as an interventionist attempt to control the country politically through friendly governments. More importantly, Greek media representation of the Marshall Planners aimed at promoting the multitude of individual interests in an overly fragmented political environment. This often pitted the Embassy and the Mission against the factions of the Greek political world, causing friction in an overly delicate cooperative environment.

Conclusion

The aid program that the Economic Cooperation Administration set out to accomplish in Greece can be described as a relief and rescue effort in tandem with a brutal civil war which acted as a hindrance for formative reconstruction projects, followed by a rushed effort to implement a recovery program in an increasingly polarized and militarized global environment. For the first two pivotal years of the Marshall Plan during which Greece struggled to preserve itself on the democratic side of the Iron Curtain, reconstruction came second to the fight against the communist-led Democratic Army. During that time, the use of economic aid provided through the ERP was directed to the needs of the armed forces and not for projects that would bolster long-term socioeconomic development. Exemplifying this phenomenon was correspondence between the Greek government and the U.S. Embassy in Athens in February 1950, well past the heyday of the Marshall Plan aid program, which announced the "initiation of the construction of the energy grid of the country" through the construction of five hydroelectric dams.[19] However, by the time the Civil War was concluded and Greece was attempting to make up for lost time in the race for reconstruction, U.S. foreign policy would shift gears, especially after the outbreak of the Korean War, and follow a more rigid course as indicated by NSC-68.

While the Marshall Plan was not meant to be a countermeasure for communism in Europe, for Greece it had this very effect, considering that it was the aid appropriated through the ERP that established the armed forces as a formidable bulwark against the advance of communism in the Balkans. Greece would not have to wait until the summer of 1950 and the outbreak of the Korean War to experience the qualitative change and the intensification in the ideological economic and psychological pressure to tackle communist proliferation. While from the Korean War onwards "problems of military security would [formally] take over from economic reconstruction at the head of US priorities in Europe. [...] The ECA men on the ground [in Greece] had already decided [...] that there was no conflict between defense and the ERP objectives: it was just a matter of bending the existing policy goals to the new requirements.[20] The policy, inaugurated after the onset of the Korean conflict, continued to promote the core ideals of the Marshall Plan, injecting, however, the element of militarism and circumscribing the principles of corporate capitalism and market economics. Thus the new guidelines as interpreted by David Ellwood indicate that:

1. Marshall aid and military assistance are good for you because they give you—as Europeans—a fighting chance to make Europe strong enough to discourage any aggression.
2. This strength can only be achieved through unity. As separate, rival powers, the nations of Free Europe are weak, are dangerously exposed.[21]

These new guidelines were a far cry from the original principles presented by the Office of Information of the Office of Economic Cooperation Administration. However, they had always been underlying principles in media representations of the Marshall Plan in Greece and remained unwavering from the outset of the European Recovery Program in both the presentation and application of the aid program.

Notes

1 The European Recover Program (ERP), as the Marshall Plan was officially titled, was operated by the Economic Cooperation Administration (ECA). During the four year period, Congress granted and the ECA administered $13,224.1 billion, $11,736.2 billion in grants, and $1,487.9 billion in loans. (U.S. Agency for International Development, *U.S. Economic Assistance Programs Administered by the Agency for International Development and Predecessor Agencies, April 3, 1948-June 30, 1970* (Washington, D.C.: AID Office of Statistics and Reports, June 1971), 16, 22, 68–77.

2 RG, 469, Office of Information, Office of the Director, Subject Files 1949–53, Box 6 (National Archives and Records Administration) as indicated by Hans-Jürgen Schröder, "Marshall Plan Propaganda in Austria and West Germany" in *The Marshall Plan in Austria*, ed. Gunter Bischof et al., vol 8., Contemporary Austrian Studies (New Brunswick, NJ: Transaction, 2000), 214.

3 U.S. Agency for International Development, *U.S. Economic Assistance Programs*, 16, 22, 68–77.

4 There is extensive bibliography on the Greek Civil War including the books by D. Close, ed., *The Greek Civil War, 1943–1950: Studies of Polarization* (London: Routledge, 1993), Andre Gerolymatos, *Greek Civil War and the Origins of Soviet American Rivalry, 1943–1949* (New York: Basic Books, 2004).

5 "Greece Aid 'Ample' to Win Civil War," *New York Times*, 14 December 1947.

6 Barry Machado, *In Search of a Usable Past: The Marshall Plan and Post-war Reconstruction Today* (Lexington, VA: George C. Marshall Foundation, 2007), 65.

7 "Years of Partnership—The Story of Greek-American Cooperation Since the War," prepared by the United States Information Service, 10. Also, "U.S. Aid to Greece in Food Bulks Big: AMAG

Summary of its work Also Shows Major Works in Roads and Waterways," *New York Times*, 27 June 1948.

8 "Years of Partnership," 14. It is important to note that Greece was the largest per capita recipient of Marshall Plan Aid and received, in Marshall Plan Aid alone, $706.7 million for the four-year period of the Marshall Plan. Source: U.S. Agency for International Development, *U.S. Economic Assistance Programs*, 16, 22, 68–77.

9 State Department Aide Memoire, 21 October 1949, Hellenic Ministry of Foreign Affairs, Diplomatic and Historical Archives Service, Central Files, 1949, File 24, sub file 3.

10 "Greece: Military Phase," *Christian Science Monitor*, 18 February 1948, 18.

11 "Dollars Are Not Enough," *New York Times*, 5 March 1948.

12 Also see Bernadette Whelan, "Marshall Plan Publicity and Propaganda in Italy and Ireland, 1947–1951," *Historical Journal of Film, Radio and Television* 23.4 (October 2003): 311–28, David W. Ellwood, "The Propaganda of the Marshall Plan in Italy in the Cold War Context," *Intelligence and National Security* 18.2 (2003): 225–36

13 A partial collection of the publication can be found at the Hellenic Literary and Historical Archive in Athens.

14 Machado, *In Search*, 68.

15 "U.S. Voluntary Agencies Occupy a Distinct Place in Greek Life," *Boston Sunday Globe*, 6 June 1948. The agencies indicated are the American Farm School, the American Joint Distribution Committee, the American Near East Foundation, and the American School of Classical Studies, as well as the Gennadius Library, Anatolia College, Athens College, the Congressional Christian Service Committee, Cooperation for American Remittances to Europe, the Council of Jewish Women, the Greek War Relief Association, Pierce College, and the Rockefeller Foundation.

16 The director of USIS in Athens was First Secretary of Embassy George W. Edman.

17 The USIS offices were in Ioannina, Lamia, Larissa, Komotini, Tripoli, Florina, and Piraeus. Many of the USIS centers provided English lessons as well. (Έντυπο «Ελεύθερος Κόσμος» Αριθ. 1, Ιούνιος 1952 σελ. 26–27).

18 Machado, *In Search*, 60.

19 Letter of the G. Theotokis to Paul Porter, 17 February 1950, Ministry of Foreign Affairs, Marshall Plan Archive, File 4, sub file III, section 2. All five hydroelectric plants were completed by 1956, marking one of the successes of the industrialization effort in Greece.

20 David Ellwood, "'You too can be like us': Selling the Marshall Plan—American Propaganda during the European Recovery Program," *History Today* 48 (October 1998): 33.

21 Ibid.

Section III:

The Marshall Plan in Austria: Myth, Moloch, and Memory

Barbara Stelzl-Marx

Marshall Plan Dead Ends and Anti-USIA Campaigns:

The Soviet Economic Propaganda Campaign in Austria

The Soviet occupying power in Austria from the beginning viewed the Marshall Plan as an enemy from abroad. The United States, after all, adopted the allocation of aid as a concerted measure against a further spread of communism. Furthermore, Moscow's economic policy towards the country divided into four parts could hardly have differed more from that of the United States. Thus it was precisely in this area that a clash of the two Cold War rivals manifested itself especially clearly. As the Soviet Union and, subsequently, the Communist Party of Austria (KPÖ) explicitly rejected the Marshall Plan, the Austrian federal government equally vehemently supported it. Thus a long-lasting conflict over the European Recovery Program (ERP) was pre-programmed. Fierce propaganda battles were the result.

Soviet Economic Policy in Austria

In Austria, the Soviets also pursued the economic aim of obtaining reparations for the immense losses they had suffered in terms of industrial potential during the Second World War as well as obtaining "compensation."[1] During the period of occupation, the material wealth of the Eastern Zone was therefore removed by means of "private" plundering through the evacuation of industrial and commercial installations with the help of the Soviets' own removal crews, or via the confiscation of entire firms regarded as "German property." In this context, national interests regarding reparations and the rebuilding of the Soviet economy were of primary importance; however, averting a concerted destabilization of the liberated country was of some concern as well.[2] Stalin's "donation of peas" to the starving Vienna population or the donation of millions for the reconstruction of the Vienna State Opera House are just two examples of this.[3]

Furthermore, the Kremlin had already anticipated an eventual armed conflict with the West; therefore, it wanted all the more quickly to be in a position where it could compete economically with its potential Western enemy in the Cold War. In Austria, the Soviet policy of exploitation was felt particularly heavily given that the dismantling of industry was, in fact, removing the Austrian postwar economy's means of existence. Western and Eastern Zones were drifting apart economically and socially.[4]

With regard to Soviet economic policy in Austria, one can differentiate between three partially overlapping phases.[5] The first began in April 1945 and lasted until early summer 1946. This military phase was dominated by "war booty and operations for trophies," marked by plunder, dismantling, and the necessity of supplying the occupying troops, but also the granting of Soviet aid in the form of foodstuffs. The widespread practice of carrying out the dismantling quickly, yet not removing the dismantled goods for weeks, thereby risking irreparable damage, contributed additionally to the resentment felt by the Austrian population.[6]

In the second phase, the emphasis shifted from the focus on booty to the exploitation of regular production. Simultaneously to the dismantling operations, the Soviet occupying force began to set up an ex-territorial economic corpus. The Potsdam Agreement of August 1945—although it was never officially recognized in Austria—and Order No. 17 from High Commissar Vladimir Kurasov, retrospectively dated to 27 June 1946, served as the legal basis. The following three columns ultimately constituted the Soviet economic empire in Austria:[7]

- The Soviet Mineral Oil Administration (SMV), which was founded in October following the failure of negotiations regarding a Soviet-Austrian Crude Oil Administration (SANAPHTA). The OROP, later ÖROP (Austrian-Russian Oil Products, or PLC for Crude Oil Products of Austrian and Russian Origin), which was, however, a public limited company according to Austrian law, took over the production of its raw material. The crude oil fields of the SMV were located exclusively in Lower Austria.[8]
- The Soviet Danube Steamship Company (DDSG), which was called into being as the administration firm for the property in the Soviet zone of occupation that was confiscated on 2 February 1946.[9]
- The Administration of Soviet Property in Austria (*Upravlenie Sovetskim Imushchestvom v Avstrii*, abbreviated to USIA, originally USIVA), which came into being up as a result of Order No. 17.[10] It took over the administration of all facilities located in the Soviet zone that were to be regarded as "German property"[11] in accordance with the Soviet definition.[12] The Austrian government had henceforth no influence at all on the confiscated businesses. According to Soviet figures, in 1953 the USIA alone encompassed 436 businesses, of which 231 were in the field of industry. In addition, more than 3,100 residential houses, schools, hospitals, barracks, churches, and other economic and residential buildings were under its control.[13] Furthermore, from 1950 onward, so-called USIA shops were set up, their number rising by 1955 to a total of 126 stores.[14] This retail business, which stood outside Austrian trade law, negated for the most part the domestic tax and customs regulations, as a result of which the prices of Austrian stores could be overbid.[15]

The negotiations for the transfer fee for the Soviet economic complex, which was ultimately agreed on in the Moscow Memorandum, and the deliveries to the Soviet Union over the coming years fell in the third phase. The price Austria paid for this was (too) high: not only was the USIA complex ultimately overpaid,[16] but the agreed upon transfer deliveries of crude oil were considerably higher than the actual value of the SMV businesses in 1955.[17]

The Soviet occupying force was clearly aware what a negative effect the plundering as well as the organized dismantling had on the mood of the populace. With a feeling of cultural superiority that belied their actual impotence in this area, the Austrians jeered, "*Uhra, Uhra, nix kultura*!"[18] Exchanges such as "What time is it?"—"I don't have a watch; the Russians stole it," which a TASS reporter overheard while standing in a queue, were regarded by the Soviet side as alarming.[19] Unsurprisingly, the political departments of the army, among others, knew the "anti-Soviet" adaptation of the Lord's Prayer. Although—or perhaps because—the aforementioned infringements accorded with the truth, at least one person from Lower Austria was imprisoned because of the dissemination of this "prayer":[20]

> Our generalissimo, who art in the Kremlin,
> Tedious be thy name,
> Debauched be thy empire,
> Thy will be done in Russia, but not in Austria.
> Give us this day our daily peas
> And forgive us our European culture,
> As we forgive those who plunder us,
> And don't let us go to the dogs
> But deliver us from the Red Army, Amen![21]

The Marshall Plan in Soviet Eyes

Shaped by Nazi propaganda, but also by bad experiences with the Red Army at the end of the war, a picture of the "bad Russian" and the "good American" quickly established itself among the population.[22] This contrasted starkly with the reputation that the Soviet occupying force wanted to disseminate about itself: "The Red Army liberates, the Red Army helps!" claimed a poster from the early post-war period.[23] The particularly negative image of the Russians, however, offered the United States the ideal opportunity to apply propaganda leverage in this matter. It accordingly stylized the economic question as an image question, which ultimately manifested itself in the Marshall Plan.

One of the United States' central aims regarding Austria was to break the economic monopoly of Soviet businesses with the help of the Marshall Plan and at the same time to strengthen the industry in the Western Zones. ERP aid allocated to the Eastern Zone was, like Austrian economic contact with Eastern Europe, subjected to strict controls. As a result, SMV and USIA received until 1955 little aid from the Marshall Plan. As part of an ex-territorial Soviet economic corpus, they were subjected *de facto* to an ERP embargo.[24] Up to October 1950, a total of only 16.5 percent of ERP funds, by 1955 around 19 percent, were allotted to the Soviet zone of occupation.[25]

At the same time, with the help of the Marshall Plan the development of alternative industries in western Austria took place, above all in those branches in which the USIA dominated the market, such as glass, chemicals, and metals.[26] In this way, the Marshall Plan contributed to the shift in regional focus to the West.[27] The economic reunification of eastern and western Austria was, therefore, to last years following the signing of the State Treaty.[28]

The bilateral agreement of 2 July 1948 between Austria and the United States on participation in the Marshall Plan was met unsurprisingly with protests by the Soviet occupying power and the KPÖ. On 13 August 1948, the Soviets filed an official protest with the Allied Council, but their initiative was doomed to failure from the outset. For the bilateral agreement to be rejected, a unanimous resolution would have been necessary.[29] In contrast to Poland and Czechoslovakia, whose entry had been blocked by the Soviet Union in 1947, Austria was not excluded from the ERP.[30]

Also during later sessions of the Allied Council, the Soviet delegates repeatedly protested against the Marshall Plan. They regarded it as an "unscrupulous intervention on the part of the Americans in Austrian affairs" and criticized the "slave-like conditions of Austrian payments for the 'Marshall deliveries.'"[31] One of their main arguments was that the ERP aid would not serve the restoration of an independent Austrian economy, but the "transformation of the Western Zones of Austria into an American military-strategic base." From the Soviet perspective, this would lead to a "covert militarization" of the country.[32]

Furthermore, the Soviets brought economic considerations into play. The Marshall Plan, they said, would bring Austria "under the control of American monopolies" transforming it into a "lucrative market for seasoned goods of poor quality." The United States would also exploit "strategic raw materials at low prices."[33]

The Soviets criticized the successive increase in exports to Western Europe, in particular to West Germany. Thirty-four percent of exported raw materials and energy went to countries of the "capitalist West," while only 9 percent was exported to people's democracies. According to estimates of the Economic Section of the Allied Commission from the beginning of 1954, this would have "extremely negative consequences for Austria's manufacturing industry, which was highly dependent on exports."[34]

Statements from Austrian politicians were also interpreted in the same way. The internal report to the Central Committee of the Communist Party of the Soviet Union (CPSU) mentioned above commented as follows on the statement of Transport Minister Karl Waldbrunner that in Austria nothing could have been achieved had it not been for Marshall Plan aid: "That is a valuable admission. It demonstrates that the USA only implements the Hitlerian plans to convert Austria's economic apparatus for the fulfilment of the military requirements of imperialist Germany."[35] On this topic, KPÖ propaganda spoke of a "loss of Austrian sovereignty" and the preparation of a "new Anschluß" by means of the strengthening of economic ties to Germany.[36] A further argument was that Austria would—in contrast to the Moscow Declaration—sacrifice Austrian independence for economic control by the United States.[37] Innumerable counter-strikes against the enemy image of the Marshall Plan as the symbol of U.S. imperialism were pre-programmed.

Communist Propaganda against the Marshall Plan

All available means were used in the propaganda campaign initiated by Moscow and directed against the ERP. Thus Soviet newsreels reported on protests of Austrian workers against the Marshall Plan. Broadcasts from Moscow railed against the ERP.[38] The main mouthpieces of the Communist propaganda on the ground were the daily *Austrian People's Voice* (*Österreichische Volksstimme*), the central organ of the KPÖ, and the Soviet occupation organ, the *Österreichische Zeitung*, an Austrian newspaper. The Soviets' polemical views were also visualized on countless posters.

In contrast to its stance on earlier Western aid programs, the KPÖ involved itself more actively in the anti-ERP propaganda and brought—in agreement with the Soviets—the following arguments in particular into play. These criticisms included 1) the loss of Austrian sovereignty, 2) the one-sided attachment of Austria to the West with the aim of political and military incorporation, 3) the Marshall Plan as a "present" that actually had to be purchased by the recipient, 4) the import of spoiled and surplus U.S. goods of poor quality, which could in many cases be produced in Austria itself, 5) the decline in manufacturing production, including Austria's degradation to being merely a deliverer of raw materials to the Western powers, 6) the excessive prices for ERP imports that could be obtained more cheaply from Eastern Europe, 7) the impossibility of increasing rations for normal consumers as the immediate result of the expensive food imports from overseas, and 8) the insufficient allocation of dollars as a drawback of the aid.[39]

In general, warnings were made about a "Marshallization" of Austria, which would lead to an "enslavement" of the working class and a loss of sovereignty.[40] On this point, Moscow's diction paralleled that of the Austrians. Soviet reports always talked of a "Marshallization of the Austrian economy" (*marshallizaciya avstriiskoi ėkonomiki*)[41] that should be prevented if at all possible.

"American Aid ... Who helps Whom?"

One of the main communist arguments against the Marshall Plan consisted of defaming the economic aid as a "present that had to be purchased" by the recipient. One example of this Soviet approach is the report of a former economic expert from the Soviet part of the Allied Commission. In the report, he informed Moscow about a commentary in the *Trade Union Review* (*Gewerkschaftliche Rundschau*) from April 1953. In the commentary, the "American millions received by Austria in the framework of the 'Marshall Plan'" were praised "because they must not be paid back." His assessment was as follows: "Such a declaration testifies to a subjective approach to the question and to a desire to ingratiate oneself with the USA." It was, he continued, namely "this important question, which is connected with the use of those funds that were generated from the sale of American goods, on which there was an intentional silence."[42]

Criticism of the ERP was directed at the extensive advertising campaign carried out by the United States and the Austria federal government, which promoted the Marshall Plan as a largely free aid program. According to one of the ad campaign posters, "4/5 of Austria's bread rations are a present from the American aid. Austria's federal government uses the money that you pay for this in order to help the needy."[43] The message of another poster, which portrayed food ration cards, a shilling note, and a girl eating, was similar: "60 percent of your rations are a present from the American aid for Austria. The money that you pay for this stays in the country—Austria's government uses it to help the needy."[44]

The communist response to this was expressed in the form of posters, too. One such poster read, "American aid ... Who helps whom?"[45] Thereupon, the left hand of a man identified as an American by the U.S. flag on his wristbands tenders various goods. At the same time, however, a vast stream of dollars flows out of Austria and into his right hand, which, contorted into a claw, is meant to express greed. According to the poster's message, the "aid" benefits first and foremost the United States.

Inflation in the Marshall Countries

A further point of criticism expressed in communist propaganda was directed at the reduced purchasing power in the "Marshall countries." The cause of this reduction was seen as the import of U.S. surplus foods of poor quality, which for the most part could have been produced in Austria itself. Resulting from this, in the estimation of the KPÖ, was a downturn in manufacturing production, for which reason Austria would be increasingly relegated to being a deliverer of raw materials to the Western powers.[46]

In 1951, Die Sowjetunion im Bild (The Soviet Union in Pictures) released a corresponding poster, which attacked the enormous price increase that made "Austrian workers' lives" difficult. Due to the ERP, the Austrian population "for the same money" for which it could buy a full loaf of bread in 1947, was apparently only able to buy two-thirds in 1949 and merely one-third in 1951. The poster also graphically demonstrated this "theft of the real wage" by means of a suit jacket and a pair of shoes.[47] Underneath the image, the poster's text read:

> As a result of the Marshallization of Austria, enormous price increases make life difficult for Austrian workers. Labor productivity is as high today as before the war. But everything is more expensive; all prices are rising, whether it's food, clothing, fuel, rent or other things! Unemployment is increasing, and Austria's raw materials are exported in crude form! By using all possible excuses, by means of various pacts and "aid," more and more of the real wage is stolen from the working population and used to finance a new war.[48]

In contrast to this, the Soviet economy was booming and had almost halved prices for food, clothing, and mass-produced articles by means of four price cuts between 1947 and 1951: "As a result," it was emphasized, "the purchasing power of the Soviet people increased in 1951 by 301.5 billion rubles. While at the same time in all capitalist countries the prices increased and an arms race took place, the Soviet state improved the life of workers and constructed gigantic peace projects."[49]

Similar arguments were used by the KPÖ in its campaign for the elections to the National Council on 22 February 1953. A leaflet printed by the communist publishing house Globus systematically fuelled fear of price increases and a simultaneous devaluation of wages: "Inflation in the Marshall countries: on 18 September, the English pound was abruptly devalued by a third at the insistence of the Americans. The English socialist government[50] immediately increased the price of bread and flour. All other prices are rising rapidly. Twenty-three Marshall countries followed suit and also devalued their currencies." The KPÖ warned that the Austrian "Marshall government" was also planning something similar: "Now, before the elections," the government would deny

> that it will also devalue the shilling, but remind yourselves: just twelve hours before the Law for Currency Protection, the ÖVP [Austrian People's Party] and the SPÖ [Social Democratic Party of Austria] denied that they had such plans. But then they cheated hundreds of thousands of their savings! A new devaluation of the shilling means: a rapid rise in prices, the devaluation of all wages, salaries and pensions, inflation. Only an election victory of the left block can protect us from this. Defend yourself against the devaluation as long as there is still time: vote for the left block![51]

The Government's Shadow Role

As the aforementioned poster demonstrates, the U.S. aid program played a decisive role in the election campaign. The KPÖ characterized the governing parties of the ÖVP and SPÖ as a "Marshall government" that was merely a puppet of the United States. The argument is particularly clearly expressed in a poster which reads: "Vote for an independent government! Vote communists and left-wing socialists!" Upon it, two Americans equipped with a sack of dollars cast a shadow over Austria. The shadow constitutes the outline of the embracing SPÖ and ÖVP. A sign next to it explains the symbolism of these shadows: "The current Austrian federal government only plays a shadow role."[52]

As a counter-model to the Marshall Plan, the KPÖ envisaged a package with the following three columns: a move away from the United States, concentration on one's own resources with regard to economic restructuring, and foreign economic cooperation with Eastern European states. The KPÖ regarded it as its duty to lead the way out of the dead end of the Marshall Plan.[53]

USIA Campaign: Pros and Cons

Just as intensively as the various Soviet propaganda organs in Austria fulminated against the Marshall Plan, they emphasized the achievements of the communist economic empire. An example of this is the poster "This is How the Strunin Family Lives," which *Die Sowjetunion im Bild* published in 1950.[54] The question must be asked, however, whether the propagated image of the everyday lives of individual members of the Strunin family actually appealed to a postwar Austrian public, or whether this gray poster with photos of Mr. Strunin at the workbench and Mrs. Strunin in the kitchen didn't, in fact, provoke the opposite effect rather than the desired one.

Even the employees of the USIA and SMV firms, who were composed of an above average proportion of KPÖ members, devoted themselves to their own campaigns. These campaigns manifested themselves above all in the form of lectures, exhibitions, cinema shows, and theatre performances as well as in the setting up of libraries and the founding of sports teams. Beginning in 1947, an annual soccer tournament was staged between oil firms. A particularly high propagandistic value was ascribed to the SMV company newspaper *Der Erdölarbeiter* (*The Oil Worker*). In 1949, the newspaper already appeared once a week with a print run of 6,000 copies.[55]

In secret reports, however, Soviet authorities themselves had to confess that much was in a state of disorder at the USIA firms. Rapid drops in sales on the domestic market and the inability of most businesses to compete led from 1950 onward to a deterioration of their financial well-being. Many products continued to lag behind those of Austrian firms in terms of quality. According to internal criticism, this would dilute the "efficiency of the measures put into place by the democratic [that is, communist] organizations." In this way, the poor conditions of countless properties belonging to the USIA constituted "the reason for continual accusations [that were] laid at the door of the USIA and the KPÖ by reactionary elements."[56]

Outwardly, no mention was made of this—justified—criticism. The Soviet occupying force reacted all the more touchily when "imperialist" attacks on their economic policy took place. A particularly illuminating example of the U.S. propaganda directed against the USIA is a poster stamped with a "USIA cow." While the cow gloats over eastern Austria, she is milked by a small, red, unfriendly-looking communist. The message here is unmistakable: the Soviet occupation zone is being devoured by the USIA; the profit, however, symbolized by the milk, flows into Moscow's bucket.[57]

The *Arbeiter-Zeitung* (*Workers' Newspaper*) under the leadership of its editor-in-chief Oscar Pollak attacked various aspects of the Soviet occupation in Austria particularly aggressively. His editorials were credited not only with eloquence, but also with real political power. As a "newspaper that has the heart to do something," the SPÖ organ denounced, for example, violations by Red Army soldiers—referred to as the "unknown"—in postwar Austria. In 1950, the *Arbeiter-Zeitung* started a regular campaign against Soviet economic enterprises in Austria. "Depletion and Record Extraction Like under the Nazis"[58] or "The Communist Profiteers and Tax Evaders"[59] were characteristic headlines.[60] In the 7 July issue, the newspaper addressed the propaganda battle between the KPÖ and the *Arbeiter-Zeitung*:

> A few days ago, the Communists threw several communist oil workers, whom they cursed and accused of treason, espionage and sabotage, out of the Communist Party. Those expelled were also accused of having been linked to the *Arbeiter-Zeitung*. In fact, the *Arbeiter-Zeitung* did not have anything to do with these people. Anyone who goes to the oil region and speaks to the oil workers or reads the letters that they write to us can find out what the *Arbeiter-Zeitung* writes. We are publishing a small selection of them today.[61]

The Soviet occupying force reacted to these attacks with, among other things, the poster "Technological 'Miracle': American Typewriter" from 1952. On the poster, journalists such as Editor-in-Chief Pollak, who was identified by name, form the keys of a typewriter, with which they produce the "USIA agitation" of the *Arbeiter-Zeitung*. This typewriter, sarcastically referred to as a "Technological 'Miracle'," is operated by the hairy hand of an American, as the dollar sign on his cufflink unmistakably shows. Pollak and other journalists from the *Arbeiter-Zeitung* are in this way discredited as puppets of the United States, which exploits them—according to the poster—for their criticism of the USIA.[62]

Conclusion

In spite of Soviet protests, Austria became the only country that was partially under Soviet occupation to receive Marshall Plan aid.[63] The result was a fierce propaganda war, albeit one which the Soviets were certainly unable to decide in their own favor. On the one hand, their economic policy, characterized by dismantling resources and removing them from regular production, in no way led to the anti-ERP propaganda falling on fertile ground. On the other hand, the palpable successes of the Marshall Plan torpedoed the communist attempt to justify the socialist planned economy as a superior model.[64]

The aforementioned "USIA cow" is a telling example of how important the propaganda surrounding the Marshall Plan was in the East-West conflict of the Cold War. Both superpowers employed it as an integral part of their respective foreign policies and used it as an instrument for their worldwide rivalries. In the microcosm of Austria, another decisive component can be added: not only did the "USIA cow" milked by Moscow graze in the Soviet occupying zone, but she also received an intensive "concentrated feed" indirectly from the Marshall Plan. According to Günter Bischof, the Soviet Union removed roughly the same amount from its zone as the United States pumped into Austria via the ERP.[65] Ultimately, the "food chain" was completed.

Notes

1 On reparations and the economic reorganization of the Soviet zone of occupation in Germany, see, for example, Norman N. Naimark, *Die Russen in Deutschland: Die sowjetische Besatzungszone 1945 bis 1949* (Berlin: Propylaën, 1997), 181–258. The research for this piece was carried out in the context of Austrian Program for Advanced Research and Technology (APART) of the Austrian Academy of Sciences at the Ludwig Boltzmann Institute for Research on War Consequences, History Cluster. I am very grateful to Mr. Markus Feigl for making posters from the Vienna City and Regional Library (Wiener Stadt- und Landesbibliothek, WStLB) available to me and to Mr Alex J. Kay for translating the text into English.

2 Oliver Rathkolb, "Sonderfall Österreich? Ein peripherer Kleinstaat in der sowjetischen Nachkriegszeit 1945–1947," in *Gleichschaltung unter Stalin? Die Entwicklung der Parteien im östlichen Europa, 1944–1949*, ed. Stefan Creuzberger and Manfred Görtemaker (Paderborn: F. Schöningh, 2002), 353–73, here 361–64.

3 Barbara Stelzl-Marx, "Erbsen für Wien: Zur sowjetischen Lebensmittelhilfe 1945," in *"Österreich ist frei!" Der Österreichische Staatsvertrag 1955: Beitragsband zur Ausstellung auf Schloss Schallaburg 2005*, ed. Stefan Karner and Gottfried Stangler (Horn: Berger, 2005), 54–57; Stefan Karner and Peter Ruggenthaler, "Unter sowjetischer Kontrolle: Zur Regierungsbildung in Österreich 1945," in *Die Rote Armee in Österreich: Sowjetische Besatzung 1945–1955. Beiträge*, ed. Stefan Karner and Barbara Stelzl-Marx (Graz: Verein zur Förderung der Forschung von Folgen nach Konflikten und Kriegen 2005), 105–48, here 144.

4 Roman Sandgruber, "Das wirtschaftliche Umfeld des Staatsvertrages," in *Die Gunst des Augenblicks: Neuere Forschungen zu Staatsvertrag und Neutralität*, ed. Manfried Rauchensteiner and Robert Kriechbaumer (Vienna: Böhlau, 2005), 359–78, here 364f.; Barbara Stelzl-Marx, "Die 'Wiedervereinigung' Österreichs. Kontinuität und Wandel," in ibid., 187–222; Wilfried Aichinger, "Die Sowjetunion und Österreich 1945–1949," in *Die bevormundete Nation: Österreich und die Alliierten 1945–1949*, ed. Günter Bischof and Josef Leidenfrost (Innsbruck: Haymon, 1988), 275–92, here 277–79.

5 Dieter Stiefel, on the other hand, takes the view that there were two phases, without specifically factoring in the stage of transfers fixed in the 1955 State Treaty. Because Austria paid "reparations" to the Soviet Union until 1964, however, a three-tier subdivision seems to be reasonable. See Dieter Stiefel, "Coca-Cola kam nicht über die Enns: Die ökonomische Benachteiligung der sowjetischen Besatzungszone," in *"80 Dollar": 50 Jahre ERP-Fonds und Marshall-Plan in Österreich, 1948–1998*, ed. Günter Bischof and Dieter Stiefel (Vienna: Ueberreuter, 1999), 111–32, here 116.

6 Aichinger, "Die Sowjetunion und Österreich," 277f.

7 Otto Klambauer, "Ein Überblick über Entwicklung und Organisation des USIA-Konzernes," in *Die USIA-Betriebe in Niederösterreich: Geschichte, Organisation, Dokumentation*, ed. Otto Klambauer, Ernst Bezemek, Studien und Forschungen aus dem Niederösterreichischen Institut für Landeskunde (Vienna: Selbstverlag des NÖ Istituts für Landeskunde 1983), 1–79, here 4–27.

8 Walter Martin Iber, "Die Sowjetische Mineralölverwaltung (SMV) in Österreich 1945–1955: Sowjetische Besatzungswirtschaft und der Kampf ums Öl als Vorgeschichte der OMV," Ph.D. diss., Graz University, 2008.

9 Waltraud Brunner, "Das Deutsche Eigentum und das Ringen um den Österreichischen Staatsvertrag," Ph.D. diss., University of Vienna, 1976, 139.

10 Analogue organizations also existed in Czechoslovakia, Hungary, East Germany, Finland, Bulgaria, and Romania. See Stiefel, "Coca-Cola kam nicht über die Enns," 119.

11 See Hans Seidel, *Österreichs Wirtschaft und Wirtschaftspolitik nach dem Zweiten Weltkrieg* (Vienna: Manz'sche Verlags- und Universitätsbuchhandlung, 2005), 346.

12 On the definition of "German property," see Brunner, "Das Deutsche Eigentum," 3–6.

13 Russian State Archive for Contemporary History (hereafter: RGANI), F. 5. op. 28, d. 224, 70–78, here 70, Report of the Head of the Department for Domestic Questions of the Apparatus of the High Commissar, A.G. Kolobov, on political work in USIA and SMV businesses [dated no later than 9 June 1954], reprinted in: *Die Rote Armee in Österreich: Sowjetische Besatzung 1945–1955. Dokumente. Krasnaya Armiya v Avstrii. Sovetskaya okkupaciya 1945–1955. Dokumenty*, ed. Stefan Karner, Barbara Stelzl-Marx, and Alexander Tschubarjan (Graz: R. Oldenbourg, 2005), Document no. 113.

14 RGANI, F. 5, op. 28, d. 331, 329–33, here 329, Report of A. Kurmazenko on USIA businesses, 25 November 1955, reprinted in *Die Rote Armee in Österreich*, ed. Karner, Stelzl-Marx, and Tschubarjan, Document no. 116.

15 Seidel, *Österreichs Wirtschaft*, 471.

16 Ibid., 477f.

17 Iber, "Die Sowjetische Mineralölverwaltung," 161–67.

18 Information kindly provided by Elisabeth Marx, Graz, 23 February 2008.

19 Foreign Policy Archive of the Russian Federation (hereafter: AVP RF), F. 07, op. 10, p. 154, d. 13, 2110, Report of the TASS reporter Lisin to the responsible head of TASS, N.G. Pal'gunov, on the political-moral state of affairs in Austria following the liberation, 29 May 1945, reprinted in *Krasnaya Armiya v stranach Central'noi Evropy i na Balkanakh. Dokumenty i materialy 1944–1945*, ed. Institut Voennoi Istorii Ministerstva Oborony Rossiyskoi Federacii et al., Russkiy Archiv: Velikaya Otechestvennaya Voina, vol. 14 (3–2) (Moscow: Terra, 2000), 667–71.

20 Russian State Archive for Social and Political History (hereafter RGASPI), F. 17, op. 128, d. 118, 213–20, here 214–15, Report of the deputy leader of the 7th Department of the Political Administration of the CGV, Mudrikov, on Soviet propaganda in Austria and other incidents, 7 August 1946.

21 Archive of the Ludwig Boltzmann Institute for Research into War Consequences (AdBIK), Ingrid Meixner Collection, Graz. In the Soviet documents there is a verbatim Russian translation of this version.

22 On this, see also Ingrid Fraberger and Dieter Stiefel, "'Enemy Images': The Meaning of 'Anti-Communism' and its Importance for the Political and Economic Reconstruction in Austria after 1945," ed. Günter Bischof et al.in *The Marshall Plan in Austria*, vol. 8, Contemporary Austrian Studies (New Brunswick, NJ: Transaction, 2000), 56–97.

23 A facsimile can be found in Karner and Stangler, *"Österreich ist frei!,"* 61.

24 Andrea Komlosy, "The Marshall Plan and the Making of the 'Iron Curtain' in Austria," in *The Marshall Plan in Austria*, vol. 8, Contemporary Austrian Studies, ed. Günter Bischof et al. (New Brunswick, NJ: Transaction, 2000), 98–137, here 119–24.

25 Klaus Eisterer, "Österreich unter alliierter Besatzung 1945–1955," in *Österreich im 20. Jahrhundert: Ein Studienbuch in zwei Bänden, Vom Weltkrieg bis zur Gegenwart*, vol. 2, ed. Rolf Steininger and Michael Gehler (Vienna: Böhlau, 1997), 147–216, here 162.

26 Stiefel, "Coca-Cola kam nicht über die Enns," 123; Iber, "Die Sowjetische Mineralölverwaltung," 150f.

27 Stiefel, "Coca-Cola kam nicht über die Enns," 123; Sandgruber, "Das wirtschaftliche Umfeld des Staatsvertrages," 365.

28 Stelzl-Marx, "Die 'Wiedervereinigung' Österreichs," 214f.

29 Wilfried Mähr, *Der Marshallplan in Österreich* (Graz: Styria, 1989), 112–15.

30 Jill Lewis, "Dancing on a Tight-Rope: The Beginning of the Marshall Plan and the Cold War in Austria," in *The Marshall Plan in Austria*, vol. 8, Contemporary Austrian Studies, ed. Günter Bischof et al. (New Brunswick, NJ: Transaction, 2000), 138–55, here 144.

31 AVP RF, F. 066, op. 31, p. 149, d. 29, 3, Cover letter from M. Gribanov to A. Vyshinskii on the transmission of the draft of a text on the Soviet rejection of the Marshall Plan for the session of the Allied Council, 12 March 1950.

32 AVP RF, F. 066, op. 31, p. 149, d. 29, 4–6, Draft of a text on the Soviet rejection of the Marshall Plan for the session of the Allied Council, [12 March 1950].

33 Ibid.

34 RGANI, F. 5, op. 28, d. 221, 2–20, Report from A. Michailov on the USA's economic policy in Austria and its influence on the Austrian economy, 16 January 1954. The report was submitted to the Central Committee of the CPSU by order of the Soviet High Commissar. See RGANI, F. 5, op. 28, d. 221, 1, Cover letter from Kraskevich on the transmission of the report on American economic policy in Austria, 16 January 1954.

35 Ibid.

36 Mähr, *Der Marshallplan in Österreich*, 108f.

37 Lewis, "Dancing on a Tight-Rope," 144.

38 Hans-Jürgen Schröder, "Marshall Plan Propaganda in Austria and Western Germany," in *The Mar-*

shall Plan in Austria, vol. 8, Contemporary Austrian Studies, ed. Günter Bischof et al. (New Brunswick, NJ: Transaction, 2000), 212–46, here 231.

39 Mähr, *Der Marshallplan in Österreich*, 108–10.

40 Schröder, "Marshall Plan Propaganda," 231.

41 See, for example, RGANI, F. 5, op. 28, d. 221, 2–20, Report from A. Michailov on the USA's economic policy in Austria and its influence on the Austrian economy, 16 January 1954.

42 Ibid.

43 WStLB, Poster collection, P-6516.

44 WStLB, Poster collection, P-3594.

45 WStLB, Poster collection, P-6537.

46 Mähr, *Der Marshallplan in Österreich*, 109.

47 WStLB, Poster collection, P-6795.

48 Ibid.

49 Ibid.

50 The "English socialist government" referred to here was, in actual fact, a Conservative government led by Prime Minister Winston Churchill.

51 WStLB, Poster collection, P-111835.

52 WStLB, Poster collection, P-1434.

53 Schröder, "Marshall Plan Propaganda," 231f.

54 WStLB, Poster collection, P-6775.

55 Iber, "Die Sowjetische Mineralölverwaltung," 122f.; Wolfgang Mueller, "'Die Kanonen schießen nicht ... Aber der Kampf geht weiter': Die Propaganda der sowjetischen Besatzungsmacht in Österreich im Kalten Krieg," in *Die Rote Armee in Österreich*, ed. Karner and Stelzl-Marx, 339–62, here 344.

56 RGANI, F. 5. op. 28, d. 224, 70–78, Report of the Head of the Department for Domestic Questions of the Apparatus of the High Commissar, A.G. Kolobov, on political work in USIA and SMV businesses [dated no later than 9 June 1954], reprinted in *Die Rote Armee in Österreich*, ed. Karner, Stelzl-Marx, and Tschubarjan, Document no. 113.

57 ÖNB, Poster collection.

58 "Die Russen beschleunigen die Ausbeutung unserer Ölfelder: Raubbau und Rohölförderung wie unter den Nazi," in *Arbeiter-Zeitung*, 16 May 1950, p. 4.

59 "Die kommunistischen Preistreiber und Steuerhinterzieher: Eine sozialistische Anfrage wegen der volksdemokratischen Benzinpreiserhöhung," in *Arbeiter-Zeitung*, 7 June 1951, p. 1.

60 Iber, "Die Sowjetische Mineralölverwaltung," 144f.

61 "Briefe aus dem USIA-Paradies: Was die Zistersdorfer Erdölarbeiter schreiben," in *Arbeiter-Zeitung*, 7 July 1951, p. 2.

62 WStLB, Poster collection, 6818–1952.

63 Ferdinand Lacina, "Der Marshall-Plan—Ein Beitrag zur Übergangswirtschaft Österreichs," in *"80 Dollar,"* ed. Bischof and Stiefel, 17–20, here 17f.

64 Schröder, "Marshall Plan Propaganda," 233.

65 Günter Bischof, *Austria in the First Cold War, 1945–1955: The Leverage of the Weak*, Cold War History Series (London: 1999), 87 and 102. Seidel's estimate of the cost of the "quasi-reparations" at $1.832 million is even higher than that of Bischof, and he contrasts it with the foreign aid received during the first postwar decade to the tune of $1.92 million. See Seidel, *Österreichs Wirtschaft*, 467. On this, see also the contribution from Gerald Stourzh, "Der österreichische Staatsvertrag in den weltpolitischen Entscheidungsprozessen des Jahres 1955," in *Der österreichische Staatsvertrag 1955: Internationale Strategie, rechtliche Relevanz, nationale Identität* (*The Austrian State Treaty 1955: International Strategy, Legal Relevance, National Identity*), ed. Arnold Suppan et al. (Vienna: Verlag der Österreichischen Akademie der Wissenschaften, 2005), 965–96, here 989.

Ramón Reichert

Culture and Identity Politics:

Narrative Strategies in Austrian Marshall Plan Movies

Even after its discontinuation in 1952, the Marshall Plan has been a symbol of identity for the Austrian self-image of postwar reconstruction and the rhetoric of a new beginning. The embedding of the Marshall Plan in Austrians' collective memory was made possibly to a large extent by the way it was staged in the media. The subsequently explored films *Gute Ernte* (1950) and *Wunden Vernarben* (1952) were commissioned by the Austria Newsreel as explicit propaganda films for the European Recovery Program (ERP).

Popularization of Productivity

In the United States, the Economic Cooperation Administration (ECA), an independent federal administrative agency, was created to oversee the distribution and spending of Marshall Plan aid. Within the ECA was an information division that was responsible for the dissemination of facts about the Marshall Plan in Europe.[1] The purpose of the division was two-fold. First, it intended to instruct and educate Europeans about how Marshall aid was being used and could be used in the future. Second, it worked to make the U.S. efforts visible to all Europeans and foster appreciation for these efforts.[2] This was done by means of films, posters, radio broadcasts, concerts, and even puppet shows. Within each participating Marshall Plan nation was a country mission. These missions each had a team of American and foreign bureaucrats who assessed the political and economic situation of the country, proposed recommendations and made comments on ECA policies, and conducted negotiations about recovery operations within the country.[3] The ECA emphasized investment over consumption because it hoped to create self-sustaining European economies that could stand on their own and continue the program of reconstruction without further funding from the United States.[4]

Part of this effort to create a self-sustaining Europe was dependent upon the publicity efforts of the Information Division. Whereas propagandizing American citizens seemed too subversive, doing so in Europe was acceptable, if not necessary, because of communist efforts to undermine the ERP.[5] The European effort was also considerably better funded than that in the United States because the ECA abroad received 5 percent counterpart funds to pay its administrative costs. Counterpart funds consisted of money levied by each Marshall Plan nation to match U.S. donations. This money was generally used for reinvestment and for infrastructure improvements within the country.

The goal of the ECA in Europe was to make "clear to as many people as possible the fundamental purposes of the Marshall Plan as an expression of American foreign policy," as well as to dramatize "the contributions being made through it to European recovery."[6] It was hoped that the workers in Austria and in all ERP countries would know how the new productive techniques and technology provided by Marshall dollars was helping them to be more productive. Thus the European factory worker should understand how new methods of production could increase the industrial output of his country. U.S. management and its principles, instruments, and methods was considered the ultima ratio of *scientific management* that was superior to all other methods and which, together with the Organization for European Economic Cooperation (OEEC) that had been established by the United States and European governments, was going to guarantee and promote the economic rebuilding of Europe on the hegemonic basis of U.S. management methods.[7] In contrast to the rationalization paradigm of the 1920s, the key concept of *productivity* was to be used to overcome U.S. isolationism in favor of a comprehensive interventionism of U.S. management methods. The propagation of *productivity* according to U.S. performance targets was to be supported at an institutional level by national productivity centers.[8]

It was not enough simply to instruct nations' governments on the utilization of the funds. There also need to be an outreach to the citizens of Europe if the program was to be successful. It was hoped that the farmer in southern Italy would know how the new farming techniques and technology provided by Marshall dollars was helping him to be more productive. Similarly, the factory worker in Germany should understand how new methods of production could increase the industrial output of his country. The idea behind this education campaign was that the ECA could reach adults, fifteen percent of whom were illiterate, by educating their children. Because the impact of the Marshall Plan was less visible than such former aid programs as Lend-Lease, publicity was necessary to make this U.S. effort visible. Whereas donations of U.S. military supplies during the war were quite observable, internal and economic improvements brought about by the investment of Marshall dollars were not so easy to see, unless one was a banker or an economist.

Aside from making the ERP visible, the ECA hoped also to evoke a feeling of appreciation among its transatlantic recipients. While it did not want to give Europeans an inferiority complex by making them think they could not recover without U.S. aid, the United States did not want its generosity to go unnoticed. The ECA reminded Europeans in various ways that each American citizen was giving up two months salary to fund the Marshall Plan. Also, materials coming into Europe were often labeled with "ERP" or "For European Recovery—Supplied by the United States of America."

It was Article 2 of the Economic Cooperation Masterplan, signed by all the countries involved, that allowed for both the United States and the individual national governments to engage in the dissemination of information. A section of the Masterplan signed with Austria reads: "The Governments of the United States of America and Austria recognize that it is in their mutual interest that full publicity be given to the objectives and progress of the joint program for European Recovery

[... the] wide dissemination of information [...] is desirable in order to develop the sense of common effort and mutual aid which are essential to the accomplishment of the objectives of the program."[9]

Though this Austrian document may not speak for the whole of Europe, it is worthwhile to examine because Austria was particularly hard hit by ECA efforts due to the high levels of communist activity there after the war.[10] While the Information Division was initiated in 1948, it started out slowly. This slow start was due in part to the assumption that local information agencies would, to a significant extent, work to educate their people about the Marshall Plan. However, a December 1949 poll in the *New York Times* showed that many Europeans thought U.S. aid was suspicious and questioned U.S. motives in providing it. This suspicion was exacerbated by anti-Marshall Plan propaganda that charged the United States with seeking to "enslave Europe," "foment war," "create unemployment," "dump American surpluses," "exploit downtrodden labor," and "effect military penetration of sovereign nations."[11]

Because the European branch of the ECA was funded by 5 percent counterpart funds, it was never at a loss for monetary support. This allowed it to churn out large amounts of high quality information with little regard for expenditure. Its high budget allowed the Information Division to use film, a rather expensive medium, for the dissemination of information. The Paris Film Unit, which was the central location for ECA filmmaking, was composed of some of the most prominent members of the U.S. and European film community. According to Stuart Schulberg, who was chief of the Unit from 1950–1951, the Paris Film Unit grew "into a compact, efficient organization. Together they formed a multi-lingual international team able to plan and supervise films all over Western Europe."[12]

Paul Hoffman, the chief of the ECA Office in Washington, pointed out the "psychological warfare" of the Information Service: "To run the ECA without a strong information arm would be as futile as trying to conduct a major business without sales, advertising and customer-relations departments."[13] He summarized the concept of the information politics of the ECA in the following demands: first, to make clear to as many people as possible the fundamental purposes of the Marshall Plan as an expression of U.S. foreign policy, and second, to dramatize the contributions being made through it to European recovery. The primary scope of the Information Service's duties "to utilize every possible material and psychological means to create a respect, for the American attitude and purposes, and thereby to vitiate the propaganda of competing political philosophies."[14]

Gute Ernte (Austria 1950)

The documentary film *Gute Ernte* addressed the rural youth. It was directed by the prominent documentary filmmaker of Austrian postwar reconstruction, Georg Tressler, who worked as film officer of the ECA Mission during the implementation of the Marshall Plan.[15] From *Gute Ernte* (1950) to *Hansl und die 200.000 Kücken* (1952), *Traudls neuer Gemüsegarten* (1952), *Ertragreicher Kartoffelanbau* (1951, honored at the Documentary Film Festival Venice), *Ein interessanter Nachmittag* (1952), *Wie die Jungen sungen* (1954), *Rund um die Milchwirtschaft* (1954), and *Keine Sorge Franzl* (1955), all of Tressler's Marshall Plan movies are deliberately educational. They are supposed to impose economic efficiency, to promote identification with productivity increases, and to encourage positive evaluations of U.S. economic aid for the wider urban as well as rural population. The eleven documentary and educational films, which Tressler made for the Austrian Productivity Center[16] (*Österreichische Produktivitäts-Zentrum*, or ÖPZ), not only propagated the ideas and politics of U.S. economic aid, but were also influenced by the image and sound rhetoric hegemonically spreading in postwar Austria.[17] Tressler broke with the rigid form of documentary filmmaking by adding short acted scenes to his films.

In *Gute Ernte*, Tressler shows sports and entertainment programs hosted by the U.S. Army for Austrian rural youth. The American *reorientation* of Austrian rural youth was institutionalized through the "4-H Club," a rural youth organization. The film explains the importance of the symbolism of 4-H and allows insight into the various educational programs like vocational training, counseling, establishment of model businesses, itinerant libraries, and research institutions. The misogynist gender politics of *Gute Ernte* can be seen at the beginning of the film in the portrayal of "Liesl." As an allegorical personification, she represents the ignorant youth and is thus used as a leitmotif in the film. The film's commentary emphasizes that the 4-H-Club is "not at all political," in order to then literally quote the four rules of membership.

A further contrast is then introduced, that of old and young, as the meaning of 4-H is explained. In some cases, the contrast is expressed through the forms of adults, infants, or adolescents. In other cases, this contrast between old and young is not applied to people, but to the flora (for example, the spring landscape in *Wunden Vernarben*, Ö 1952). 4-H stands for *head*, meaning "independent thinking" (fading of boy/machine with a masculine connotation), for *heart*, meaning "love of nature and home" (fading of "Liesl" with a feminine connotation), and for *hands*, meaning the capability of using machines and tools. At this point, the cinematic argumenation introduces a gender-specific metalevel. The sequence of images is hierarchical: the hands of the boys are of primary importance because they work the machines (suggesting technical advancement/modernity), whereas the hands of the girls are secondary and are also rhetorically introduced as less important by an off-camera voice. Female hands, with a capacity for house and garden work, are secondarily productive. Female work ("suitable for girls") is emphasized as extraordinarily exclusive, and it is "reserved for the female members of 4-H." The fourth H stands for *health* (physical well-being) and subordinates the lifestyle of adolescents to the bio-political interests of the state ("future generations"). The seemingly unavoidable installment of discipline in young people reminds one of the Hitler Youth and the reconciliation of head, hand, and heart in Fritz Lang's pre-fascist Taylorist film *Metropolis* (Germany 1927).

The film ends with so-called "economic counselors" of the Ministry for Agriculture, trained in model businesses, visiting the agricultural research institute of the youth organization. Another film about the Ausrian 4-H Clubs is called *Fest-tage der Jugend* (Austria 1950) and was commisioned by the Austrian Newsreel and Film Production Company (Österreichischen Wochenschau- und Filmproduktions K.G.) Although this film is similar in structure, it is more factual in that it presents the brochure *What are the 4-H-Clubs*?, and it also more of a traditional documentary because the main part of the film recounts the activities of the animal show of the Upper Austrian 4-H Club in Wels.

Although with its leitmotifs *Gute Ernte* turns to one of the key issues of postwar reconstruction, that is, up-to-date methods for increasing productivity, in the film traditional gender representations remain fixed. The stereotypically repeated male interest is presented through the association with topics such as new agricultural machines, modern livestock breeding methods, and ways to increase harvest yields through the use of chemicals; counter to that, femininity is related to an interest in sewing, knitting, cooking, the improvement of growing vegetables, and the importance of hygiene.

One of the already mentioned structural characteristics of the cinematic style of *Gute Ernte* is the contrast of "old/young" or "adult/child." It is multilayered and also classified according to other dichotomies, such as the differences between "Taylorist/non-Taylorist" and "knowledge/ignorance." This construction of the child as "ignorant" and "inexperienced" is well-suited to the cinema, for children were frequently addressees and recipients of Marshall Plan movies. The youthfulness of the actors is also allegorically interrelated beyond each single film, insofar as the relationship of childlikeness to National Socialism is one of relative innocence, and it also stands for a new political malleability of the population. Here Tressler masterly translates the expectations of the U.S. administration into an image politics of "good" postwar reconstruction work. Thus the representatives of the ECA Mission assumed that the young target group of the pro-U.S. achievement pedagogy was more open towards the films than all other target groups. These findings are based on the socio-economic theory popular at the time, according to which facism "had to" result from the depression of 1930 and the resulting high unemployment rate. According to this economic theory, the mere economic upturn in Austria would hinder the development of facism.

As in most films dealing with postwar reconstruction, in *Gute Ernte* the recipients are also addressed beyond the diegetic and situated in an absolute off-screen location, in a voice over, which can be compared to an objective and omniscient gods' voice. Normative comparisons were thus emphasized both visually and acoustically through commentary. The existence of a non-diegetic commentary demands objectivity and ubiquity, comparable to a god's voice, which both overlooks and foresees the complete narrative structure. I understand narration as the chronological sequence of a causal and final interconnectedness of the actions of a character in a defined space, told from a certain perspective. This strategy to plausibly organize cinematic images through narration is a fundamental principle of *Wunden vernarben*.

Wunden vernarben (Austria 1952)

The ÖPZ-produced film *Wunden vernarben* (*Wounds Heal*) deals directly with U.S economic aid and free supplies of seeds and fertilizers. The setting and topic of the film is rural Austria. The film opens with images of the "old" Austria; two sequences are shown. The first assembles images of ruins; the second adopts the message of an irrevocably outdated method of agriculture by showing a farmer with a hand plow and horse and a sower. This is a visual reference to the soil and peasant aesthetic of National Socialist documentary films, and it is given a specific connotation through the use of words such as "old," "toil" and "grind." The war itself is neither visually nor vocally cited; instead, the war is made anonymous as a catastrophic natural force. The destruction of the "old" is introduced as a force of fate overtaking Austria, which does not refer to a perpetrator, but only creates victims: "more than 12,000 farms destroyed"; "the impoverished fields," "the lost years." This status as victims turns all farmers into "small farmers," forming a (religiously) punished community through an inexplicable force of fate. The image of the "old" Austria is managed in one harsh cut: we hear a fanfare and see a ship in a harbor. While "old" Austria was staged through long takes and static shots, the frequency of cuts now increases rapidly, resulting in a dynamic change of images (embarkation of seed, fertilizers, and livestock; a stream of grain is poured into the ship's hold; staple goods are staged to show the enormous dimension of the supplies.) The rapid sequence of images creates a homogenous overall rhythm of various activities and creates the image of a mechanical organism like a production line. This is accompanied by the off-screen commentary of a male voice: "Like everywhere, the Marshall Plan also brought relief here." Until the very end, the commentary keeps the real origin of the shippings secret; this can be reconstructed only through the written signs on the objects themselves.

In *Wunden vernarben*, technical machines and tools have a privileged position among the cinematic objects. They often fill the complete cinematic space as main characters of the cinematic image; they represent the crucial element of productivity and of the affluence promised by it. The presentations and description of objects and procedures and the visual and auditive linking of the terms "ERP" and "Marshall Plan" are remarkably dense in *Wunden vernarben*. Both terms serve the establishment of cinematic coherence and plausibility. In addition, the food supplies are stamped with phrases in such as "Furnished U.S.A.," sailing on a ship eloquently named *Friendship Train* from New York harbor with the Statue of Liberty in the background, on which gigantic building machines for the draining of land stamped Buckeye/Ohio/U.S.A. or Booth Macdonald are seen. In the film scences showing delivery of supplies, the respective goods are also used as a surface for publicity, for the placement of various logos of the country of origin. The diversity of writing and names shows that the relief supplies coming to Austria from various parts of the United States. The relief action is thus also given excessive meaning in terms of territory.

The generous presentations of agricultural machines, which is meant to represent the "new" Austria, is commented on by an off-camera voice: "The first delivery of the ERP was an important milestone for Austria" and "mechanization and motorization are the most important conditions for economical work." This statement is followed by the image of a farmer and his two sons sitting on a tractor. The tractor substitutes for the horse in the first frame as the sons take up their fathers' legacy. The theses put forward and their analysis are suggested through causal connection between image and sound: rationalization, productivity, and efficiency, the primary norms propagated by the Marshall Plan movies, are purposefully associated with other elements, such as scientific approach (microscope, laboratory), youthfulness (boys), the United States (writing), and democracy (Statue of Liberty). The naturalization of the culture is visualized in various ways: youthfulness connotes advance; mountain landscapes connote timeless tradition and rural values; and ripe corn connotes economic success.

Another technique for establishing cinematic coherence is the use of analogy and drawing parallels between image and sound. The off-camera commentary of *Wunden vernarben* says: "From the remote valleys of the Alps, milk flows once again to the consumer centers," as the image shows the transport of milk buckets with the help of a funicular from a mountain into a populated valley. This analogy leads to a double parallel: the cultural and artificial is naturalized, while the natural appears artificial. Another time-related opposition is that of "then and now" or "past and present": in *Wunden vernarben*, the off-camera commentary contrasts the "funicular making connections easier" with the "long marches of the past."

After a dynamically cut sequence of images about the other (that is, minor) options of the ERP (school system, draining, storage of grains), which is synchronized with a massive historical commentary in a euphoric tone ("30,000 new silos will be created"), the film leads once again to the contrast of old/new and then/now and thus recalls the prologue. We see images of the harvest festival, of a celebrating rural youth organization, commented on from off-screen with "where there used to be poverty and grind, cheerfulness has arrived." Both in the prologue and the epilogue, the framework narration is that of rural images, following the visual culture of National Socialist documentaries.[18] The last image, a film still, which shows an affluent farmhouse in the foreground of a monumental mountain landscape, is accompanied by the normative statement: "The ERP help has alleviated the lot of the farmers' burden." The film still makes an analogy of this sentence by naturalizing values such as "fate," "tradition" and "values" ("the lot" in the off-screen commentary) through the metaphorical image of the mountains. The farmhouse appearing before this metaphorical image of the mountain recalls the first sequence of images, where the image of rural ruins was the starting point of the narrative structure. The mechanization of the rural way of life through the ERP is harmonized in images of traditional constructions of identity. The image politics of *Wunden vernarben* promises to heal all ambiguities of technical modernization—with the ideal image vocabulary of National Socialist documentaries.[19] For this, the mountains serve as the appropriate projection surface. In their monumental grandeur, their everlasting worth, they appear as a guarantor of naturalistic explanations of the world. In the end, the final image is used as a justification of the successful "healing process" already heralded by the title *Wunden vernarben*.

When the Western Allies crossed the borders of the "Third Reich" with their armies, they not only brought cameramen who filmed the events, but had already produced films and specific plans for an extensive information campaign. During the postwar era in Europe, television did not yet play a great role in the politicization of popular culture. Cinematic reorientation was exclusively sustained by 16 mm films in non-theatrical distribution format. Films were expected to explain the complex coherences of the economic aid program, the European Recovery Program, commonly known as the Marshall Plan (1948–1952), in a more illustrative and, thus, more understandable way. By doing so, the films not only appealed to men, but also to women, children, and illiterates. Cinematic images were regarded as an indispensable weapon in the struggle for societal imagery. Film was intended to appeal to a wider audience within a growing group of moviegoers and to spellbound more intensely the viewer, particularly those who, such as people in rural areas, had never seen a film before.

Film was attractive for three reasons. First, it promised a large audience in a growing society of moviegoers.[20] Second, it held the viewer's attention. As a report of the Austrian mission pointed out, "The medium meets the spectator seated and is almost certain of finding him there at the end of the performance, something radio cannot assure."[21] Third, for those living in the rural parts of Europe who had never been exposed to motion pictures before, film would leave a lasting impression. Films were often shown in rural villages by means of mobile theatre units. In Greece, a showboat traveled to the isolated Greek islands carrying the message of the Marshall Plan through film. The ÖPZ newsletter *Produktivität* which had been launched in July 1950, first mentioned U.S. films in ÖPZ archives that offered practical information concerning managerial and technical issues in its fourth number in October 1950 in an article titled "Large Selection of Technical Films."[22] As early as spring 1951, 100 film projectors were set up in Austria in cooperation with the ECA mission in Vienna to "permit the films to be shown at the workplace."[23] In addition, the films were also made available to be shown in Viennese cinemas. The film service also had two film trucks so that the films could be shown throughout the provinces upon request. These film trucks were purchased and fitted out in 1952. These ÖPZ mobile cinemas made a crucial contribution to the educational drive to popularize productivity among the general public. It was only with the use of the film trucks that we can speak of a decisive turning point in the comprehensive popularization of *productivity.* Evidence of this is seen in the large number of visitors and the socially diverse audiences that extended beyond the company's immediate environment. The films also addressed the non-working public, above all housewives, by tackling issues such as increasing efficiency within the home and by providing consumer advice. By building up the film office and developing a network of projector sites and the mobile cinema, the ÖPZ also became a central institution for promoting efficiency outside a business context.

Notes

1 Gerd Hardach, *Der Marshall-Plan: Auslandshilfe und Wiederaufbau in Westdeutschland, 1948–1952* (Munich: Deutscher Taschenbuchverlag, 1994), 54; see also Michael Schönberg, "Amerikanische Informations- und Medienpolitik in Österreich, 1945–1955," PhD. diss., University of Vienna, 1975.

2 Albert Hemsig, "The Marshall Plan's European Film Unit 1948–1955: A Memoir and Filmography," *Historical Journal of Film, Radio and Television* 14.3 (1994): 269–74.

3 Ferald J. Bryan, "George C. Marshall at Harvard: A Study of the Origins and Construction of the Marshall Plan Speech," *Presidential Studies Quarterly* 21.3 (1991): 489–507.

4 Jacqueline Mac Glade, "The U.S. Technical Assistance and Productivity Program and the Education of Western European Managers 1948–1958," in *Missionaries and Managers: American Influences on European Management Education 1945–1960*, ed. Terry Gourvish and Nick Tiratsoo (Manchester: Manchester UP, 1998), 67; see also Kurt Tweraser, "The Politics of Productivity and Corporatism: The Late Marshall Plan in Austria 1950–1954," in *Austria in the Nineteen Fifties*, vol. 3, Contemporary Austrian Studies, ed. Günter Bischof et al. (New Brunswick, NJ: Transaction, 1995), 91–115.

5 See Wilfried Mähr, *Der Marshallplan in Österreich* (Graz: Styria, 1987).

6 See record group 511.63/2-1252, Department of State to the Officer in Charge of the American Mission Vienna, 12 February 1962–. USIE Country Paper. 1951–1952; 511.63/4-1050. Department of State to Officer in Charge of American Mission in Vienna, 7 April 1950, National Archives and Records Administration, Washington.

7 Peter Weiler, "The United States, International Labor and the Cold War: The Breakup of the World Federation of Trade Unions," *Diplomatic History* 5.1 (1981): 1–22.

8 Glade, "U.S. Technical Assistance," 13.

9 511.63/5–1551. U.S. Legation, Vienna, to Department of State, 15 May 1951. Subject: Development of Psychological Offensive by U.S. Information and Cultural Media in Austria, National Archives and Records Administration, Washington, D.C.

10 Michael Rogin, "Make my Day! Spectacle as Amnesia in Imperial Politics," in *The New Historicism Reader*, ed. Aram Veeser (London: Routledge, 1984), 229–54.

11 See Hannes Hofbauer, *Westwärts: Österreichs Wirtschaft im Wiederaufbau* (Vienna: Verlag für Gesellschaftskritik, 1992).

12 Stuart Schulberg, "Making Marshall Plan Movies," *Film News* 10 (September 1951): 10.

13 Harry Bayard Price, *The Marshall Plan and Its Meaning* (Ithaca, NY: Cornell UP, 1955), 242.

14 Alfred Hiller, "Amerikanische Medien und Schulpolitik in Österreich, 1945–1950," PhD. diss., University of Vienna, 1974, 174.

15 Robert Buchschwenter, ed., *Georg Tressler: Zwischen Auftrag und Autor* (Vienna: Filmarchiv, 2003).

16 With over 1,300 titles, the ÖPZ film archive presents a resource which is not only unique in Europe but also extremely informative for contemporary history. The ÖPZ, a partner institute of the Deutsches Rationalisierungskuratorium (German Rationalization Committee), held the monopoly on the educational representation of productivity which went beyond an organizational context in the 1950s. It arose as a direct result of the United States' economic Marshall Plan aid, as well as Austrian reconstruction projects. From the beginning, the construction of a specialized library (with approximately 7,000 books in 1960) and a comprehensive film distribution service was pushed through. A further emphasis was the organization of the "technical assistance" of the Austrian study mission in the United States and Western Europe. Participants in such journeys—such as unionists—count among the multipliers of the following "wave of Americanization." From 1950 to1960, the ÖPZ supervised 258 trips to the United States for 1,477 people and 198 trips to Western Europe for 1,054 people. At that time, what counted were selected exemplary branch analyses, exhibitions, seminars, conferences as well as special commercial projects, the erection of model work shops and the maintenance of research, training, and advice posts.

17 Ramón Reichert, "Die Popularisierung der Produktivität: Die Filme des Österreichischen Produktivitätszentrums 1950–1987: Ein Beitrag zur Diskussion um den Film als historische Quelle," *Relation* 2.7 (2000): 69–128.

18 Ramón Reichert, "Einleitung," in *Kulturfilm im Dritten Reich*, ed. Ramón Reichert (Vienna: Synema, 2005), 7–15; see also Elisabeth Büttner and Christian Dewald, *Das tägliche Brennen, Eine Geschichte des österreichischen Films von 1945 bis zur Gegenwart* (Salzburg: Residenz, 2002).

19 Ramón Reichert, "Documentary Film in Austria," in *Encyclopedia of Documentary Film*, ed. Ian Aitken (London: Routledge, 2005), 141.

20 Ramón Reichert, "Re-education Seen through Film," *Historical Journal of Film, Radio, and Television* 26 (2006): 67–75; see also Reinhold Wagnleitner, "Die kulturelle Reorientierung Österreichs nach dem Zweiten Weltkrieg," *Zeitgeschichte* 11 (1984): 326–44.

21 Ramón Reichert, "The Popularization of Productivity: The Industry Films of the Austrian Productivity Center, 1951–1959," in *Conference Proceedings: The Seventh Biennial National Labour History Conference*, ed. Canberra Austrialian National University (Canberra: Austrialian National U, 2001), 214.

22 "Große Auswahl an technischen Filmen," *Produktivität* 6 (1950): 6.

23 "Europäisches Wiederaufbauprogramm," *ERP-Aktualitäten* 87 (1951): 10.

Christoph Höllriegl

Visualizations of the Marshall Plan in Austria Based on the Former Film Collection of the Austrian Trade Union Federation

On the occasion of the sixtieth anniversary of the Marshall Plan, six trailers of cuttings from fourteen selected films were shown at the two-day conference *Images of the Marshall Plan: Film, Photographs, Exhibits, Posters* in Vienna, Austria, in 2008. Some of them were analyzed. The selections of the films that were presented were chosen on the basis of parameters of Marshall Plan films according to the filmography compiled by Linda R. Christenson.[1] They also included films that were financed, promoted, or distributed by other services such as the United States Information Service (USIS) Vienna.[2] Films selected for discussion at the conference were made before 1956 and were not limited to films exclusively produced in or for Austria.

This article should be seen as a complement to the trailers and films on the DVD and accompanying website to further scholary papers; it is neither a comprehensive analysis of the selected films, nor a film review.[3] It makes no claim to completeness because a comprehensive analysis of all relevant films and facts that should be taken in consideration is impossible. Even the attempt to define the necessary terms including "solidarity" or "everyday life and culture in the past" and an interdisciplinary scientific discourse would take more than a lifetime.[4] Actually, new approaches should be developed and new questions should be raised to inspire further research.

About the Film Collection

In 1945, the trade union movement in Austria had to start from scratch. At the initiative of some shop stewards of the former free trade unions, socialist, communist, and Christian Social trade unionists agreed in April 1945 to found the Austrian Trade Union Federation (*Österreichischer Gewerkschaftsbund*, or ÖGB) which would operate above the party level. The ÖGB asked for nationalization of the key industries to help the national economy to recover, and the ÖGB was, until 1949, a member of the Communist-dominated World Trade Union Confederation.[5] Neither fit the approach of the Marshall Plan.

George C. Marshall invited representatives of national trade union confederations to Paris on 8 October 1948 to discuss administration of the Marshall Plan. Marshall wanted close cooperation between national governments and trade unions. The first president of the ÖGB, Johann Böhm, assured Marshall of the ÖGB's support, consisting of marketing and promotion of the Marshall Plan and also Marshall Plan film programs.

The Marshall Plan film program began as the ÖGB got the temporary license to run cinemas and traveling movie shows in Austria beginning in 1949. There were different restrictions in Austrian provinces for the licenses, probably depending on the occupants. The educational center of the ÖGB was allowed to show only educational, technical, cultural, and unionized films at a distance of three to four miles from the next cinema; the ÖGB held these licenses until 1979.[6]

Lost and Found

In the years 2004 and 2005, the media department of the ÖGB (originally founded as an institution for the educational work of the ÖGB) became a separate organization. The archives of the department held more than 20,000 different film titles, including about 1,500 roles of 16mm films in German, Slavic, English, Italian, and Greek. The oldest film dates from 1931. Corresponding technical equipment also still existed, although most of the projectors in stock were not operational.

The USIS Vienna provided 1,242 copies of the 16mm films (consisting of 324 different titles) for the ÖGB and chose to donate some of its remaining 16mm films to the ÖGB archive because the USIS Vienna's archives had been closed years before.[7] By 2005, only one copy of most films remained. It's most likely that the media department of the ÖGB had lent films to other institutions and organizations. Unfortunately, a couple of film sources or data of origin are still missing. For instance, it is not clear how *Spiel der Wirtschaft* made its way in the archive of the ÖGB (see the section "The Game of the Economy" below).

One intention of the reorganization in 2004/05 was to reduce the number of 16mm films to those titles relevant to the ÖGB and not available as DVDs to rent. As a result, eighty-one films can be categorized as Marshall Plan films according to the parameters of the Marshall Plan filmography by Linda R. Christenson. At least two films had been listed in February 2002 as missing: *Spiel der Wirtschaft*, by director Max Diekhout (Germany 1950, August Rittig Film Production, Munich-Geislgasteig) and *Reichtum der Wälder* by director Albert Quendler (Austria 1950, Schönbrunn Film Production, Vienna; English working-title *Forestry in Austria*).[8] Seven films can also be found in the former archive of the Austrian Productivity Center (*Österreichisches Produktivitäts-Zentrum*, or ÖPZ). The ÖGB was one of the four Austrian social partners that founded the ÖPZ in 1950.[9]

Today, the 16mm film archive not relevant to the ÖGB is maintained by me at the request of teachers and historians. Several Marshall Plan films have been made accessible to students and scientists by simply filming the screen and transferring the video material to a DVD. In addition, research and interdisciplinary scientific analyses have been made for some of the films. Marshall Plan films have been analyzed for comparison. These analyses shed light on social change and (labor) solidarity based on the model of the *Systeme transitiver Solidariät* (systems of transitive solidarity; see the section "The Game of the Economy" below).[10]

Creating Symbols

First, because Austrian workers played an important role during the peaceful reconstruction of the country and in the struggle against communism, the research addressed the extent of showings of Marshall Plan films within the educational work program of the ÖGB.[11] Unfortunately, the ÖGB data do not indicate the number of movie screenings. The activity reports from the years 1945 to 1964 describe movie screenings under the following terms: regular films, narrow-movie-screenings with films from other distribution centers, feature films, cultural films, documentary films, or advertising films.[12]

The ÖGB was first of all a film distributor for shop stewards and functionaries across Austria. Moreover, wear spots on the film material (for example, condition of the perforation, scratches, patchy spots, and so forth) do not indicate use because abrasions can occur through unprofessional and careless use of film projectors. It is also unclear whether the extant films are originals or just copies of originals. Interviews with former projectionists brought no substantial insights. They simply remember showing films (supposedly also Marshall Plan films). Their procedure was simple. Projectionists started with the weekly or monthly review (*Wochen- oder Monatsschau*). Afterwards, one feature film was shown. It is also not clear whether the reviews shown first had been weekly reviews distributed by USIS Vienna or the monthly reviews *Erschaut-Erlebt* of the ÖGB. Thirty-eight sequels of the monthly reviews had been produced and screened from 1957 on, but not one of them mentions the Marshall Plan. On the other hand, the weekly reviews distributed by USIS Vienna promote the Marshall Plan even after 1952. The former projectionists complained about the heavy and unwieldy screening equipment. They also reported a lack of interest by Austrians living in rural regions. From 1960 on, the interest declined. One reason for this drop was the emergence of television in Austria. According to Heidemarie Schumacher, cinemas lost their function as a public meeting point for collective musing, and the cultural-industrial production of illusion and excitement was relocated to private homes. Before that, according to Schumacher, masses of people visited the (Hollywood) cinemas—not the screenings of the ÖGB—as a consequence of (world) economic crises. By going to the movies, they fled—for a short period of time—from everyday life, unemployment, or poor living conditions.[13] In addition, people from rural regions simply liked to consume the media of film, without preference for a particular content, as film director Georg Tressler explains. According to Marshall McLuhan, the media itself was the message, not the message of the filmmakers. According to Tressler, the motivation to watch films in cinemas would have been significantly less if "moving pictures" and cinemas had not been totally new in certain regions of Austria. Tressler also admits that films did not have to be blockbusters; entertaining the audience was sufficient.[14]

In 1952, Beatrice and Georg Tressler played a leading role (writing the film script and directing) in the making of *Einsteigen bitte!* Among others, the famous Austrian actor Helmuth Qualtinger took part in the film. The film was initiated by the ÖGB and produced for advertising purposes. In the *International Labour*

Film Catalogue from June 1956,[15] the film is described as a semi-documentary with great human interest. The film starts with a train pulling into the station and tells the stories of the travelers, who do not know each other. Reviews show how they still are connected with each other through their memberships in their union, how they need the union, and how the union needs them and all the other people who are fighting for a better future.[16] The film was shown at the First International Labours Film Festival in Hamburg in 1954 and won the Labour World's Screen award.[17] Two years later, Georg and Beatrice Tressler's film *Wie die Jungen sungen ...* was released (see the section "Multicultural, But Stereotyped" below). In Brussels, Tressler received an award for the best film for the unification of European countries. In Austria, the film also received praise.[18]

The train (among other vehicles) as a symbol for means of transport, for movement, but also for stagnancy, appears not only in the beginning of *Einsteigen bitte!* (see Image 1), but can be found in many (Marshall Plan) films like *Spiel der Wirtschaft* (see the section "The Game of the Economy" below) and *Strom der Berge* (see the section "Made in and for Austria" below) and brings the exhibition *Train of Goodwill and Peace* from 1950 in mind.[19] On the other hand, the National Socialist regime also knew how to use vehicles as symbols.[20] For example, taking into account that a marching army was the predominant image for symbolizing movement, the Marshall Plan filmmakers switched from marching soldiers to modern means of transportation in order to highlight the speed of reconstruction.[21]

Image 1: *The Train as Symbol*
Source: *Bitte einsteigen! film still.*
(all the 45 images listed in this text can be found on the DVD in the backpocket of this volume)

For years following the official end of the Marshall Plan, the ÖGB and filmmakers continued to produce and distribute films that did and did not mention the Marshall Plan. The distributions of other films from USIS Vienna also continued.[22] The distribution of 16mm films from USIS Vienna to the ÖGB continued until 1962. In addition, the end of the Marshall Plan in Austria did not mean the end of counterpart funds. In 1961, the United States and Austria agreed on the transfer of counterpart funds to the independent administration of Austria.[23] Therefore, it is theoretically possible that further films were financed and supported during a long period of time after the official end of the Marshall Plan. Thus those films could also be treated as Marshall Plan films.[24] According to Bettina Fritzsche, the danger of overhasty categorization should be avoided.[25] Moreover, as Jürgen Kriz asserts, order and safety, like the concentration on well-known categories, kills creativity and change.[26]

With the continued and increasing interest in the Marshall Plan and its films, much interest in the missing films has developed. Attempts have been made to explain social change in Austria since the end of World War II. With little chance for new insights, no attempts have been made to analyze already described and interpreted Marshall Plan films from various points of view.[27]

Excursus: The Making of (Reconstruction)

Since its advent, cinema has become an integral part of different scientific disciplines, but applying scientific methods to film was difficult in the past.[28] However, if a film is used merely as a source, for example to endorse historical events, film documents (including films available online) are a suitable and easy means to support historiography. The preoccupation with film faces greater difficulties, however, when the medium itself is at the center of cognitive interest and an extensive analysis if, for example, its effect on social change is to be explored.[29] On the one hand, a film tells a story by means of words and pictures that a scholar can analyze. On other hand, according to Werner Faulstich, it establishes its own story as well, such as in reference to its production, the film industry, actors and directors, or genres.[30] The same is true for the trailers created to promote the films (see trailers on the DVD).

To research all the information concerning the background of a film's evolution is a difficult task, especially with historical films because many of the films contain neither opening nor closing credits with relevant information.[31] Thus the abstract basic model of emitter and recipient with encoding and decoding is as insufficient as an analysis of picture, text, content, or language as well as research on reception in spite of various standardized methods of analysis to trace the impact of a film.[32] From an interdisciplinary point of view, a film is anchored somewhere in history and in society, and it is examined as a solitary document that reveals little of the times, the society, or the social changes.[33] Furthermore, media, according to Frank Hartmann, cannot be examined by its content either; cinema cannot be explained by describing a film. Analytical descriptions of a film are also insufficient for producing substantial understanding.[34]

The whole question of the influence of Marshall Plan films, particularly the effects on human beings' behavior, is a continuing debate. According to Gillian Dyer's *Advertising as Communication*, the problem of gauging the influence of Marshall Plan films as advertising for lifestyles, consumerism, new production methods, and so forth is multi-faceted and can be approached from a number of perspectives; there are different answers, and there is a vast literature on that subject as well.[35] All approaches will reveal different aspects of a film. The focus lies not in finding the most appropriate method, because, according to Johann August Schülein, the functional plurality and heterogeneity of the philosophy-of-science discussion make specific access possible. Investigators are encouraged to try various approaches.[36] "There have been studies which have tried to detect any difference in impact on different age groups, on the different sexes or between the different media. Some of the research into advertising's effects has investigated the change in people's attitudes, values or behavior brought about as a result of exposure to advertisements."[37] According to Dyer, sociological and psychological researchers prefer to study the effects upon children because they are vulnerable to propaganda, and some researchers have examined films' effects, that is, whether they inform, fulfill needs, or give satisfaction to individuals.[38]

Each film is embedded in a continuum along a timeline and is seen in the context of artistic styles and modes of its period. European filmmakers were influenced by other films and other film artists, especially from Hollywood.[39] According to Werner Faulstich, the postwar period was very important for international film culture, which reached its climax and exceeded its limits as higher aesthetic standards were established.[40]

The impact of a (historic) film on the consumer is essentially dependent upon its chronological placement. From a present-day perspective, it is only theoretically possible to reconstruct the chronological anchoring. In addition, a film cannot be treated as a reliable or accurate record of historic events because of the wide range of artistic compositional devices.[41] One has to be skeptical, because a film is liable—according to Judith Mair and Silke Becker—to invent inaccurate facts for the recreation of true events.[42]

To understand film as medium, asserts Thomas Slunecko, is not merely to understand the protagonists or to link their actions with the events of the day; the film constantly opens the sphere of its function by constituting the function in a dynamic way at the very same time.[43] Furthermore, a film does not have the same impact on every culture or society due to the interaction between the film and the cultures of the people in the audience shaped by their social, political, religious/symbolic, ecological, and economic realities, together with their existing media. Because Marshall Plan films were distributed in many different countries, cultures, societies, or systems and subsystems and were translated and presented in various languages, the resulting analyses and results can vary accordingly, especially concerning the films' impact on their audiences. Science has to consider, according to Bettina Fritzsche, differences among media users, such as, for example, the presentation of Marshall Plan films to an audience of entrepreneurs or workers in the course of a trade union event, and the programming itself is a matter of re-education versus re-orientation.[44]

Today, the question is whether it is possible to analyze historical films with new methods and theories.[45] Referring to the documentary method of Ralf Bohnsack, the analysis should, according to Fritzsche, focus on social pre-experiences that are determined by, for example, characteristics of the generation, the milieu, or gender. For this reason, the analysis of media use in the context of daily activities and power structures cannot be limited to the question of how the text is interpreted or how the interpretation is connected to ideology. According Fritzsche, the theory of production is based on a reconstruction of everyday life and from knowledge that comes with experience.[46] In other words and according to acting coach Lee Strasberg, "In the scene I have got to behave this and that different way. What would motivate me to behave this and that way?"[47] Conversely, the question would be, "What motivates the audience, the individual person, to behave according to the message in the film?" When the filmmaker has a certain effect he or she wishes to produce in the audience, according to Martin Baltes and Rainer Höltschl, the filmmaker later has to create situations, characters, images, and a composition that directly results in the desired effect,[48] even though, according to Georg Tressler, a documentary film reconstructs a universe and, therefore, implies a message that could not be invented.[49]

For instance, the film *Traudl's neuer Gemüsegarten* from 1952 has, according to Tressler, only one message: do not eat so many dumplings, and your health will get better.[50] This message is a rather simple one. In order to analyze the film's impact on the audience, one has to interview people who are both witnesses to history and have actually seen the film, although statements of witnesses to history are, according to Oliver Rathkolb, not necessarily reliable.[51] But according to the documentary method, sequences or frozen images out of the film can be analyzed and meaningful comparisons can be found. In the northern part of Lower Austria, films of the former ÖGB archive had been shown in the villages. Pictures from that area shot in 1964 look very similar to the advice given in a film about planting a vegetable garden, witnessed by the formation of flowers and vegetable patches, the garden fence, and the footpaths (see Images 2 and 3). The wife of a former projectionist says in an interview that she built her vegetable garden in the same way that her mother had. Sadly, whether the projectionist or his wife have ever seen the film could not be discovered. Tressler himself identifies the crop system presented in the film as common sense. The message was important to him. However, according to Daniel Wildmann, the message is quite similar to those of National Socialism: the health of the nation is determined by the behavior of a single person and demonstrated by the individual body.[52] Although the message is rather simple, according to Mair and Becker, it may be aimed at the postwar generation, a generation not burdened with ideological reservations.[53]

Image 2: *Advice for Planting a Vegetable Garden, 1952*
Source: *Traudl's neuer Gemüsegarten film still.*

Image 3: *Garden Designed According to Mother's*
Source: *Photo by Hermine Stagl, Lower Austria, in 1964.*

In this film, Tressler also intended to transform the local residents into actors, documenting their lives.[54] But one has to keep in mind that dumplings were regarded by hard-working construction workers in urban regions as essential food for survival. But for people who did not need so many calories, dumplings were regarded as unhealthy food.

Sandra Schulberg asks why contemporary scholars should review the films made by U.S. and European filmmakers more than fifty years ago and whether film can effect widespread social change, as the Marshall Plan filmmakers thought.[55] First of all, the message to eat fewer dumplings is still relevant today. Moreover, the film *Blick auf Europa* (see the section "Absolute Marshall Plan" below) gives the answer to the first part of the question, suggesting we should remember from time to time, and the answer to the second part of the question can be found in the film *Spiel der Wirtschaft* (see the section "The Game of the Economy" below).

Absolute Marshall Plan

According to Brian Angus McKenzie:

> The Marshall Plan provided the United States with an unprecedented opportunity to intervene in the affairs of Western Europe. It was not only an effort to reconstruct European economies; the plan was also an attempt by the United States to reorder European society. From chicken farming to class relations, the United States deployed the Marshall Plan in an attempt to provide economic and technical assistance that would end class conflict, cement peaceful European relations, check the rise of communism, and promote American interests.[56]

The purpose of the Marshall Plan film program was also to document the destruction of European countries and to promote the Marshall Plan itself.[57] According to Victoria de Grazia, some of the counterpart funds went to the Economic Cooperation Administration's (ECA) Film Unit, "which in the hands of talented teams of European filmmakers produced about 200 documentary-style movies from 1949 to 1953."[58]

The film *Blick auf Europa*, probably a shortened German dubbing of *The Hour of Choice* directed by Stuart Legg (1951) and distributed by USIS Vienna (see trailer 1 on DVD), proclaims as best free trade in the shape of free supply and free demand wherein everyone can buy with his or her money whatever is most pleasing. Shown, among other items, is a luxury car (see Image 4). The members of the audience immediately envision, according to Martin Baltes and Rainer Höltschl, their dreams, purchasable for money, but unaffordable in reality. At the cinema, the audience continues to dream, and even their frustrations evaporate as they dream of better living standards.[59] The picture of the luxury car can be interpreted, according to Georg Vobruba's methodology, as an excessive demand for consumption of prestigious goods and as consumption for amusement, which is characterized as unproductive consumption by Karl Marx. This consumption is a proof of acquired success.[60] The Marshall Plan has proven its potential, and the Europeans have made their contribution to the reconstruction. But according to Milton and Rose Friedman, technological development in particular has strongly influenced perception. Assuming cinema is the precursor of television, and according to Milton and Rose Friedman, Marshall Plan films demonstrate a standard of living the poor are unable to achieve by honest labor.[61] To moderate the excessive demand encouraged by the film *Blick auf Europa*, the question of how all this might be possible, considering the recent devastation in Western Europe, arises (see Image 5). Pointing out that maybe remembering this unpleasant memory from time to time is valuable, the films of the Marshall Plan warn of communism. According to Noam Chomsky, while nobody considered the Soviet Union a military threat, nevertheless Western policy after World War II immediately focused on Soviet hegemony and containment.[62]

Image 4: *Luxury Car for Everybody*
Source: *Blick auf Europa film still.*

Image 5: *Remember from Time to Time*
Source: *Blick auf Europa film still.*

Although the American characters living in the United States in *Uncle Jim and Aunt Mary* pay higher taxes in order for the old world to rebuild, the film builds a bridge of solidarity between Americans and Europeans. According Paul M. Zulehner et al., solidarity is, in general, the ability or competence of a human being to advocate for the common good and a just disposition of opportunities in life. Accordingly, human beings are aware of the necessity of solidarity, with solidarity being stronger from a close range rather than a distant one. However, says Franz M. Wuketits, cooperative solidarity or altruistic behavior among creatures has a higher probability within familial relationships.[63]

At the start of the Marshall Plan, however, there were some barriers to be faced; *Die ersten Europäer* from 1950 broaches the issue of artificial borders between the European countries leading to ebbing trade.[64] The gates close and the train wagons are sealed. According to the film, no country could recover from the consequences of the war on its own. Thus there is no other choice this time for avoiding misfortune. The Marshall Plan was depicted as the U.S. spark to ignite the European engine; ships and trucks, along with trains and ships, become symbols for motion as well as strength. The ship as symbol is also utilized on a poster "Europe—All Our Colors to the Mast."[65] A comparable poster with similar symbolic content was printed by the Austrian Trade Union Federation in December 1958 as a new year's wish for a better life in 1959, this time with the Austrian flag displayed in the image.[66]

How the Marshall Plan effectively works in practice is explained in the 1951 film *Die entscheidenden Jahre* which reports on the economic reconstruction of Europe.[67] The film explained to 270 million people in Western Europe that the Marshall Plan was by no means a loan, but a gift of the American people. The tractor donated by the United States is, in many cases, the symbol for the assistance in support of the agricultural economy, as well as a symbol for motion and progress. The farmer in the film, Marcel Roubiere, does not understand, however, why he should pay for his tractor if it was a gift from the United States. Simple animations explain that the tractor was presented to the French people by the American people. Marcel's money is deposited in the special counterpart funds (see Image 6) and is used to finance house building, hydropower plants, the energy sector, road construction, new machineries, and so on. Thus the Marshall Plan secures achievements in all the European countries (see Image 7). The film explains the Marshall Plan in an easily understood style for France, although probably the film was used for the same purpose in various countries. What is missing, however, is that fact that the Marshall Plan also benefited the U.S. economy.

Image 6: *How Counterpart Funds Work*
Source: *Die entscheidenden Jahre film still.*

Image 7: *Screen of Results of Counterpart Funds.*
Source: *Die entscheidenden Jahre film still.*

Made in and for Austria

Among other examples, the film *Vom Erz zum Stahl* (see trailer 2 on DVD) shows the effects of the Marshall Plan in Austria: investments of the European Recovery Program in heavy industry (the film was distributed by USIS Vienna). Extensive investments were made, for example, in new excavators for the iron and steel industry. The key industry of the Austrian economy desperately needed modern machines for mining at the main iron ore field in Styria and to transport the material to the steel industry companies in Donauwitz and Linz. The heart of the modern conveyor system was the electric power engine and control units. In *Strom der Berge* from 1950, Austrians learn of the future source of electricity for the power engines and control units. The English version is known under the film title *The Invisible Link.*[68] A foreman of a group of cement-workers explains in Austrian dialect (see Image 8) that Kaprun is going to be the biggest hydropower plant in Austria, producing electricity for the valleys and towns. Because electricity creates jobs through the use of electric machines (see Image 9) and brings a higher level of comfort at home, electric power for Austria was the most important infrastructure project. Scenes illustrate the ease and value of such technology, for instance, electrically operated dung-pumps for mountain farmers are so easy to handle that even girls can operate them (see Image 10). An electric hoist makes plowing in the mountains easier. A young man shows how easy it is to operate such a cable-plow (see Image 11). Similar to *Reichtum der Wälder* (see below), the film shows that nature can be more easily controlled with the help of electric power and new machines. Filming and cutting techniques may also remind viewers of the mountain films made between 1924 and 1954 by director Arnold Fanck and by actress and later director of the National Socialist regime Leni Riefenstahl.[69]

Image 8: *Narrator Explains in Austrian Dialect*
Source: *Strom der Berge film still.*

Image 9: *Electricity Creates Jobs in Austrian Industries*
Source: *Strom der Berge film still.*

Image 10: *Easy to Operate Dung-Pumps*
Source: *Strom der Berge film still.*

Image 11: *Plowing in the Mountains*
Source: *Strom der Berge film still.*

The film *Reichtum der Wälder* (see film on DVD), with the English working title *Forestry in Austria*, asks at its beginning if the country can succeed by the time the Marshall Plan ends, two years hence.[70] The answer is yes if Austrians can activate all their power and use the richness of their country. In the corresponding image in the film, one can see a calendar page with the year 1950 and a reversing train loaded with wood. The young Austrian farmer has chosen to carry out the aforementioned program.

The Austrians in the film are members of the 4-H Clubs, which are supported by the United Sates.[71] A chainsaw operated by one person increases productivity in the forestry industry. The use of the transportable chainsaw saves twenty minutes. Two workers with a traditional saw need fifteen minutes for one tree. The single operator chainsaw fells a tree in only five minutes (see Image 13). A detonation for constructing new transportation roadways through the woods symbolizes the Marshall Plan. The explosion argues for a better life instead of death and perdition (see Image 14). New cable cranes and tractors symbolize activity and progress (see Image 15), over-emphasized when an oxcart gets left behind. Nature can be controlled for economic profit through modern technology. In addition, new scientific insights make it possible to recycle wood waste and to produce fiberboard (see Image 16). As a consequence, fiberboard totally changed the production of furniture. In 1952, the ÖGB, the Vienna Board of Trade, and the City of Vienna together founded the cooperation for *Soziale Wohnkultur* (social cultivation of home decor), which organized furniture exhibitions and offered particularly cheap installment plans to enable workers to purchase the furniture.[72]

Image 12: *Youth Carries Out the Aforementioned Program*
Source: *Reichtum der Wälder film still.*

Image 13: *A One-Operator Chainsaw*
Source: *Reichtum der Wälder film still.*

Image 14: *Symbol for the Marshall Plan*
Source: *Reichtum der Wälder film still.*

Image 15: *Oxcart Gets Left behind Tractors*
Source: *Reichtum der Wälder film still.*

Image 16: *Fiberboard for Furniture*
Source: *Reichtum der Wälder film still.*

A different branch of the forestry industry produced modular homes for the markets in Israel, Australia, and South America (see Image 17). In contrast to fiberboard production, however, the modular home was not a booming business in Austria. The film finishes with the note that the Marshall Plan ends in the year 1952 and poses the question, "Is this going to be our end, too?" The answer is, "No, it is not. It has to be the beginning." A train decorated with an Austrian banner and a white flag moves forward.

Image 17: *Modular Homes for Export*
Source: *Reichtum der Wälder film still.*

The *Monthly Review of the USIS Vienna* from the year 1954 (*USIS Monatsschau aus FOX tönende Wochenschau*) humorously presents the productions of skis in the town Ried im Innkreis (Upper Austria). The title of the short film is *Ski from Austria*. With the help of the Marshall Plan, the Fischer Company, one of the major producers of laminated skis in Europe, was able to increase its productivity and number of exports. Fischer's laminated ski is promoted as an Austrian product of high quality: it is does not break, even when a man uses the ski as a seesaw (see Image 18).

Image 18: *Demonstration of Laminated Ski's Strength*
Source: *Monthly Review of the USIS Vienna film still, 1954.*

The *Monatsbericht in Bild und Wort* (produced in cooperation with Movietone News, Volume 1, Number 12, from the year 1950, about the European reconstruction progress) identifies summer and winter tourism as the most important source of foreign currency in Europe. Therefore, financial aid from the Marshall Plan is used to enlarge winter sports resorts and to modernize hotel buildings. The money primarily supports smaller tourist hotels, making skiing cheaper so more and more people can afford the excitement of winter sports. All over Europe, people start to go on vacation trips. Traveling becomes the most joyful but unexpected aid for devastated Europe. It also marks the start of mass tourism in Austrian summer and winter sports resorts and documents the interdependency of Western Europe in regard to sources of foreign currency. The highlight is an open-topped luxury car in the middle of snow-covered mountains (see Image 19, Image 4).

Image 19: *A Convertible Luxury Car*
Source: *Monatsbericht in Bild und Wort film still, 1950.*

Scientific Management—Even in Sports

The film *Wenn jemand eine Reise tut ...*" (Crown Film Unit) from the year 1951 (see trailer 3 on DVD) reports on the mutual visits of experts from the United States to Europe and vice versa. U.S. specialists come to Europe to explain new industrial machines. European economic experts (from Great Britain) visit the United States to study more efficient work methods. A buttonhole sewing machine attracts the attention of the European visitors. The simply designed machine can sew seven button holes in fourteen seconds. Only one worker is needed to operate simultaneously two sewing-machines (see Image 20). Even more impressive to the Europeans is the speed in the shirt-ironing section, achieved by a simple division of labor. Specifically, every shirt is ironed and folded by work groups consisting of three female workers. All in all, they finish over 600 shirts per day. The employees are paid by the number of finished shirts, the payment for one shirt being negotiated with the union. A higher productivity level results in higher wages.

Image 20: *Time Measurement*
Source: *Wenn jemand eine Reise tut ... film still.*

The major difference between U.S. and European working processes is clear at the end of each day. Almost all workers have their own car. Mass production produces a higher standard of living, characterized by more amenities and more leisure time. For instance, as a golfer prepares for his next shot, he does not have to stoop down because a special machine places the ball on the tee (see Image 21). The film par excellence praises scientific management; Fordism becomes evident in the *USIS Monatsschau* aus *Fox tönende Wochenschau* 1955. A report for sports fans about a cooking competition, organized by the Ladies of the Austrian-American Society, presents a modern electric kitchen and household equipment. A fashionably dressed woman from the United States uses modern electric cooking machines (see Image 22). In contrast, the Austrian competitor appears in traditional dress, her assistant: a wooden spoon (see Image 23). Fortunately, due the jury's serious indigestion, the cooking competition ends in a draw.

Image 21: *Advantage for Golfer*
Source: *Wenn jemand eine Reise tut ... film still.*

Image 22: *Modern Electric Cooking*
Source: *USIS Monatsschau film still, 1955.*

Image 23: *Austrian Cooking Assistant*
Source: *USIS Monatsschau film still 1955.*

Both films seem to be accurate documentations of U.S. practices, though humorously exaggerated. According to McKenzie, European workers saw in the films American workers owning houses, cars, and appliances (compare Image 4). According to McKenzie, "All these, they were told, could belong to them if they emulated American practices."[73] As McKenzie argues, for French workers this way of life was a fantasy because the Marshall Plan had not increased the standard of living or the wages of workers. U.S. public diplomacy created an image of the American way of life as an utopia of gratified individuals leading lives of mass consumption and then promised it to the Europeans.[74] For this reason—according to Neil Postman—slogans and symbols were created that enable the audience to adopt a comprehensive self-perception.[75]

Division of work and piecework brought advantages, but removed the last remnants of individual responsibility, according to Jeremy Rifkin.[76] Rifkin concludes that routine work weakens human brainpower. Richard Sennet apparently agrees that relying upon mechanical intelligence dulls the mind.[77] Still no one can deny that modern labor-saving devices make household work and leisure activities easier and more productive, except perhaps the frivolous golf ball-to-tee device.

Fear and Loathing in *Metropolis*

In contrast to many other films, the 1952 German dubbing of the film *Der Mensch und die Maschine* (see trailer 4 on DVD) shows quite clearly humankind's fear of enslavement through machinery (see Image 24).[78] However, there are no industries where machines have not proven their advantage and changed human beings' needs. The division of work, which assigns each worker exactly what he or she needs at exactly the moment the worker needs it (just in time), is given as a prime example of well-conceived organization (see Image 25). No matter how far mechanization will develop, human skills and knowledge will always be necessary to build and operate the machines. Although the demand for unskilled workers will decline, the demand for skilled and specialized workers will increase. Of course, the worker should receive a fair share of the advantages gained by a more efficient use of means of production. This is the message of the film.

Image 24: *Fear of Enslavement*
Source: *Der Mensch und die Maschine film still.*

Image 25: *"Just in Time" Production*
Source: *Der Mensch und die Maschine film still.*

The film is an attempt to answer an old question, "Does technological development reduce or even destroy employment in the long run?" According to Neil Postman, technology is ideology in itself,[79] and according to Ulrich van Suntum, the question was posed by David Ricardo as far back as 1821, and he arrived at the same conclusion: technological development will—at least temporarily—lay off workers. However, as van Suntum notes, many academics in the field of economic science argue that new technologies create new jobs at the same rate as they destroy the old.[80] Every sectoral or technical change merely demands—as the film states—that the workforce adjust its skills just as government makes regulative and political adjustments.[81] The answer to the social question in industrialized societies has been the creation of the social welfare state.[82] In a similar way, Karl Marx asked whether technological development has relieved any human being of his or her everyday travails and concluded that this is by no means the purpose of capitalist machinery;[83] Jeremy Rifkin even posited the factory without humans. Here technology should already have made the human being disappear or at least create a human-machine hybrid.[84]

Anyone who is familiar with Fritz Lang's 1927 science fiction classic *Metropolis* will hardly discover anything new in either *Der Mensch und die Maschine* or Rifkin's factory without humans. The silent film is set in a city of the future, megacity Metropolis. Atop everything are the rulers of this highly industrialized city, with the workers at the very bottom. In between, a class of technocrats assures the frictionless operation of the machinery while the sons of the ruling class enjoy the pleasures of the eternal gardens. In a rare encounter, they are introduced as brothers to an unbelieving group of workers' children. To meet the growing dissatisfaction among the workers, the conceiver and effective ruler of the city has the hybrid human machine built, an artificial being resembling the charismatic Maria (see Images 26 and 27), who the workers hold in high esteem. Maria is, however, unaware of the deep grudge the human machine's constructor holds against her and the latter's plans to use the human machine to instigate a workers' revolt in his revenge scheme aimed at the destruction of Metropolis. Having successfully manipulated the workers to destroy the city's machinery, the human machine calls for ultimate destruction: the world going to hell. In the heat of battle, the workers, as well as the rulers and keepers of the machinery, realize they have been misled. The conclusion: the heart has to be the mediator between head and hands.[85]

Image 26: *Machine Resembling the Charismatic Maria*
Source: *The image was taken by Christoph Höllriegl during the public performance of Metropolis at an event of the Austrian petition Sozialstaat Österreich, held at the Stephansplatz in Vienna on 3 April 2002.*

Image 27: *The Human Machine Maria Is Built*
Source: *The image was taken by Christoph Höllriegl during the public performance of Metropolis at an event of the Austrian petition Sozialstaat Österreich, held at the Stephansplatz in Vienna on 3 April 2002.*

Multicultural, but Stereotyped

Georg Tressler in his 1954 film *Wie die Jungen sungen ....* (see trailer 5 on DVD), intentionally or not utilizes the idea of childhood as, according to Neil Postman, containing a vision of the future in that children are living messages delivered to the future; however, these messages cannot be experienced by the adults at present. This premise is a complete contradiction of the 1950 film *Let's Be Childish.*[86] In comparison to cinema in the 1950s, today's television communicates, according to Postman, neither a sense of the future nor a sense of the past. Thus everything shown on television nowadays is experienced as taking place at the exact moment of its viewing, hence speech is needed, Postman says, to establish reference to its evolution.[87] Furthermore, Postman describes education as a continuation of politics through gentle means.[88]

The films that were shown in the course of *Diagonale—Festival des österreichischen Films* in Graz (Styria) in 2000 encouraged younger Austrian critics, according Uli Jung, to attempt new interpretations in the very same year, especially in regard to the current political situation of Austria forty-six years after the film's completion.[89] These events once again clarified that understanding, analysis, and interpretation of older films can be accomplished only in reference to time.[90]

The beginning of *Wie die Jungen sungen ...* humorously deals with lingual differences. Being asked a question in French by a student (subtitles with German translation), a bus driver points out he only speaks German. The student says that the bus driver wouldn't speak German but "*wienerisch*," a local Viennese dialect.

A vendor of fruit (portrayed by the very popular Austrian actor and entertainer Heinz Conrads) then offers "*prima Maschanska*," an expression for a variety of apples, incomprehensible to anyone unfamiliar with the term. Subsequently, an Austrian girl, a Hungarian boy, an American boy, an African boy, and a Swedish girl are the film's main characters as pupils at the *Lycée Francais de Vienne*. Communication is, at first, established with gestures and facial expressions, especially during meals. Gradually, the Austrian girl and the African boy start befriending each other (see Image 28) with the other pupils following suit; all are finally able to communicate with each other in German (!) in the film, not in French as would be the case in real life at the *Lycée Francais de Vienne*. Furthermore, national characteristics and stereotypes are dramatized, exemplified by a German boy being mistaken for American due to the boy's plaid shirt (see Image 29) and by a dark-haired girl in a dirndl, who is Australian, *not* Austrian. A map of Europe is then shown with the pupils' countries tagged (see Image 30); with the narrator remarking that, unfortunately, not all countries are participating, the camera pans to the Soviet Union, which is—maybe in a slight exaggeration—further accentuated by being a darker color than Western Europe (see Image 31).

Image 28: *African Boy and Austrian Girl Become Friends*
Source: *Wie die Jungen sungen ... film still.*

Image 29: *National Stereotypes Are Dramatized*
Source: *Wie die Jungen sungen ... film still.*

Image 30: *Map of Western Europe*
Source: *Wie die Jungen sungen .. . film still.*

Image 31: *Camera Pans to the Soviet Union*
Source: *Wie die Jungen sungen ... film still.*

In contrast to the critique offered in the year 2000, the film can only be understood not as aiming at a forced understanding among Western European countries in the French language, but at international understanding of nations as a principle; the presentation of the African boy has to be seen as reference to the—at that time still stumbling—Civil Rights Movement in the United States. This reference to the U.S. Civil Rights Movement, emphasized by Albert Hemsing, who worked for the Marshall Plan Film Division, resulted in Tressler's shortening scenes that included the boy.[91] The subtle reference to the Cold War is based on an internationally shared understanding throughout Europe and serves as a contribution towards peace rather than as an enhancement of ideological differences—a point of view quite in opposition to other Marshall Plan films.[92] The disintegration of national characteristics depicted here in a clichéd manner through the highly exaggerated styles of fashion confuses the original message of the film and might revive the stereotyped ideas about culture promoted by National Socialism.

White Stallions and the Debate Regarding *Porgy*

According to McKenzie, the literature on the Marshall Plan and its films is already extensive, and there are many conceptions of Americanization; he uses the term "Americanization" to refer to the social, political, economic, and cultural changes achieved through modernity and promoted by the United States. Nevertheless, for McKenzie the different conceptions of Americanization complicate the use of the term today.[93] Europeans established American culture long before the Marshall Plan; with the Marshall Plan, American culture became global, extending at least to Western Europe. It is not the purpose of this essay with the benefit of hindsight to raise again the discussion about the terms "Americanization" or "culture" because there is no consensus about the definitions; certainly, one may quarrel endlessly about the terms, and today there are more than two hundred different conceptions of the term "culture."[94] But it is clear that American culture was in the past and is at present more than competition between U.S. companies and brands. For example, today the Austrian energy drink producer Red Bull, after actively expanding its business to North and South America as well as Australia starting 1997, is a serious competitor to the dominant U.S. Coca-Cola company.[95] The German discount store chain Aldi is establishing itself in the United States and putting the market leader Wal-Mart under pressure.[96]

Cultural exchange has occurred between the United States and Austria in both directions and still occurs today (see trailer 6 on DVD). The film *Weisse Hengste aus Wien* (produced after 1950) starts with a voiceover spoken by Austrian *Kammerschauspieler* (a term of honor for accomplished actors) Josef Meinrad. For once, Austrians can witness how they are viewed in the United States and realize the great amount of gratitude they owe to their Spanish Riding School.[97] The film shows the Lipizzaner horses parading for U.S. General George C. Patton in St. Martin, Upper Austria, on 7 May 1945 (see Image 32). Additionally, Patton provided the School's horses with the protection of the U.S. Army in the form of a military escort for the return of the mares and foals that were located in Czechoslovakia to Vienna, thus conserving a piece of eighteenth-century Vienna. The horses are presented as living monuments and Vienna as a shining center of European culture exemplified in the waltz and baroque art. The horses used in the Spanish Riding School in Vienna are Lipizzaner stallions. Usually of a dark-brown color when born, they start changing to white at the age of about four years. Education of the horses is achieved by benevolence rather than violence; every horse has to develop an enthusiasm for the exercises and has to acquire and refine courage, safety and cooperation, natural balance, and grace. Its performance and achievements are, in the end, a perfection of nature.

Image 32: *Lipizzaner Parading for U.S. General George C. Patton*
Source: *Weisse Hengste aus Wien film still.*

New triumph awaited the Lipizzaner horses in the new world, after being invited to the United States in 1950. Crossing the ocean for the first time, they showed their artistry at the annual Horse Show at Madison Square Garden in New York. For a critical audience used to excellence, the unique display of Austrian horsemanship was a most impressive and successful event. The applause was reserved for not only the fabulous horses—the last of a breed that once carried Julius Caesar into battle—but also the men who dedicated their lives to preserving the remnant of a classical art form at the Spanish Riding School of Vienna.[98]

In another case, the Vienna state opera (situated in the house of the Vienna *Volksoper* at the period due to the extensive damage of the State Opera building) saw the first European guest performance of the U.S. ensemble in Vienna (see Image 33) touring the musical *Porgy and Bess* (originally an opera written by George Gershwin in collaboration with DuBose Heyward and Ira Gershwin) on 9 September 1952. The film (distributed by USIS Vienna, sound: music, black and white, 30 min.) is dedicated to the American artists bringing *Porgy and Bess* to Austria, an American folk opera telling the story of beggar Porgy strolling Catfish Row in Charleston, South Carolina, with his goat-cart at the turn of the century, and of his love for easygoing Bess. It tells of his disappointment upon her leaving him and his loyalty driving him to search for her.

Image 33: *Dancers in Blackface*
Source: *Porgy and Bess film still.*

The film shows the artists rehearsing at Vienna's *Raimundtheater*, promenading through Vienna in company of the goat, participating in the city's everyday life, and admiring its sights. It shows clips of the glamorous state opera premiere at the Vienna *Volksoper*, of a successful charity concert at the *Mozartsaal* of the Vienna *Konzerthaus* and finally an evening at a *Heuriger* (as the traditional wine taverns of Vienna are called), where waltz and jazz tunes unite into one harmony. Thus the guests will never forget—beyond the gratitude to the Austrian audience—the city of Vienna, its people, and its music. The film's profits were entirely dedicated to the Austrian charity *Künstler helfen Künstlern* (Artists for Artists).

According to an interview by John Ardoin, William Warfield, one of foremost interpreters of the role of Porgy, who in 1952 sang the part, said, "When I sang *Porgy* in Vienna, only the principals were black. The chorus and the dancers were all made up to look black."[99] As Ardoin argues, the world was still not ready to accept *Porgy* because "many blacks' acceptance in their struggle for equal rights during the 1950s and 1960s were offended by the portrayal of their race represented in *Porgy*."[100] According to James Standifer, the opera was performed in Copenhagen in Danish on 23 March 1943 with an all-white cast. When the opera was a great success, the National Socialist occupiers ended the show because they did not like an American work of any kind to be performed.[101]

The two films, together with *Wie die Jungen sungen ...* and *Mozart's Reise durch Amerika* (see next section), seem to defy using particular films to explain cultural exchanges or cultural hegemony. Rather, additional films produced or distributed in the course of the Marshall Plan film program or by the USIS have to be consulted to draw relevant and significant conclusions, keeping in mind that Hollywood-produced films definitely had more influence on cultural development in Europe.

Back to Austrian Roots

The film *Mozart's Reise durch Amerika* of 1956, which was not distributed by USIS Vienna, came out just one year after the treaty of Austria and tries to get to the bottom of increased productivity. It again exemplifies the exchange of cultures in ways similar to the films discussed in the previous section.[102]

Starting with the words "legends are like clouds," which disappear and reappear, this legend is as old as the world and states that every human being gets a whistle from God that he is able to play. Although Mozart was born a long time ago, even today marionettes play tunes from his opera *Zauberflöte*. Mozart is seen as a marionette that is going to the United States together with his professor and will have many experiences there (see Image 34). At first, the United States seems to Mozart to be too large because he lives in a small and old Austrian town, Salzburg, where everything is manageable and where everything is not measured in seconds and human beings still have time but are not dominated by time. Mozart asks for to slow down in protest to the new production methods in the United States that are presented in many Marshall Plan films, and Mozart hopes to rest between two parked cars (see Image 35).

Image 34: *Marionette in LIFE Magazine*
Source: *Mozart's Reise durch Amerika film still.*

Image 35: *Looking for a Place to Rest in Manhattan*
Source: *Mozart's Reise durch Amerika film still.*

In an idealized U.S. wilderness landscape, Mozart comes into contact with a little African-American boy. Both are frightened at the beginning, but at the end they become friends through Mozart's music (see Image 36). Later, Mozart watches two drifters shown in the characteristic cowboy-style of Westerns produced in Hollywood, who attempt to rob a girl. Again, it is the sound of Mozart's music played by a whistle that fascinates the listeners, here, the two drifters (see Image 37). Thanks to the music, the girl has the chance to escape. The whistle makes it possible for the two drifters and the girl to attend a concert and listen to Mozart's music (see Images 38 and 39). The conclusion of the film is that Mozart and the marionettes were initially scared of the United States, but after their visit they don't want leave. The question is poetically posed, "Was it just a dream in which the little African-American boy, the two drifters, and the girl meet Mozart? Do they learn something that they did not know before, and are they dreaming about playing a flute themselves?" Legends are like clouds that float in and out of compositions and have no end.

Image 36: *Becoming Friends through Mozart's Music*
Source: *Mozart's Reise durch Amerika film still.*

Image 37: *Drifters Try to Rob a Girl*
Source: *Mozart's Reise durch Amerika film still.*

Image 38: *Drifters at Mozart's Concert*
Source: *Mozart's Reise durch Amerika film still.*

Image 39: *Making Eye Contact with the Drifters*
Source: *Mozart's Reise durch Amerika film still.*

The same is true for the Marshall Plan: the help still continues in one way or another long after its official end and will never end. The Americans who fought and were based in Europe also learned something of the Europeans. They took back to their homeland, something like Mozart's music, a new interest in leisure and restfulness as a counterpart to the scientific management in the world of employment and relaxation (see the section "Scientific Management —Even in Sports").

The Game of the Economy

In the 1950 film *Spiel der Wirtschaft* (see film on DVD), several children sit on a beach and discuss coal. A boy and girl sitting high on a dune (see Image 40) comment to a black haired boy playing with a piece of black coal that the coal is dirty.[103] The black haired boy (see image 41) says that the coal is worth more than gold. Between questions and answers, the film shows the different industries and workstations where the parents of the children are working as coal miners, farmers, woodworkers, fishers, technicians, car makers, and textile workers. They all produce products that are needed by the others. Coal is necessary for the steel industry as well as for heating houses and flats; wood is needed to block up drives in coal mines and to build roof trusses; food products are needed by everybody. The film shows wires, transformers, and generators, as well as electrical household and medical appliances made by Siemens in Berlin, Germany; production of trucks in Württemberg, Germany; and flocks of sheep in Germany. German wool is not sufficient to supply the quantity that the German weaving mills need; additional wool has to be imported from Africa, India, and Australia, but there are too few German machines to process and too little coal to pay for the imported wool. All these conditions point to the need for U.S. help in the framework of the Marshall Plan. For example, worn-out machines in the mining industry are replaced and new tractors are purchased for agriculture and farming to increase productivity, resulting in more and cheaper products. The Marshall Plan will end in 1952; then Germany itself must be able to pay for imports by exporting its products. In that manner, one country helps the others in Western Europe to recover their economies as fast as possible.

Image 40: *Boy and Girl Sitting on a Sand Dune*
Source: *Spiel der Wirtschaft film still.*

Image 41: *Boy Sits Down on the Dune*
Source: *Spiel der Wirtschaft film still.*

At the end of the film, all the children are sitting on the beach (see Image 42), and one boy shows the others a brochure with the title *Wir bauen auf!* (see Image 43). The children decide to enlighten their parents at home about the outcome of their debate, which is the functionality (game) of the economy and the solidarity between the different industries and their workers and between societies in which the labor is divided.

Image 42: *Children Are Sitting Together*
Source: *Spiel der Wirtschaft film still.*

Image 43: *Brochure Wir bauen auf!*
Source: *Spiel der Wirtschaft film still.*

The film was used in 2005 for comparing respectively contrary elements to the explanation of the development of solidarity between parents and their children based on my model of *Systeme transitiver Solidarität*, developed on the basis of the qualitative research method on human development and, especially, on the documentary method of interpretation of pictures and films, narration, and today's commercials and within group discussions, in accordance with the ideas of Ralf Bohnsack.[104] The approach can be explained, on the one hand, with hypothetical behavior and, on the other, with real solidarity between human beings within systems and subsystems as well as from systems to subsystems. The primary purpose is to research not only possible logical patterns and respective attitudes of the structure of differentiated solidarity behavior, but also the process of transformation prompted by emotions and feelings and the process itself (see Image 44).[105]

Image 44: *Systems of Transitive Solidarity*
Source: *Author's own figure.*

Today, the cohesion of generations and systems and the respective subsystems in a knowledge-based society or the society of options can be explained better by the dynamic functional model of conscious and unconscious solidarity than by social solidarity according to Émile Durkheim—even if the model creates a theoretical heterogenic society of options in which the concrete form of real solidarity behavior is blocked out.[106]

Analysis of a commercial for the Vienna Insurance Group (*Wiener Städtische Versicherung AG*) that aired in 2005 reveals the message that parents, when they retire or get sick in their old age, cannot count on their children's help. For that reason, parents should decide to look for a private pension fund in addition to the Austrian public pension system.[107] According to Milton Friedman, such insurance satisfies only the need for safety. Nevertheless, it is evident today that the need for additional insurance has grown and the cohesion between parents and their children has been greatly weakened.[108] The commercial attempts to introduce a regression to former characteristics of self-organized microstructures apart from social welfare states or well developed social systems close to the principle of solidarity. At the same time, the commercial suggests changes in the behavior of human beings and in the relationships between them. According to Konrad Paul Liessmann, the consciousness of human beings changes much the same way the economy dynamically changes.[109]

To put it simply, hypothetically the attributes between the cohesion of parents and their children are (A) the parents' care of their children to satisfy their primary needs, (B) the parents' care of their children to satisfy their secondary needs, and (C) the children's care of their parents in old age. These attributes refer to the past when children were raised in an atmosphere of conscious solidarity by human beings or societies and this was passed on to the next generation and then became unconscious solidarity in the sense of human beings behavior (see Image 45).[110]

Image 45: *Conclusions of Commercials and Films*
Source: *Author's own figure.*

The Vienna Insurance Group's commercial suggests to parents that the attributes of the children have changed and are different today (D instead of C). If the commercial influences the parents' emotions and if the commercial's message fits with the personal feelings of the parents, the consequence of that unconscious solidarity is transformed to conscious solidarity and the attributes are adjusted: A is continuous, B is replaced by E (additional private pension funds), and D is the converse of C (children do not take care of their parents in old age which is acceptable). What follows is that the adjusted and changed attitudes become unconscious solidarity in the future. That hypothetical change cannot only be compared with today's commercials, but also with historical commercials or films to explain the social change in human behavior in previous decades.[111]

The results of the analysis of the commercial were compared with the scenes of the dialogue among the children of *Spiel der Wirtschaft* based on the film's argument that children played an important role in enlightening their parents about the role of, for example, solidarity after World War II. There had to be a strong solidarity between children and their parents, as well. Former soldiers who had become disabled during World War II, wives who were widowed, and orphans needed someone to take care of them—both their basic needs (food, housing, heating, and so forth) and their financial ones. The first way to meet these needs was to give them help within the framework of the Marshall Plan. The second was through the Austrian social security system, especially through publicly funded pensions in which the active workers pay for the pensions of already retired workers. Pension funds on the capital market were not standard; and as late as 2000, the European Commission asked Austria to open the publicly funded pension system because this released billions of dollars into the free capital market.[112]

A result of the analysis in *Spiel der Wirtschaft* is a focus on the debate of the children emphasizing the correlation of different products and that through the division of labor, solidarity is needed for the cohesion between not only children and their parents, but also between the different industries and countries. According to Kurt Imhof, the capitalistic economy creates partitions of industries and status groups including, for example, dress regulations, which are masterfully avoided in the film by setting the debate on the beach with the children wearing swimwear.[113]

The message of the film in a wider sense is, according to Horst Pöttker, that the most important cohesion in complex societies depends on the conscious mercy of different industries, professions, and countries and that everybody is attuned to each other.[114] However, a common emergency—rebuilding Europe after World War II, for example—promotes solidarity behavior, but it is not true solidarity because after the end of the common emergency the solidarity disappears as fast as it came. In the case of a common emergency, an increased amount of insight shows that a collective egoism emerges to bring fulfillment of individual egoism.[115]

To put it simply, attribute A means solidarity of the children in relation to the professions of their parents, B stands for the partitions of industries and status groups, and C is the solidarity between the workers in the industries within which they working. The message of the film as described above shows its impact on the audience in that A is continuous, C is replaced by D (all professions and countries are dependant on the other), and instead of B, E is launched (children enlighten their parents about D). As a result, the former attribute B is weakened. Said another way, children play a role in teaching their parents about B and D, where solidarity across borders, professions, and generations is more important. The most important message of the film is, however, the dependence of every human being on the different branch-specific products; therefore, the solidarity between workers of all industries and agriculture is necessary for a fast rebuilding (reconstruction) of the European economy.

The conclusion of a comparison of the film and commercial is that the results of the analysis of the film cannot address the hypotheses created by the analysis of the Vienna Insurance Group's commercial. However, the analysis of the film encourages further research seeking to compare respective contrary elements to cover the hypotheses of both texts. Even though the analyses of films are very time consuming, the results of the research must not be understood as the real reflection of an absolute objectivity, but as a possible model of conscious cognitive perception of human beings on whom films unleash the impact of their placed messages.[116]

Recent results of the analysis of *Spiel der Wirtschaft* seem to be important for today's European Union because, according to Danute Hübner, many people argue that the solidarity between the member states has been weakened through enlargement and the inclusion of Central and Eastern European countries.[117] However, without a minimum dimension of resilient solidarity, according to Zulehner et al., human lives of fairness, lived in liberty and peace, are unimaginable both in the European Union and the globalized world.[118]

Conclusion

The first goal of this essay was to serve as a complement to the trailers and films on the DVD and to further scientific papers; the second was to stress some symbols used or created by filmmakers, whether intentionally or not, in Marshall Plan films, which have been identified as a result of analyses of selected scenes. At the essay's beginning, films were discussed which explain the Marshall Plan and its efforts exclusively and its contribution in general to Western European economies. Afterwards, the focus turned to Austrian films; formerly missing films were mentioned which were produced for and in Austria. Following a debate about scientific management and new production methods, the cultural exchange was put in the foreground, but not in such a way as to raise again the whole tired discussion of "Americanization" and "culture." Rather, two films were compared illustrating the value of looking at different films in order to examine the era of their creation by analyzing historic films or posters that are contemporary with them on the basis of the qualitative research method on human development, through the documentary method of interpretation of pictures and films and narrations, and within group discussions. The approach can be explained, on the one hand, with hypothetical solidarity behavior which was necessary for rebuilding Europe, and on other hand with real solidarity between human beings within systems and subsystems as well as from systems to subsystems because the world has changed during the last six decades, just as the behavior of human beings has changed individually, too. Hence, the cohesion of generations, systems, and the respective subsystems in a knowledge-based society or the society of options can be better explained by a dynamic functional model of conscious and unconscious solidarity than by social solidarity according to Émile Durkheim—even if the explanation acts to create a theoretical heterogenic society of options in which the concrete form of true solidarity behavior is hastily blocked out.

This essay's primary message to scholars is to research not only possible logical patterns and respective attitudes of the structure of differentiated solidarity behavior at present and in the past, but also the process of transformation prompted by emotions and feelings and the process itself. Therefore, this essay doesn't make a claim to completeness because a comprehensive analysis of all relevant films and facts and advanced methods and theories (some of which were not even mentioned and which should be taken in consideration) is impossible. The way the films are described in this essay and were shown at the conference intentionally stressed that analyses of each and every Marshall Plan film makes less sense in the long run, despite the fact that the results of such analyses are necessary for further research. However, the approach today should turn to putting the results of all completed analyses—and there already many—logically together, drawing new conclusions and spurring further research. The whole question of the influence of Marshall Plan films, particularly the effects on human behavior, is a continuing debate, but investigators are encouraged to try various approaches. Actually, this essay points out uncommon approaches and new questions intended to inspire further research. Though respectful of the results of earlier research, this essay encourages further inquiry, especially in the sciences, which will enable historians, sociologists, economists, and others to measure the impact of the Marshall Plan films on social changes over the last decades in more detail and to examine the current argument that a "new" Marshall Plan could very quickly boost economies on each side of the Atlantic Ocean that are today weakened by the global financial crisis.

Notes

1 Linda R. Christenson, "Marshall Plan Filmography," 2002, George C. Marshall Motion Pictures, http://www.marshallfilms.org/mpf.asp, accessed 26 December 2006.

2 Compare with, for example, Rainer Rother, "Selling Democracy," in *Selling Democracy: The Films of the Marshall Plan,* booklet to the DVD edition (Bonn: German Federal Agency for Civic Education in co-operation with the Federal Film Archive, the German Historical Museum, and the Berlin International Film Festival (Germany: bhp artworx postproduction, KMS Kafitz Medienservice, 2006), 7–25, 10. Compare also with Sandra Schulberg, "What Was the Marshall Plan?", in *Selling Democracy: Films of the Marshall Plan*, 3rd ed., vol. 3 (November 2008), http://www.sellingdemocracy.org/whatwas.html, accessed 5 January 2009.

3 Compare to Uli Jung, "Der nachträgliche Vorläufer, Georg Tresslers Filme in der Primär- und Sekundärrezeption," in *Halbstark, Georg Tressler: Zwischen Auftrag und Autor*, ed. Robert Buchschwenter and Lukas Maurer (Vienna: Filmarchiv Austria, 2003), 179–85.

4 Compare to Paul M. Zulehner et al., *Solidarität, Option für die Modernisierungsverlierer*, 2nd. ed. (Innsbruck: Tyrolia, 1997), 51 et seq. See also Helene Karmasin and Matthias Karmasin, *Cultural Theory: Ein neuer Ansatz für Kommunikation, Marketing und Management* (Vienna: Linde, 1996), 21 et seq.

5 Anton Zapotocky, "Ideele und organisatorische Aufgaben der einheitlichen Gewerkschaften," *Gewerkschaftlicher Nachrichten-Dienst* 1, ed. Fritz Klenner (15 Nov. 1945): 2–5, here 2.

6 This refers to the activity report 1945–1947 and the annual activity reports 1948–1964 of the Austrian Trade Union Federation (Vienna: Verlag des ÖGB, 1948–1965); source: archive of the ÖGB.

7 Quantity and titles refer to fragments of contracts about agreements and terms of grants between the United States Information Service, Vienna and are also from the Former Special Project and the ÖGB of 16 September 1963, in the possession of the author.

8 Linda R. Christenson, "Missing Films," Marshall Plan Filmography, February 2002, George C. Marshall Motion Pictures, http://www.marshallfilms.org/mpfdetail.asp#missingfilms, accessed 26 December 2006.

9 Ramón Reichert, "Useful Images: The Industry Films of the Austrian Productivity Center 1951–1959," in *Work—Organisation—Struggle: The Seventh National Labour History Conference, Held at the Australian National University, Canberra, 19–21 April 2001*, ed. Rosemary Webb et al. (Canberra: Australian Society for the Study of Labour History, Canberra Region Branch, 2001), 209–15.

10 Christoph Höllriegl, "Systeme transitiver Solidarität," unpublished working paper, Vienna University of Economics and Business Administration, 2005.

11 Compare to Oliver Rathkolb, *Washington ruft Wien: US-Großmacht und Österreich, 1953–1963* (Vienna: Böhlau Verlag, 1997), 201 et seq.

12 This refers to the annual activity reports 1948–1964 of the Austrian Trade Union Federation (Vienna: Verlag des ÖGB, 1949–1965), source archive of the ÖGB.

13 Heidemarie Schumacher, *Fernsehen fernsehen: Modelle der Medien- und Fernsehtheorie* (Cologne: DuMont, 2000), 102. Compare to Ralf Vollbrecht, *Einführung in die Medienpädagogik* (Weinheim: Beltz Verlag, 2001), 36 et seq.

14 Martin Baltes and Rainer Höltschl, *Absolute Marshall McLuhan, Mit einem biografischen Essay von Philip Marchand*, ed. Klaus Theweleit and Rainer Höltschl (Freiburg: orange-press, 2002), 93. Compare to Neil Postman, *Die Verweigerung der Hörigkeit, Lauter Einsprüche*, trans. by Reinhard Kaiser (Frankfurt/Main: S. Fischer, 1988), 31. Georg Tressler, Personal interviews by Frank Mehring and by Linda R. and Eric Christenson in Berlin, Germany, on 15 February 2004, copies in the possession of the author.

15 *International Labour Film Catalogue: A World Survey of Films for Labour Audiences* (Brussels: n.p., 1956).

16 *Einsteigen bitte!*, 1952, sound: German, black and white, 61 min., film by *Österreichischer Gewerkschaftsbund*, director: Georg Tressler, actors: Helmuth Qualtinger, Fred Weis, Evi Servaes, Kurt Eilers, Marcell Kuzniarsky, Fritz Heller, Hans Hais, and Gisa Wurm, narrator: Hannes Schiel, script: Beatrice and Georg Tressler, Dr. Heinz Scheiderbauer, ÖGB, camera: Sepp Riff, production management: Walter Hoessig, music: Prof. Friedrich Witeschnik, cutting: Georg Tressler, sound: Georg

Niebisch, copies: Listo-Film-Wien. Compare to Ralph Eue, "Schmeichelkunst für die gute Sache," in *Halbstark*, ed. Buchschwenter and Maurer, 31–47, 40 et seq.

17 Internationales Institut für Arbeiterfilme, *Internationaler Arbeiterfilm-Katalog*, 1st. ed. (Brussels: n.p., 1956), 75–76.

18 Tressler, Personal interviews.

19 Hans-Jürgen Schröder, "Marshall Plan Propaganda in Austria and Western Germany," in *The Marshall Plan in Austria*, ed. ed. Günter Bischof et al., vol. 8, Contemporary Austrian Studies (New Brunswick, NJ: Transaction, 2000), 212–46, here 217.

20 *Die Macht der Bilder—Leni Riefenstahl, Preisgekrönte Dokumentation einer umstrittenen Regisseurin*, 31 July 2002, 197 min., VZ-Handelsgesellschaft, script: Ray Müller et al.

21 Schumacher, *Fernsehen fernsehen*, 73 et seq.

22 Compare to Tressler, Personal interviews; Schulberg, "What Was the Marshall Plan?"

23 Compare to Rathkolb, *Washington ruft Wien*, 141; Kurt Löffler and Hans Fußenegger, "The Acitivities of the ERP Fund from 1962 to 1998," trans. by Mel Greenwald, in *The Marshall Plan in Austria*, ed. Bischof et al., 15- 97.

24 See Mauthausen Komitee Österreich, *Unser(?)Amerika, Austro-amerikanische Blitzlichter im Zuge der US-Wahl 2008* (Vienna: ÖGB-Verlag, 2008).

25 Bettina Fritzsche, "Mediennutzung im Kontext kultureller Praktiken als Herausforderung an die qualitative Forschung," in *Die dokumentarische Methode und ihre Forschungspraxis, Grundlagen qualitativer Sozialforschung*, ed. Ralf Bohnsack et al. (Opladen: Leske + Budrich Verlag, 2001), 27–42, here 40.

26 Jürgen Kriz, *Chaos, Angst und Ordnung: Wie wir unsere Lebenswelt gestalten*, 2nd. ed., vol. 42, Transparent (Göttingen: Vandenhoeck & Ruprecht, 1998), 24.

27 Compare to Schröder, "Marshall Plan Propaganda in Austria and Western Germany," 221 et seq.; Eue, "Schmeichelkunst für die gute Sache," 31–47.

28 There are many Marshall Plan films and others available online at the website Deutsches Historisches Museum, http://www.dhm.de/filmarchiv/marshall-plan-filme, accessed 19 January 2009.

29 Compare to Victoria de Grazia, *Irresistible Empire: America's Advance through Twentieth-Century Europe* (Cambridge, MA: Belknap, 2006), 554.

30 Werner Faulstich, *Medienwissenschaft* (Paderborn: Wilhelm Fink Verlag, 2004), 121. Compare to Bettina Mathes, "Reproduktion," in *Gender@Wissen, Ein Handbuch der Gender Theorien*, 1st. ed., ed. Cristina von Braun and Inge Stephan (Cologne: Böhlau Verlag, 2005), 81–99, here 82.

31 Vilém Flusser, *Medienkultur*, ed. Stefan Bollmann, 3rd. ed. (Frankfurt/Main: Fischer Taschenbuch Verlag, 2002), 90 et seq.

32 Schumacher, *Fernsehen fernsehen*, 168. Compare to Burkhard Schäffer, *Generationen—Medien—Bildung: Medienpraxiskulturen im Generationenvergleich* (Opladen: Leske + Budrich Verlag, 2003), 117; Philipp Mayring, *Qualitative Inhaltsanalyse, Grundlagen und Techniken*, 8th ed. (Weinheim: Beltz Verlag, 2003), 11 et seq.; Jürgen Bortz and Nicola Döring, *Forschungsmethoden und Evaluation für Human- und Sozialwissenschaftler*, 3rd. ed. (Berlin: Springer Verlag, 2002), 332 et seq.

33 See Postman, *Die Verweigerung der Hörigkeit*, 35.

34 Frank Hartmann, *Mediologie, Ansätze einer Medientheorie der Kulturwissenschaften* (Vienna: Facultas Verlags- und Buchhandels AG, 2003), 16.

35 Gillian Dyer, *Advertising as Communication*, 1982 (London: Routledge, 1995), 73. Compare to Michael Kunczik, *Public Relations, Konzepte und Theorien*, 4th. ed. (Cologne: Böhlau Verlag, 2002), 101 et seq.

36 Johann August Schülein, *Die Logik der Psychoanalyse, Eine erkenntnistheoretische Studie* (Giessen: Psychosozial-Verlag, 1999), 165.

37 Dyer, *Advertising as Communication*, 75.

38 Ibid.

39 Compare to Georg Tressler, Personal interviews; Müller, *Die Macht der Bilder—Leni Riefenstahl.*

40 Werner Faulstich, *Filmgeschichte* (Paderborn: Wilhelm Fink Verlag, 2005), 119 et seq.

41 Compare to Gerhard Schult and Axel Buchholz, *Fernseh-Journalismus: Ein Handbuch für Ausbildung und Praxis*, 5th. ed. (Düsseldorf: List, 1997).

42 Judith Mair and Silke Becker, *Fake for Real: Über die private und politische Taktik des So-tun-als-ob* (Frankfurt/Main: Campus Verlag, 2005), 240.

43 Thomas Slunecko, *Von der Konstruktion zur dynamischen Konstitution, Beobachtungen auf der eigenen Spur* (Vienna: Facultas WUV Universitätsverlag, 2002), 81. In addition, compare to Peter L. Berger and Thomas Luckmann, *Die gesellschaftliche Konstruktion der Wirklichkeit, Eine Theorie der Wissenssoziologie*, trans. Monika Plessner, 17th ed. (Frankfurt/Main: Fischer Taschenbuch Verlag, 2000), 74f.; Konrad Paul Liessmann, *Philosophie des verbotenen Wissens, Friedrich Nietzsche und die schwarzen Seiten des Denkens* (Vienna: Zsolnay, 2000), 105f.; Michael Hauskeller, *Versuch über die Grundlagen der Moral* (Munich: C.H. Beck, 2001), 78.

44 Compare to Fritzsche, "Mediennutzung im Kontext kultureller Praktiken als Herausforderung an die qualitative Forschung"; Rother, "Selling Democracy."

45 Compare to Hartmann, *Mediologie*; Kurt Imhof et al., ed., *Mediengesellschaft, Strukturen, Merkmale, Entwicklungsdynamiken*, 1st. ed. (Wiesbaden: VS Verlag für Sozialwissenschaften/GWV Fachverlage, 2004); Sarah-Jayne Blakemore and Uta Frith, *Wie wir lernen, Was die Hirnforschung darüber weiß*, trans. Hella Beister (Munich: Deutsche Verlags-Anstalt, 2006).

46 See Fritzsche, "Mediennutzung im Kontext kultureller Praktiken als Herausforderung an die qualitative Forschung," 36 et seq.

47 *Dennis Hopper, Spiel (oder stirb)*, German dubbing by alias film Sprachtransfer, English version, *Dennis Hopper - Create (Or Die)*, Germany/USA, 2003, director: Ariane Riecker and Henning Lohner.

48 Baltes and Höltschl, *Absolute Marshall McLuhan*, 86.

49 Eue, "Schmeichelkunst für die gute Sache," 34.

50 Tressler, Personal interviews.

51 Compare to Oliver Rathkolb, Interview, in *Die Erfindung Europas, (un)erwartete Folgen des Marshallplans*, documentary, Vienna, 2008, director: Reichhold Christian.

52 Daniel Wildmann, *Begehrte Körper, Kostruktion und Inszenierung des "arischen" Männerkörpers im "Dritten Reich"* (Würzburg: Königshausen & Neumann, 1998), 18.

53 Mair and Becker, *Fake for Real*, 202.

54 Eue, "Schmeichelkunst für die gute Sache," 34.

55 Sandra Schulberg, "The Relevance of Marshall Plan Films Today," in *Selling Democracy: Films of the Marshall Plan* vol. 3/3rd. ed. (November 2008), http://www.sellingdemocracy.org/relevance.html, accessed 5 January 2009.

56 Brian Angus McKenzie, *Remaking France: Americanization, Public Diplomacy, and the Marshall Plan*, vol. 2, Explorations in Culture and International History Series (New York: Berghahn Books, 2008), 3.

57 Compare to Schulberg, "The Relevance of Marshall Plan Films Today."

58 De Grazia, *Irresistible Empire*, 348; compare to McKenzie, *Remaking France*, 3.

59 Baltes and Höltschl, *Absolute Marshall McLuhan*, 82.

60 Karl Marx and Friedrich Engels, *Das Kapital, Kritik der politischen Ökonomie*, vol. 1, 6th. ed. (Hamburg: Verlag von Otto Meissner, 1909), 535. Compare to Georg Vobruba, *Jenseits der sozialen Fragen, Modernisierung und Transformation von Gesellschaftssytemen*, 1st. ed. (Frankfurt/Main: Suhrkamp, 1991), 51f.

61 Milton Friedman and Rose Friedman, *Die Tyrannei des Status Quo (Munich: Wirtschaftsverlag Langen-Müller/Herbig, 1985)*, 203 et seq.

62 Noam Chomsky, *Neue Weltordnungen, Vom Kolonialismus zum Big MAC*, trans. Michael Haupt (Leipzig: Europa Verlag, 2004), 66.

63 Compare to Zulehner et al., *Solidarität*, 89; Franz M. Wuketits, "Ethologie," in *Psychologie, Eine Einführung, Grundlagen, Methoden, Perspektiven*, 2nd. ed., ed. Jürgen Straub et al. (Munich: Dtv, 1998), 201–22; Èmile Durkheim, *Über soziale Arbeitsteilung, Studie über die Organisation höherer Gesellschaften* (Frankfurt/Main: Suhrkamp Taschenbuch, 1992), 101 et seq.

64 *Die Ersten Europäer*, 1950, sound: German, black and white, 24 min., script: Dr. Wolfgang Frank, camera: Herbert Körösi, Wolfgang Krimmel, and Maurice Brunet, sound: Alfred Fuchs and Fritz Michelis, narrators: Dr. Georg Eilert, Heinz Ladiges, and Manfred Steffen, Real-Film-Studio Hamburg and Atelier Stordel Hamburg, music: Erich Bender, director: Gert Stegemann, distributed by USIS Vienna.

65 Sandra Schulberg, "Poster Archive—Marshall Plan Posters," in *Selling Democracy: Films of the Marshall Plan* vol. 3/3rd. ed. (November 2008), http://www.sellingdemocracy.org/posters.html, accessed 5 January 2009.

66 Verlag des Österreichischen Gewerkschaftsbundes, ed., *Wandkalender 2009, Kalenderblatt für Jänner 2009*, 1st. ed. Auflage (Vienna: ÖGB-Verlag, 2008).

67 *Die entscheidenden Jahre, Bericht über den wirtschaftlichen Wiederaufbau Europas*, 1951, sound: German, black and white, 21 min., script: Stuart Legg, edited by Lewis Linzee, music: Jack Beaver, produced by Gaumont British Picture Corporation Ltd, London, U.K., distributed by USIS Vienna.

68 *Strom der Berge* (*The Invisible Link*), 1950, sound: German, black and white, 15 min., director: Victor Vicas, camera: Helmuth Ashley, music: Claude Arrieu, Victor Vicas Film, distributed by USIS Vienna, available online at website Deutsches Historisches Museum, see note 28.

69 Compare to *Die Macht der Bilder—Leni Riefenstahl.*

70 *Reichtum der Wälder* (English working title, *Forestry in Austria*), 1950, sound: German, black and white, 14 min., director: Albert Quendler, camera: Elio Carniel, music: Hans Hagen, cutting: Renate Knitschke, narrator: Günther Schifter; production and script: S. H. Bloom, Schönbrunn Film Produktion, (probably not distributed by USIS Vienna). Compare to Christenson, "Missing Films."

71 Compare to Reinhold Wagnleitner, *Coca-Colonization and the Cold War: The Cultural Mission of the United States in Austria after the Second World War*, trans. by Diana M. Wolf, (Chapel Hill, NC: U of North Carolina P, 1994), 277; Eue, "Schmeichelkunst für die gute Sache," 37.

72 Thomas Karny, "Furnierter Wiederaufbau, 'Soziales Wohnen' ermöglichte Billigmöblierung nach dem Krieg," October 2005, Thomas Karny, http://www.karny.at/beitraege/zeit_beitrag_03.html, accessed 9 January 2009; "*Modernes Wohnen*," in *Die Reportage des Monats* (monthly review), *ERSCHAUT-ERLEBT, Es berichtete das Reporter-Team des Österreichischen Gewerkschaftsbundes*, episode 16, after April 1960, sound: German, black and white, 18 min., source: *ÖGB-Medienarchiv*.

73 McKenzie, *Remaking France*, 148.

74 Ibid., 13.

75 Neil Postman, *Wir amüsieren uns zu Tode, Urteilsbildung im Zeitalter der Unterhaltungsindustrie*, trans. Reinhard Kaiser, 12th ed. (Frankfurt/Main: Fischer Taschenbuch Verlag, 1999), 166.

76 Rifkin, Jeremy, *Das Ende der Arbeit und ihre Zukunft, Neue Konzepte für das 21. Jahrhundert*, (Frankfurt/Main: Campus Verlag, 2004), 147.

77 Richard Sennett, *Der flexible Mensch, Die Kultur des neuen Kapitalismus*, trans. Martin Richter, 7th ed. (Berlin: btb Verlag, 2000), 95. Compare to Max Weber, *Gesammelte Aufsätze zur Soziologie und Sozialpolitik*, 2nd ed. (Stuttgart: UTB, 1988), 61 et seq.

78 *Der Mensch und die Maschine*, 1952 (German dubbing), sound: German, black and white, 20 min., director: William Novik, German arrangement: Peter Elsholtz, Olaf Meitzner, and Freimut Kalden, *Hergestellt von der Société Française de Chronophotographie in Zusammenarbeit mit dem Film Centre-London*, French release *L'age des machines* probably of 1950.

79 Postman, *Wir amüsieren uns zu Tode*, 191.

80 Ulrich van Suntum, *Die unsichtbare Hand, Ökonomisches Denken gestern und heute* (Berlin: Springer Verlag, 1999), 289 et seq.

81 Compare to the Independent Commission on Population and Quality of Live, *Visionen für eine bessere Lebensqualität* (Basel: Birkhäuser Verlag, 1998).

82 Compare to Gertaude Mikl-Horke, *Industrie- und Arbeitssoziologie*, 5th. ed. (Oldenbourg: Oldenbourg Wissenschaftsverlag, 2000); Dirk Baecker, *Archäologie der Arbeit* (Berlin: Kulturverlag Kadmos, 2002).

83 Marx and Engels, *Das Kapital*, 593 et seq.

84 Rifkin, *Das Ende der Arbeit und ihre Zukunft*, 165. Compare to Ralph Sichler, "Neue Arbeitswelt und Autonomie, Aspekte menschlicher Selbstbestimmung im flexibilisierten Kapitalismus," in *Der flexibilisierte Mensch, Subjektivität und Solidarität im Wandel*, ed. Andrea Birbaumer and Gerald Steinhardt (Heidelberg: Asanger, 2003), 139–49, here 139; Manfred Fassler, "Handlung ohne Ende? Simulation, elektronisch verteiltes Wissen und programmierte Hybride," in *Hybridkultur, Medien, Netze, Künste*, ed. Irmela Schneider and Christian W. Thomsen (Cologne: Wienand Verlag, 1997), 300–23; van Suntum, *Die unsichtbare Hand*, 289.

85 Information about the film refers to a brochure which was distributed during the public performance of *Metropolis* at an event of the Austrian petition *Sozialstaat Österreich*, held at the Stephansplatz in Vienna on 3 April 2002, Transit Film, Thomas Sessler Verlag and Friedrich-Wilhelm-Murnau-Stiftung, the film is available on DVD by Transit Film GmbH, Munich, Germany, 2003.

86 Compare to *Selling Democracy, The Films of the Marshall Plan,* DVD edition, publishers: German Federal Agency for Civic Education in co-operation with the Federal Film Archive, the German Historical Museum and the Berlin International Film Festival (Germany: bhp artworx postproduction, KMS Kafitz Medienservice, 2006).

87 Postman, *Die Verweigerung der Hörigkeit*, 184.

88 Ibid., 33.

89 Jung, "Der nachträgliche Vorläufer," 217.

90 Lukas Maurer, "Kleine Wirklichkeiten, Über den Filmemacher Georg Tressler," in *Halbstark*, ed. Buchschwenter and Maurer, 11–30, here 13.

91 Tressler, Personal interviews; compare to *Frank Mehring, "Propaganda für die Demokratie?* Deutschland und das 'Neue Europa' in den Filmen des Marshall Plans," Deutsches Historisches Museum Berlin, http://www.dhm.de/filmarchiv/film-im-kontext/propaganda, accessed 13 January 2009.

92 Compare to *Mehring, "Propaganda für die Demokratie?"*

93 McKenzie, *Remaking France*, 4.

94 Compare to Karmasin and Karmasin, *Cultural Theory*, 21 et seq.

95 David Noonan, "Red Bull's Good Buzz," 14 May 2001, Newsweek Online, http://www.newsweek.com/id/79400, accessed 10 January 2009. Compare to Mair and Becker, *Fake for Real*, 200; Schumacher, *Fernsehen fernsehen*, 102.

96 Wolfgang Kerler, "Aldi expandiert in den USA," 17 December 2008, WirtschaftsWoche, http://www.wiwo.de/unternehmer-maerkte/aldi-expandiert-in-den-usa-381220, accessed 13 January 2009.

97 *Weisse Hengste aus Wien* (*White Stallions of Vienna*), after 1950, sound: German, black and white, 12 min., production: Peter Elgar, direction and camera: Douglas J. Baker, script: Robert Hertzberg, narrator: Raymond Johnson, cutting: Julius Edelmann, German narrator: Josef Meinrad, distributed by USIS Vienna.

98 Compare to Alice Higgins, "The Horse Show, In Prestige Event of a Record Year, the Ancient and Aristocratic Sport of Horsemanship Comes to Its Climax in New York's Madison Square Garden," 31 October 1955, Sports Illustrated Vault, http://vault.sportsillustrated.cnn.com/vault/article/magazine/MAG1130393/index.htm, accessed 10 January 2009.

99 John Ardoin, "An Interview with William Warfield," PBS Online, http://www.pbs.org/wnet/gperf/porgy/html/artists.html, accessed 16 January 2009.

100 John Ardoin, "The Great 'Porgy' Debate," PBS Online, http://www.pbs.org/wnet/gperf/porgy/html/work.html, accessed 17 January 2009.

101 James Standifer, "The Complicated Life of Porgy and Bess," *Humanities* 18.6 (November/December 1997), National Endowment for the Humanities, http://www.neh.gov/news/humanities/1997-11/porgy.html, accessed 7 January 2009)

102 *Mozart's Reise durch Amerika*, 1950, sound: German, black and white, 15 min., *Arbeitsgemeinschaft Atlantis-Film Wien, hergestellt mit Förderung des Bundesministeriums für Unterricht unter Mitwirkung des Marionettentheaters Salzburg Prof. Hermann Aicher, mit Tonaufnahmen aus der Oper* "Die Zauberflöte" *gespielt von dem Wiener Philharmonischen Orchester*, director: Rudolf Zehetgruber, camera: Wolfgang Frass, musical compilation: Bruno Uher; production management: Kurt Miksch.

103 *Spiel der Wirtschaft*, 1950, sound German, black and white, 14 min., script: Max Dickhout, music: Hans Ebert, camera: Kurt Grigoleit, C.D.K.; cutting: Werner Franz; production: Dr. August Rittig Dokumentarfilmproduktion, München-Geiselgasteig, Germany.

104 Ralf Bohnsack, "Die dokumentarische Methode in der Bild- und Fotointerpretation," in *Die dokumentarische Methode und ihre Forschungspraxis: Grundlagen qualitativer Sozialforschung*, ed. Ralf Bohnsacket al. (Opladen: Leske + Budrich Verlag, 2001), 67–89.

105 Compare to Gerhard Roth, *Fühlen, Denken, Handeln: Wie das Gehirn unser Verhalten steuert* (Frankfurt/Main: Suhrkamp Taschenbuch, 2003), 285 et seq.; Antonio R. Damasio, *Descartes' Irrtum, Fühlen, Denken und das menschliche Gehirn* (Munich: List, 1995), 50 et seq.; Bernhard Miebach, *Soziologische Handlungstheorie: Eine Einführung* (Opladen: Vs Verlag, 1991), 31 et seq.

106 Durkheim, *Über soziale Arbeitsteilung*, 283. See, too, Gertraude *Mikl-Horke, Soziologie, Historischer Kontext und soziologische Theorie-Entwürfe*, 5th. ed. (Oldenbourg: Oldenbourg Verlag, 2001), 70; Siegfried Lamnek, *Neue Theorien abweichenden Verhaltens*, 2nd. ed. (Munich: UTB, 1997), 8; Uwe Schimank, "Entwöhnung von der Lebensgeschichte, Muster biographischer Selbstreflexion in

'Ulysses' und 'Manhatten Transfer'," in *Biographische Sozialisation*, ed. Erika M. Hoerning (Stuttgart: Lucius & Lucius, 2000), 33–49, esp. 47; Johann August Schülein, "Über Veränderungen in den Konstitutions- und Reproduktionsbedingungen von Subjektivität," in *Der flexibilisierte Mensch*, ed. Birbaumer and Steinhardt, 38–57, esp. 57.

107 "Pony," commercial, 2005, Wiener Städtische Versicherung AG (Vienna Insurance Group), http://www.staedtische.co.at/privat/werbung/tv-spots/pony, accessed 9 June 2005.

108 Milton Friedman, *Kapitalismus und Freiheit* (Frankfurt/Main: Eichborn, 2002), 194 et seq.

109 Liessmann, *Philosophie des verbotenen Wissens*, 105f.

110 Compare to Kurt Lüscher and Ludwig Liegle, *Generationenbeziehungen in Familie und Gesellschaft* (Konstanz: UTB, 2003), 292.

111 Compare to Helena Flam, *Soziologie der Emotionen, Eine Einführung* (Konstanz: UTB, 2002), 17.

112 European Commission, *Beitrag der Kommission zur Sondertagung des Europäischen Rates, Eine Agenda für die wirtschaftliche und soziale Erneuerung Europas*, Lisbon, 23–24 March 2000: DOC/00/07, 28 February 2000, 11 et seq.

113 Kurt Imhof, *Die Diskontinuität der Moderne, Zur Theorie des sozialen Wandels* (Frankfurt/Main: Campus Verlag, 2006), 125 et seq.

114 Horst Pöttker, "Maßstab: Balance von Eigensinn und Fremdverstehen, Zur Analyse der Kritik an der Mediatisierung," in *Mediengesellschaft*, ed. Imhof et al., 347–62, esp. 352.

115 Compare to Rainer Zoll, *Was ist Solidarität heute?* (Frankfurt/Main: Suhrkamp Taschenbuch, 2000), 15; Zulehner et al., *Solidarität*, 51; Leopold Rosenmayr, "Frühe Erfahrungen—späte Einsichten," in *Soziologie in interdisziplinären Netzwerken*, ed. Anton Amann and Gerhard Majce (Vienna: Böhlau, 2005), 31–76.

116 Compare to Paul Watzlawick, *Wie wirklich ist die Wirklichkeit? Wahn, Täuschung, Verstehen* (Munich: Piper, 1976); Niklas Luhmann, *Soziale Systeme, Grundriß einer allgemeinen Theorie* (Frankfurt/Main: Suhrkamp, 1984); Erving Goffman, *Wir alle spielen Theater, Die Selbstdarstellung im Alltag*, trans. Peter Weber-Schäfer, 7th. ed. (Munich: Piper, 1998); Ernst von Glasersfeld, "Einführung in den radikalen Konstruktivismus," in *Die erfundene Wirklichkeit, Wie wissen wir, was wir zu wissen glauben? Beiträge zum Konstruktivismus*, ed. Paul Watzlawick, 11th. ed. (Munich: Piper, 1999), 6–38.

117 Danuta Hübner, "Expansion is Solidarity," in project-syndicate.org, March 2005, http://www.project-syndicate.org/commentary/hubner1, accessed 4 May 2005. Compare to Gerd-Christian Weniger, *Projekt Menschwerdung, Streifzüge durch die Entwicklungsgeschichte des Menschen* (Heidelberg: Spektrum Verlag, 2001), 106.

118 Compare to Zulehner et al., *Solidarität*, 17 et seq; cf. Philipp Mayring, *Qualitative Inhaltsanalyse, Grundlagen und Techniken*, 8th. ed. (Weinheim: Beltz Verlag, 2003), 11 et seq.; Jürgen Bortz and Nicola Döring, *Forschungsmethoden und Evaluation für Human- und Sozialwissenschaftler*, 3rd. ed. (Berlin: Springer Verlag, 2002), 332 et seq.

Herbert Friedlmeier, Hans Petschar, and Michaela Pfundner

U.S. Photography and the Marshall Plan

Introduction

In 1977, the U.S. Embassy in Vienna handed over a unique historical documentation to the Picture Archive of the Austrian National Library: the photographic archives of the United States Information Services (USIS) in Austria. Today the collection includes about 10,000 negatives in envelopes, sorted by numbers, and a thematic documentation on subject cards with English and German texts and handwritten notes.

In May 1945, shortly after American troops had entered Austria, the Information Service Branch (ISB) of the United States Information Services was established at Salzburg, headed by General A.J. MacChrystal. The Pictorial Section of the ISB produced and archived from 1945 to 1955 photographs for other ISB units and provided national and international agencies with pictures and documentation of all aspects of the political, economic, and cultural life in Austria.[1] While initially under military control, the Pictorial Section of the ISB was eventually transformed into a civil institution, reporting on Austria under the supervision of American press officers. A large archive was built up, which was used by Austrian and international media.

Young Austrian photographers and darkroom technicians were trained by Americans and worked from 1945 to 1955 for the USIS. It was their duty to report the progress in the Austrian economic recovery and to support the economic, social, and political measures of the United States in Austria with photographic stories. Early stories, with captions written on subject cards and on paper copies, which were produced in advance in order to allow for efficient service, prove that USIS staff members were professionally trained and observed by ISB officers. Very early photo stories informed the Austrians about Nazi crimes, followed up quickly by economic, cultural, and educational topics to support the information policy of the United States in Austria.

From 1948 onward, the same year the Marshall Plan was introduced to Europe in general and Austria in particular, Yoichi R. Okamoto led the Vienna bureau of the USIS Pictorial Section as chief of reporters and ISB staff photographers until 1964. While Okamoto can be called a chronicler of cultural life in Vienna as far as those years are concerned, he had a very sophisticated approach to industrial photography as well. In 1964, Okomato became the official photographer for President Lyndon B. Johnson in Washington, D.C., but his craftsmanship lived on in the works of his pupils.

An outstanding and highly imaginative photographer himself, Okamoto also became a teacher of young Austrian photographers in his crew like Gottfried "Jeff" Rainer, Herbert Bayer, Fritz Mayr, and Heinrich Mayr. A fine example of the

"Okamoto school" is a picture taken at the aluminum factory at Ranshofen (see Image 1). This site was part of the reconstruction plans of the ECA, which was documented in three series of photographs in August 1949, September 1952, and May 1953. Even the tubes and the chimneys and reflections in metal rolls have their charm, but a cross section view of notched aluminum roofing is a masterpiece.

Image 1: *Aluminum Factory at Ranshofen, September 1952*
Source: *US 22.495B.*

In August 1950, Yoichi Okamoto gave a report on the mission, program, and activities of the Pictorial Section for the past year.[2] According to the report of the Pictorial Officer, the mission of the Pictorial Section was "to furnish complete pictorial service to the various sections of ISB, the ECA [Economic Cooperation Administration] Mission in Austria, and other related agencies of USFA [United States Forces in Austria]."[3] The Pictorial Section serviced the following agencies:

- *Wiener Kurier* (with 18 percent of the man-hour work),
- Rot-Weiss-Rot radio station (with 16 percent of the man-hour work),
- other sections of the ISB including the Features, Publication, and Theatre and Music Sections along with the Amerikanischer Nachrichtendienst, (with 9 percent of the man-hour work),
- Information Centers of the ISB (with 21 percent of the man-hour work),
- ECA (with 27 percent of the man-hour work), and
- miscellaneous agencies, such as the International Refugee Organization, UNICEF, CARE, USFA Public Information Division, the Austrian Youth Association, Austro-American Society, and so forth.

In August 1950, the Pictorial Section of the ISB was located at the Waldheim Eberle building in Vienna, Seidengasse 3–11, with offices in Linz and Salzburg. The Pictorial Sections consisted of a main office with four staff members (the chief, Pictorial Officer Yoichi R. Okamoto; Pictorial Officer Franz Kraus, an Austrian; the Pictorial Researcher, an Austrian; and a Secretary, also an Austrian) and several other departments (Editorial Department; Staff Photographers Department; Library; Laboratories; Photocopy Department; Cutting, Pasting, and Packaging Department; Salzburg and Linz offices) with twenty-one Austrian staff members. The Mission of Economic Cooperation (MEC) and its successor organization, established on 1 January 1952, the Mutual Security Agency (MSA), oversaw the USIS Pictorial Section (see Image 2).

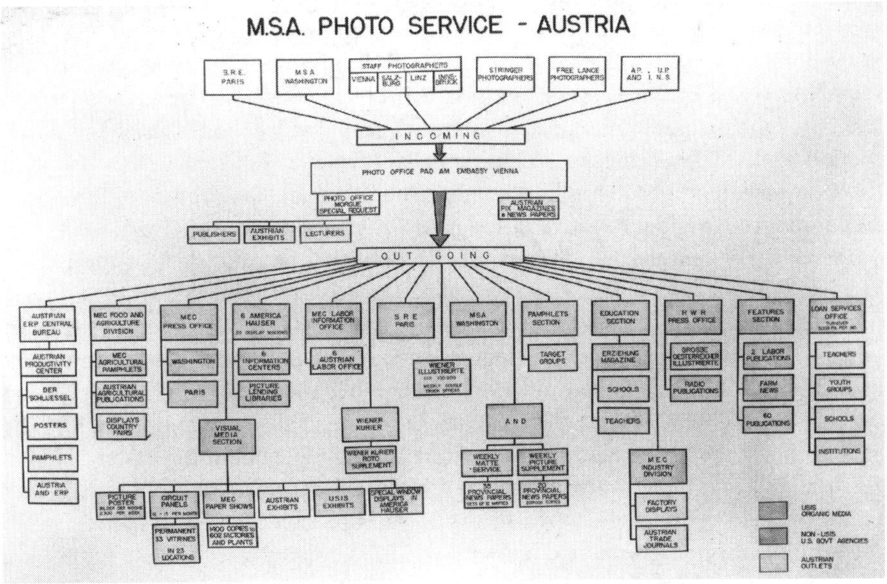

Image 2: *Organizational Model of USIS Pictorial Section Photographic Services*
Source: *US 22883 B.*

From 1950 to 1955, the Pictorial Section supported the activities of the ISB sections and, above all, the ECA Mission with an extensive documenting of Marshall Plan projects in the Austrian provinces. In the first features, the editors had already been supporting U.S. policy, even before the media campaign around the Marshall Plan began. Along with the Marshall Plan, the influence of the Pictorial Section was extended to all three Western occupation zones. Comprehensive photographic documentations of the ECA from Carinthia, Salzburg, Tyrol, and Vorarlberg were produced all over Austria and arrived in the archives. River regulations, drainage works, road building, and actions supporting Austrian tourism were documented as well as—in some cases from a humorous angle—educational programs of the United States, local festivals, and everyday life in the Austrians provinces.

Communicating Democracy in Postwar Austria

In 1952, seven years after the end of World War II, the average Austrian man and woman could be optimistic if not confident that economic recovery was finally under way. It was possible by now to find employment guaranteeing basic pay, which in turn made it possible to meet the bare necessities of life again. But Austrians could remember a recent past around the year 1947, when fears of starvation and freezing to death in unheated rooms were ubiquitous. How could anyone convince people that these times had been overcome for good?

American leaders (and probably Austrian authorities as well) accepted as a matter of fact that the various programs provided by the Marshall Plan pulled Austria and many other countries in Western Europe out of the dire straits of postwar misery. USIS photography and the messages these images communicated to the Austrian people give insight into U.S. information policy in postwar Austria.

What nowadays is referred to as the USIS photographic archives, held by the Picture Archives of the Austrian National Library since 1977, is an incomplete collection of the original photographic material provided by the Pictorial Section of the ISB and USIS subdivisions.[4] Nearly half of the material matches the focus of this essay, for those photographs document the Marshall Plan programs. Envelopes containing the original negatives are signed with the abbreviation ECA.

From 1948 onward, the *Wiener Kurier* published a good deal of the photographs. In June 1945 a weekly paper called the *Österreichischer Kurier* had been founded, but ended after a few editions. This weekly was precursor to the daily paper *Wiener Kurier* founded in August 1945, which became the most important of all media run by the USIS until 1955 when publication ceased. With circulation varying between 150,000 and 300,000 copies during the years of publication, the *Wiener Kurier* had the biggest market share for daily papers in the eastern part of Austria. Although it was also distributed in Soviet-controlled Lower Austria and provinces held by the British, two-thirds of the copies were sold in Vienna.

When ISB photographers documented ERP-funded projects from Vorarlberg to Salzburg and Carinthia, from Tyrol to Upper Austria and Burgenland, it took more media to deliver that information to local people. For example, when the ERP provided new medical equipment for clinics and infirmaries, the bi-weekly bulletin *Medizinische Nachrichten* was an appropriate place to report the story. A series of pictures showing the development of drainage systems could illustrate the *Landwirtschaftliche Nachrichten* (*Agricultural News*), while the monthly *Erziehung* was right place to print a story about classrooms newly equipped with teaching aids bought with ERP funds. When ECA/MEC pictures were published in the *Wiener Kurier* and other media, captions were generally much shorter than the original "master caption" found on the corresponding subject card in the USIS archives.

But not everybody was reading newspapers; as a matter of fact, a lot of Austrian people could not afford to buy a daily paper, a weekly, and a special magazine in the years of the late 1940s and early 1950s. This raises the issue of the effectiveness of the photographic images in shaping Austrians' perceptions. On Thursday, 21 September 1950, Clyde Nelson King, chief of the ECA Mission to Austria, together with the Austrian Social Minister Karl Maisel, was present at the Waldheim-Eberle printing shop in Vienna's 7th district (where the *Wiener Kurier* was also produced) because the second edition of the booklet *This is Freedom* came out of the printing press (see Image 3). Its subject was a report on the life of American workers, declaring them to be free from misery, pressure, and fear. The booklet was given away to private company libraries and public libraries for free. But did the message reach the European colleagues of the American worker in a time of Cold War propaganda battles?

Image 3: *Clyde Nelson King and Karl Maisel with Copies of This is Freedom, Vienna, 1950*
Source: *US 20.965 B.*

The answer may be found in certain facts. The interest of the Austrian public in this book, translated and published a year previously, was so great that a second printing was necessary. Only a month after the booklet was published, in October 1950, a series of labor strikes shook Austria, organized mostly by communist organizations, but initially undertaken by a lot of Social Democrats and independent workers, too, protesting the "4.Lohn-Preis-Abkommen" agreed upon by the Austrian government—a conflict extensively debated in Austrian contemporary historiography.

Exhibitions offered another good chance to present the successful outcomes of ERP projects. As part of the Vienna Spring Fair of 1950, Clyde N. King opened a special exhibition entitled *A Mirror for Recovery during the Past Two Years.* On

Saturday, 11 March, the day before the opening of the Vienna Spring Fair, the ECA Mission held a press conference for Austrian and U.S. reporter in the rooms of the Special ERP exhibition at the Messepalast. In his speech, Clyde N. King, chief of the ECA Mission to Austria, called the Vienna Spring Fair a "mirror for recovery during the past two years" (see Image 4). Another speaker at the meeting, which also was attended by Gen. Fry, USFA, was Minister Taucher, Ph.D., chief of the ERP's main office.

Image 4: *Clyde N. King addressing the Press Corps at Messepalast, Vienna, 11 March 1950*
Source: *US 20.678 B/C*

Image 5: *Surrounded by a Folk Group, the Chief of the ECA Mission Looks Like a Genuine Tyrolean, Kitzbühel, October 1950*
Source: *US 21.053.*

Resuming his duties as chief of the ECA Mission, King went on an ERP projects inspection tour throughout Austria from 11 to 16 October 1950. In Kitzbühel, he was awarded a Tyrolean hat (see Image 5) and entertained by performers (see Image 6). His successor as chief, Clarence Meyer, though greeted respectfully by American and Austrian officials upon his arrival at Vienna's Westbahnhof (see Image 7) was shown a "slap-in-the-face dance" upon his inspection tour in 1952. Going along with the people and joining in their fun were the rules of the game for building a positive image of American ERP representatives in Austria.

Image 6: *At the Praxmayr Coffee House in Kitzbühel, Woodcutters Present a Funny "Night Cap Dance" to ECA Chief King, October 1950*
Source: *US 21.057.*

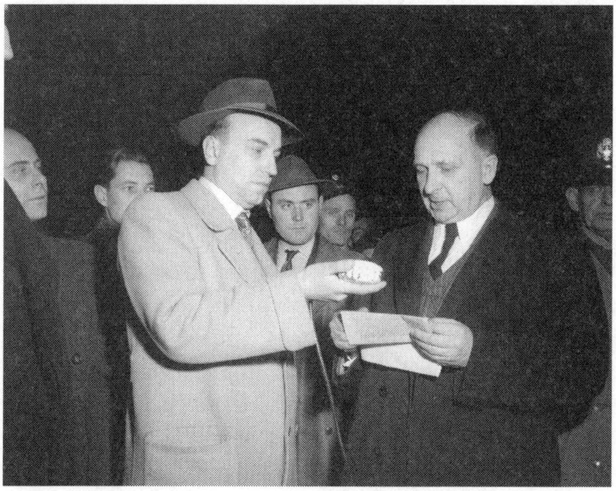

Image 7: *New Chief of the ECA Mission Meyer Arrives in Vienna, 16 February 1951*
Source: *US 21.267.*

Meyer was also the speaker at the opening ceremony of the finished Limberg embankment dam, part of the giant hydroelectric power station project, known as Kaprun. Construction work there was frequently shown in Austrian newsreels, and it attracted international attention, too. While a cameraman of the British Film Company Wessex from London was shooting in Technicolor, he was photographed by a USIS reporter, and a naturalistic painter from Linz was engaged to create the official painting of the Limberg embankment (see Image 8).

Image 8: *The Kaprun Power Plant (Limberg Dam) at the end of September 1950. A painter from Linz was ordered to make an oil painting and a carbon drawing of the Limberg Dam.*
Source: *Kaprun ECA 175/20.*

Without reading a paper, watching a film, or visiting an exhibition, everyone passing by a site would have noticed signboards. Hundreds of them bearing the ERP logo were spread all over the country: no building site, no drainage system under construction, no road repair was left undecorated (see Image 9). Even vocational schools and test orchards had their ERP signboards.

Mobile exhibitions traveling around the country were used for informational and propaganda purposes. A tractor pulling a double trailer containing a photographic exhibition of ERP projects in its interior was sent around the country. In rural areas, test drivers were allowed on the tractor and sometimes even on displayed combine harvesters. In May 1950, the Chamber of Agriculture in Upper Austria had a truck financed by the ECA for information services. The vehicle was equipped with a microphone and two loudspeakers as well as a film projector (see Image 10). Its mission was to inform farm people about the activities of ECA and to give medical advice. When the photo was taken, only one truck was in service, but putting more such trucks in operation was planned.

The most ambitious project was "The Train of Europe," consisting of six exhibition wagons traveling through Austria and communicating on a very local level the message of the European "American dream": a free Europe based on democratic

Image 9: *Road Building under Construction between Innsbruck and the Zugspitze, January 1950*
Source: *US 20.642 B.*

Image 10: *Loudspeaker Truck for Rural Information Service, Vienna, 22 May 1950*
Source: *US 20.777 B/C.*

Image 11: *Train of Europe Comes to Austria, 8 July 1952*
Source: *MEC 483/3 (US 22.003 B).*

principles and led by the U.S. economy. Text accompanying the archived photo reads, "On Tuesday, July 8, 1952 the Train of Europe crossed the Austro-Italian border at 12.30 a.m. en route to Klagenfurt, where the train is to be prepared for its 40-days showing in Austria. Leaving Tarvisio, the train travels towards Arnoldstein" (see Image 11).

The most important distribution channels for the materials provided by the Pictorial Section were the ten U.S. centers, the Rot-Weiss-Rot radio station (with its magazines), the *Wiener Kurier Bildbeilage*, and, above all the Information Office of the ECA Mission in Austria.

The Pictorial Section was completely responsible for production of the *Wiener Kurier Bildbeilage*, including the provision and selection of the picture material, editing, the use of propaganda material, layout, and follow-through to the press run in conjunction with the business manager and the American editor-in-chief. One full page per week was dedicated to promoting and publicizing the ERP.

In the organizational model of the Pictorial Section, the ECA mission formed a separate unit, which included 27 percent of the total man-hour work of the Pictorial Section, plus the work of ten stringer photographers located throughout Austria, including the Russian zone. Over 1,800 pictures per month were taken in 1950 in order to fulfil the duty of the section, which was "to see that pictures to inform the Austrian public of what ECA is doing are placed as extensively as possible to every available outlet."[5]

In his report of 31 August 1950, Okamoto outlines the editorial policy of the *Wiener Kurier Bildbeilage*, which can be taken to articulate the Policy of the Pictorial Section and the ECA mission:

1. always tell the truth in pictures;
2. U.S. propaganda should be subtle, without losing reader interest;
3. all picture stories will present a fundamental idea rather than straight reportage (i.e. so that the reader is left with a mental impression of an *idea*. Therefore an *idea* in propaganda is more apt to leave a lasting impression;
4. new, modern, and even radical approaches and uses of photo technique to carry on the American tradition of journalistic progressiveness.[6]

In comprehensive form, Okamoto summarizes an impressive policy program which was fully realized in communicating the ERP to the Austrian people. In all picture stories covering major ERP projects, two basic ideas were presented: first that the ERP helped the individual Austrian and, second, that Austrian participation in the overall Marshall Plan was important and necessary.

Picture Stories

On 5 June 1947, U.S. Secretary of State George C. Marshall gave his speech at Harvard University describing the state of the economy in most European countries as disastrous with large parts of their population on the brink of starvation. In Marshall's opinion, the "enormous complexity" of the situation would make it extremely difficult "for the man in the street to reach a clear appraisement of the situation."[7] Being at such a great distance from the troubled European countries, the American people would find it virtually impossible to grasp the real significance of the situation "merely by reading, listening, or even seeing photographs and motion pictures."[8] Marshall identified the essential elements for the success of reconstruction in his speech: understanding the nature of the problem on the part of the American people and active participation of European nations in placing Europe on its own feet economically.

In December 1947, Henry Truman proposed to the Congress of the United States a program for United States Aid in European Recovery based on the suggestions of his Secretary of State. In January 1948, the ingenious military strategist in his statement before the Senate Committee on Foreign Relations in dramatic manner outlined the political impact of the European Recovery Program and explained the U.S. interests involved:

> So long as hunger, poverty, desperation and resulting chaos threaten the great concentrations of people in Western Europe—some 270 million—there will steadily develop social unease and political confusion on every side. Left to their own resources there will be, I believe, no escape from economic distress so intense, social discontents so violent, political confusion so widespread, and hopes of the future so shattered that the historic base of western civilization, of which we are by belief and inheritance an integral part, will take on a new form in the image of the tyranny that we fought to destroy in Germany. The vacuum which the war created in Western Europe will be filled by the forces of which wars are made. Our national security will be seriously threatened. We shall in effect live in an armed camp, regulated and controlled. But if we furnish effective aid to support the now visibly reviving hope of Europe, the prospect should speedily change. The foundation of political vitality is economic recovery. Durable peace requires the restoration of western European vitality.[9]

In the following months, the organizational structure for implementing the program was built up and resulted in the foundation of the Economic Cooperation Administration. It goes without saying that the development of the Marshall Plan had enormous consequences for U.S. information policy in Austria. The Pictorial Section of the USIS produced picture stories fully in line with the political mission. One of the first picture stories, *Hunger and Distress in Austria* (February 1948), gives more or less a visual explanation of George C. Marshall's speech and places the need for help in the spectator's mind through emotional pictures and captions. The story *The Austrian Woman and the ERP* explains in a humorous manner how, more than two years later, the ERP has changed everyday life and postwar restrictions came to an end for Austrian women. The picture story *Modern Logging in Carinthia* is one example of a successful ERP project in rural Austria, dedicated to the modernization of Austrian lumber industry. The pictorial report on *The Train of Europe* finally can be seen as one of the most effective public relations initiatives of the USIS, bringing George C. Marshall's ideas—"the establishment of enduring peace and the maintenance of true freedom for the individual"—directly to the people.

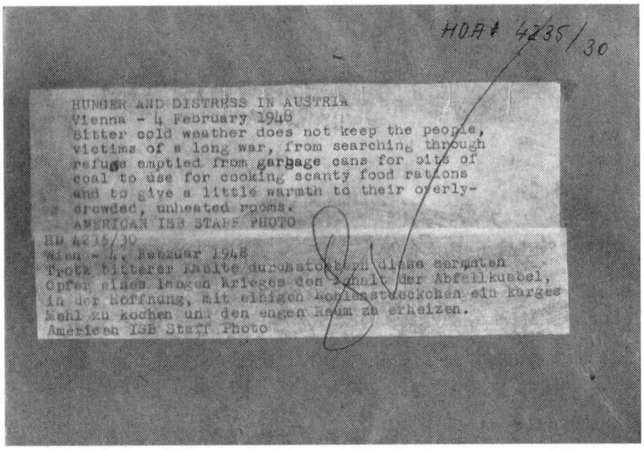

HOA 4235/30

HUNGER AND DISTRESS IN AUSTRIA
Vienna - 4 February 1948
Bitter cold weather does not keep the people, victims of a long war, from searching through refuge emptied from garbage cans for bits of coal to use for cooking scanty food rations and to give a little warmth to their overly-crowded, unheated rooms.
AMERICAN ISB STAFF PHOTO

HD 4235/30
Wien - 4. Februar 1948
Trotz bitterer Kälte durchstöbern diese armsten Opfer eines langen Krieges den [illegible] der Abfallkuebel, in der Hoffnung, mit einigen Kohlenstueckchen ein karges Mahl zu kochen und den engen Raum zu erheizen.
American ISB Staff Photo

US 4235/30
Bitter cold weather does not keep the people, victims of a long war, from searching through refuge emptied from garbage cans for bits of coal to use for cooking scanty food rations and to give a little warmth to their overly-crowded, unheated rooms.

US 4235/29
Day by day Vienna's city dumps are searched for bits of coal by the old and young alike. The small amount of coal carried home at the end of the day supplies fuel for cooking scanty rations, but is not enough to heat their cheerless lodgings.

US 4235/32a
Every bit of wood found in and around Vienna is utilized for heating and cooking, because of the lack of coal and other necessary fuel. Photo shows civilians returning from surrounding woods carrying what bits of wood they were able to gather.

US 4235/40
Exposed to the cold—hungry and destitute—this family had no place to live last winter. They worked hard all summer building this crude shanty against this winter's wind, snow and rain., unheated rooms.

US 4235/48
Home for displaced persons.

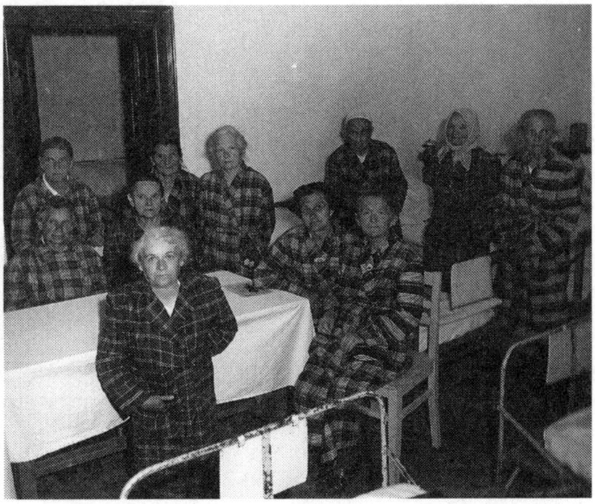

MEC 483/1 (US 22.001 B)

MEC 483/2 (US 22.002 B)

MEC 483/3 (US 22.003 B)

A Reproduction of The Train of Europe[11]

The Marshall Plan was linked with propaganda machinery for marketing the project which would help it to achieve all its aims. The massive deployment of public relations instruments was intended to guarantee favorable European opinions of the United States and to establish a positive image.
The promotion repertoire included brochures, quarterly summaries, official posters, poster and photo competitions, the "Train of Europe," and public films and lectures in the Amerika Häuser.

MEC 483/1–4 (Master caption)
TRAIN OF EUROPE COMES TO AUSTRIA
Vienna, July 8, 1952
On Tuesday, July 8, 1952 the Train of Europe crossed the Austro-Italian border at 12.30 a.m. en route to Klagenfurt, where the train is to be prepared for its 40-days showing in Austria.
The especially constructed six-car exhibition train dramatizing "Cooperation Among Free People" carries interior evidence of European problems and progress since the end of world war II.
Moving displays, special lighting, sound effects and unique press-button devices are features of the train, which will keep visitors interested from start to finish. The official opening of the train of Europe will take place in Klagenfurt on the 18th July 1952.

MEC 483/1 (US 22.001 B)
TRAIN OF EUROPE COMES TO AUSTRIA
The Train being checked through the Italian border, by Italian border police.

MEC 483/2 (US 22.002 B)
TRAIN OF EUROPE COMES TO AUSTRIA
The Train is checked through the Italian border and prepares to proceed to Austria.

MEC 483/3 (US 22.003 B)
TRAIN OF EUROPE COMES TO AUSTRIA
Leaving Tarvisio the Train travels towards Arnoldstein.

MEC 483/4 (US 22.004 B)
TRAIN OF EUROPE COMES TO AUSTRIA
The Train passes through Arnoldstein on its final trip into Austria.

MEC 483/4 (US 22.004 B)

MEC 483/5- (Mastercaption)
TRAIN OF EUROPE IN AUSTRIA
Vienna, July 18, 1952
The Train of Europe arrived in Klagenfurt on July 8, 1952 for refitting, redecoration and preparing its Austrian run, which opened in Klagenfurt's Hauptbahnhof on Friday, July 18, 1952.
This specially constructed five-car exhibition train dramatizing "Cooperation Among Free People," carries interior and exterior evidence of European progress since the end of World War II. The train, called the Train of Europe, and sponsored by the OEEC, represents the cooperative efforts of artists, technicians and workers from 14 countries and its crew consists of members of 9 different European nationalities.

MEC 483/5 (US 22.005)
TRAIN OF EUROPE IN AUSTRIA
Local Austrian workers were employed during the refitting and redecorating of the train in Klagenfurt.

MEC 483/6 (US 22. 006 B)
TRAIN OF EUROPE IN AUSTRIA
Local Austrian workers were employed during the refitting and redecorating of the train in Klagenfurt.

MEC 483/7 (US 22. 007 B)
TRAIN OF EUROPE IN AUSTRIA
Local Austrian workers were employed during the refitting and redecorating of the train in Klagenfurt.

MEC 483/5 (US 22. 005 B)

MEC 483/6 (US 22. 006 B)

MEC 483/7 (US 22. 007 B)

MEC 483/8 (US 22. 008 B)

MEC 483/9 (US 22. 09 B)

MEC 483/10 (US 22. 010 B)

MEC 483/8 (US 22. 008 B)
TRAIN OF EUROPE IN AUSTRIA
A member of the 9-man European crew, Mr. P. Porteneuve (French), Chief Technician, inspecting refitting work of the exterior lighting system.

MEC 483/9 (US 22. 009 B)
TRAIN OF EUROPE IN AUSTRIA
Train crew members inspecting refitting progress in Klagenfurt
L.t.r.: Mr. Acker, Deputy Chief, (Norvegian), Mr. Demer, Chief, (Dane), Mr. Roddam, Disbursing Officer, (British), Mr. Bortolotti, Railway Officer, (French), and Mr. Portneuve, Chief Technician, (French).

MEC 483/10 (US 22. 010 B)
TRAIN OF EUROPE IN AUSTRIA
Train crew members inspecting refitting progress in Klagenfurt
L.t.r.: Mr. Acker, Deputy Chief, (Norwegian), Mr. Demer, Chief, (Dane), Mr. Roddam, Disbursing Officer, (British), Mr. Bortolotti, Railway Officer, (French), and Mr. Portneuve, Chief Technician, (French).

MEC 483/11 (US 22. 011 B)
TRAIN OF EUROPE IN AUSTRIA
Refitting and redecoration is thoroughly discussed by members of the train's crew. L.t.r.: Mr. Acker, Deputy Chief, (Norwegian), Mr. Bortolotti, Railway Officer, (French), Mr. Roddam, Disbursing Officer, (British), Mr. Portneuve, Chief Technician, (French), Mr. Demer, Chief, (Dane).

MEC 483/16 (US 22.011 B)

MEC 483/16 (US 22.016 B)

MEC 483/16- (Mastercaption)
TRAIN OF EUROPE IN KLAGENFURT, AUSTRIA
Vienna, July 19, 1952
The Train of Europe opened its five exhibition cars to the Austrian public in ceremonies held at the Klagenfurt Hauptbahnhof at 10.30 a.m. on Friday, July 18, 1952. The blue and silver train, which shows how European integration and increasing productivity is bringing Europe's resources to full development, was welcomed by a group of Austrian and American officials and large crowds thronged the platform to visit the exhibition. After the Klagenfurt showings, ending July 21, the train moves on to Graz, Leoben, Innsbruck, Linz, Steyr, Wels, Vienna (during the autumn fair) and Salzburg.

MEC 483/16 (US 22.016 B)
TRAIN OF EUROPE IN KLAGENFURT, AUSTRIA
Hans Graf, Burgomaster [sic] of Klagenfurt speaking during the opening ceremony, held at the Klagenfurt's Hauptbahnhof on Friday, July 18, 1952.

A Reproduction of Modern Logging in Carinthia[12]

MEC 426 (Master caption)
February 1952

Until recently the transportation of lumber was limited to horsepower and the waterways. This again, limited the transportatin [sic] to certain favorable periods of time like snowfall, rains etc. That is the reason why many a tree which was cut never came to be used by people and rotted in the woods because of lack of transportation.

Considerable economic disadvantages were connected with lacking roads and loss of quality of the delivered lumber.

The most important condition for new wood transportation methods was the buildig [sic] of new roads. The new lumber transportation methods use tractors and trucks first. Other possibilities for the transportation of lumber from inaccessible areas include the cable crane, rendering possible the transport from even very remote areas and high peaks. During the last years, the so-called flying cable crane has proven to be very useful.

For transportation of lumber during the winter months, special sleds were constructed by Oberforstmeister Weiss and so-called "Strotzkoerbe" bei [sic] Revierinspektor Schnedl. With the help of these two devices, the transport of 20 cubic meters with an estimated weight of 14 tons is average.

A horsedrawn cart transports 1.5 cubic meters of lumber at a time. This means that fourteen horses would be necessary to move the same amount of lumber transported with one of the sleds at a time. The daily quantity of lumber a horse is able to move on a certain distance is about 3 to 3.5 cubic meters while the sled is able to move 80 cubic meters at the same time. A second plus is the cheaper transportation by motor vehicles. The transportation costs are cut to one fourth compared with the transportation by horsepower, and sometimes it is even lowered to one fifth of the original cost. Taking into consideration the expenses for road building and maintenance, there is still a cut of 48 percent compared with the former transportation costs.

Problems are different with cable cranes. Stable cable cranes, as they were built in the last years, are only proving economically profitable where a yearly quantity of at least 3,000 cubic meters of lumber has to be transported. However, portable cranes are much cheaper and proved to be of great economic value in the last time. This device is especially valuable in badly accessible areas even though the maintenance cost may be a little higher than that of the older device because it prevents loss of quality. The main advantage of the portable cable crane system is ensuring a high quality of lumber.

Thanks to the new wood transportation methods which also facilitate a quality increase of the delivered lumber, logging is possible throughout the whole year, while formerly it was limited to certain periods, mostly in winter. Only this way is it possible to meet the constantly increasing demands on the woodworking industry.

US 21.884-B (MEC 426/1)

US 21.885-B (MEC 426/10)

US 21.886-B (MEC 426/3)

Modern harvesting methods have also eliminated to a certain extent the danger in the life of the wood workers.

The social security and the living standard of Carinthia's almost 7,000 lumber workers is improving constantly. The owrkers [sic] are at present permanently employed; during ten months of the year they work on a contract basis, while the last two months they are receiving constant wages. Besides their wages they do also receive their share of the cut timber for fuel.

Through the building of roads, purchase of machinery and devices, erection of worker housing projects and workshops, everything of that was carried through by the help of ERP allocations, Carinthia's forestry economy was able to raise its lumber production to a yearly 1.2 million cubic meters, thus helping considerably the reconstruction of the various industries and Austrian economic life. Thanks to these improvements, Carinthia also ranks first in lumber exports, with an estimated third of Austria's whole lumber exports.

The systematic expansion of this very important branch of the industry will in the future be furthered by a special Carinthian Fair. It will be especially streamlined to a wood working industry's fair and will contain exhibitions of the most important branches of this industry like forestry, wood transportation, saw mill, furniture industry, paper industry, wood working machinery, and the lumber trade.

US 21.884-B (MEC 426/1)
MODERN LOGGING IN CARINTHIA
Diesel Caterpillar removes a 12 ton load of logs from the forests of Rubland near Paternion, Upper Carinthia.
MODERNE HOLZBRINGUNG IN KAERNTEN
Ein Diesel-Raupenschlepper befoerdert 12 to [sic] Holz aus dem Revier Rubland bei Paternion in Oberkaernten.

US 21.885-B (MEC 426/10)
MODERN LOGGING IN CARINTHIA
Load of logs being removed by means of a Caterpillar tractor, which formerly would require fourteen horses.
MODERNE HOLZBRINGUNG IN KAERNTEN
Die Fiat-Raupe ersetzt beim Holztransport 14 Pferde.

US 21.886-B (MEC 426/3)
MODERN LOGGING IN CARINTHIA
Heavy handling of logs is done by means of the modern Motormuli tractor.
MODERNE HOLZBRINGUNG IN KAERNTEN
Oesterreichischer Motormuli im Einsatz fuer Langholztransport.

US 21.887-B (MEC 426/11)

US 21.888-B (MEC 426/14)

US 21.889-B (MEC 426/15)

US 21.887-B (MEC 426/11)
MODERN LOGGING IN CARINTHIA
At Stockenboi-Graben near Paternion, Upper Carinthia, foresters measure felled trees to determine size and weight.
MODERNE HOLZBRINGUNG IN KAERNTEN
Die im Stockenboi-Graben bei Paternion, Oberkaernten, geschlaegerten Staemme werden zur Ermittlung ihres Gewichts gemessen.

US 21.888-B (MEC 426/14)
MODERN LOGGING IN CARINTHIA
Preparing logs for removal by means of the diesel Caterpillar.
MODERNE HOLZBRINGUNG IN KAERNTEN
Beladen der Schlittenkoerbe für den Abtransport mittels Fiat-Raupe.

US 21.889-B (MEC 426/15)
MODERN LOGGING IN CARINTHIA
Modern transport equipment is facilitating immediate and prompt removal of logs.
MODERNE HOLZBRINGUNG IN KAERNTEN
Moderne Transportmittel ermoeglichen den sofortigen Abtransport der Staemme.

US 21.890-B (MEC 426/20)
MODERN LOGGING IN CARINTHIA
This cable system is capable of carrying a 1,000 kg load.
MODERNE HOLZBRINGUNG IN KAERNTEN
Erst eine Belastung ueber 1000 kg gefaehrdet die Sicherheit des Seilbahnbetriebes.

US 21.891-B (MEC 426/21)
MODERN LOGGING IN CARINTHIA
Lumbermen jockey logs into position for their ride to market. Modern lumbering methods like this are helping to speed up the development of Austria's wood industry.
Staemme werden für den Transport in die Talstation fertig gemacht. Dank der modernen Transportmittel wird die oesterreichische Holzindustrie laufend mit Material versorgt.

US 21.892-B (MEC 426/23)
MODERN LOGGING IN CARINTHIA
On a mountaintop, another load of logs is prepared for their ride to market.
In der Bergstation wartet schon ein weiteres Gehaenge auf den Abtransport.

US 21.893-B (MEC 426/30)
MODERN LOGGING IN CARINTHIA
At Stockenboi near Paternion, Upper Carinthia, half sleds drawn by horses are still in use for transporting logs.
In Stockenboi bei Paternion, Oberkaernten, wird Holz noch mittels des landesueblichen Strotzfuehrwerkes transportiert.

US 21.894-B (MEC 426/33)
MODERN LOGGING IN CARINTHIA
The half sled method is inadequate because many times unfavorable stretches of road make it necessary to release drag loads, resulting in lost time and additional work.
MODERNE HOLZBRINGUNG IN KAERNTEN
Der Transport des Holzes mittels Halbschlitten ist in schwierigem Gelaende unmoeglich, sodass frueher oft Zeit verloren ging und zusaetzliche Arbeiten noetig waren.

US 21.895-B (MEC 426/34)
MODERN LOGGING IN CARINTHIA
The weight of a load removed by means of the half sled depends on the amount and condition of the snow on the road.
MODERNE HOLZBRINGUNG IN KAERNTEN
Die Holzlast, die der Halbschlitten ziehen kann, haengt von den Schneeverhaeltnissen ab.

US 21.894-B (MEC 426/33)

US 21.895-B (MEC 426/34)

US 21.896-B (MEC 426/36)

US 21.897-B (MEC 426/41)

US 21.896-B (MEC 426/36)
MODERN LOGGING IN CARINTHIA
The logging industry is enjoying a revival in Austria and is doing much to relieve the shortage of lumber for home construction.
MODERNE HOLZBRINGUNG IN KAERNTEN
Die oesterreichische Holzindustrie erlebt einen Aufschwung und traegt zur Behebung der Baustoffknappheit bei.

US 21.897-B (MEC 426/41)
MODERN LOGGING IN CARINTHIA
Foresters take time out for lunch and a smoke.
MODERNE HOLZBRINGUNG IN KAERNTEN
Waldarbeiter bei einer wohlverdienten Ruhepause.

A Reproduction of The Austrian Woman and the ERP[13]

ECA 119 (Master caption)
THE AUSTRIAN WOMAN AND THE ERP
Vienna—14 June 1950
Life is easier for women, since victuals and articles for everyday life are available in Austria again through the liberal aid of the ERP. Hardly any of the war and postwar restrictions exist anymore, and household needs are supplied by far less work than during the previous years.
DIE OESTERREICHERIN UND DAS ERP
Wien, 14. Juni 1950
Die Frauen haben es leichter, seit auch in Oesterreich wieder Lebensmittel und Artikel für [sic] den taeglichen Gebrauch dank der grosszuegigen ERP-Hilfe in ausrechendem Masse vorhanden sind. Fast alle Beschraenkungen der Kriegs- und Nachkriegszeit konnten bereits aufgehoben werden und die Fuehrung des Haushalts erfordert bei weitem nicht mehr die Muehe wie in den vergangenen Jahren.

US 20.778-B (ECA 119/1)
Have you got a headache, madam? Take this peacetime quality medicine. During the last years, the ERP has supplied 6 million dollars worth of medicines, pharmaceutical products, and raw materials to the pharmaceutical industry.
Sie haben Kopfschmerzen, gnaedige Frau? Nehmen Sie doch ein gutes Medikament in Friedensqualitaet. Das ERP hat im vergangenen Jahr fuer mehr al [sic] 6 Millionen Dollar medizinische Praeparate und pharmazeutische Praeparate sowie Rohstoffe fuer die Heilmittelerzeugung bereitgestellt.

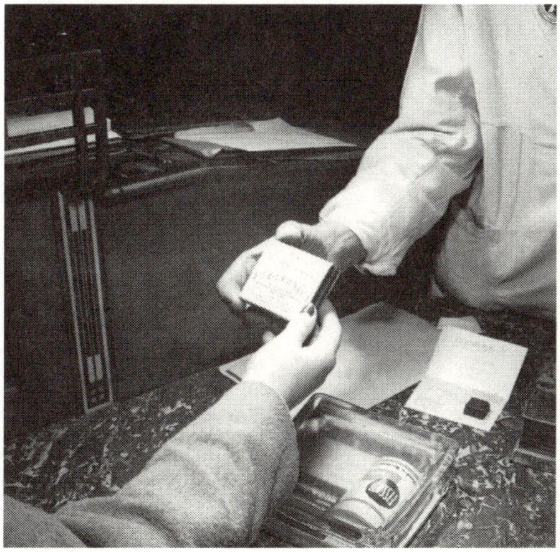

US 20.778-B (ECA 119/1)

US 20.779-B/C (ECA 119/2)
Cooking is also a pleasure again because everything required is easily available.
Auch das Kochen ist heute wieder ein Vergnuegen, da man alles Noetige leicht bekommt.

US 20.780-B (ECA 119/3)
The busy housewife, too, can keep her good looks when the adequate cosmetics are available. Through the ERP, the cosmetics industry was supplied with the necessary raw materials.
Auch die vielbeschaeftigte Hausfrau kann stets gepflegt aussehen, wenn sie geeignete kosmetische Praeparate zur Verfuegung hat. Im Rahmen des ERP wurden auch zur Erzeugung von Kosmetika die erforderlichen Rohstoffe geliefert.

US 20.781-B (ECA 119/4)
A good cigarette for a leisure house [sic] spent writing a letter is available again. Thanks to large ERP tobacco shipments (6,500 tons totaling 5 million dollars) cigarette production zoomed to a record in March.
Auch die gute oesterreichische Zigarette fuer eine besinnliche Stunde beim Briefschreiben ist wieder da. Dank der umfangreichen Tabaklieferungen des ERP (6.500 Tonnen im Wert von ueber 5 Millionen Dollar) konnte im Maerz d.J. die Zigarettenproduktion eine Rekordziffer erreichen.

US 20.782-B (ECA 119/5)
She need not be afraid of a breakdown of the power system anymore, the power supply having been secured through ERP aid: 180 million counterpart schillings helped to construct twenty power plants. During the last year, power production has been increased to about 240 million kWh.
Sie braucht keinen Zusammenbruch des Verbundnetzes mehr zu befuerchten, denn das ERP hat weitgehend dazu beigetragen, eine regelmaessige Stromversorgung zu gewaehrleisten. Fuer den Bau von 20 Kraftwerken wurden 180 Millionen Schilling vom Sonderkonto freigegeben und die Produktion von elektrischer Energie ist innerhalb des letzten Jahres um rund 240 Millionen kWh gestiegen.

US 20.781-B (ECA 119/4)

US 20.782-B (ECA 119/5)

US 20.783-B (ECA 119/6)

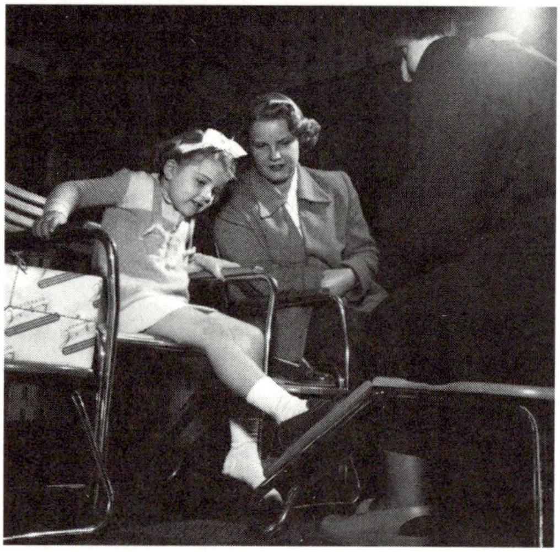

US 20.784-B (ECA 119/7)

US 20.785-B (ECA 119/8)

US 20.783-B (ECA 119/6)
In the grocery store, a peace-time display is arranged for the housewife. The sufficient supply of all kinds of food was made possible only by ERP shipments to Austria totaling 166 million dollars.
In den Lebensmittelgeschaeften biete [sic] sich der Hausfrau beim Einkauf wieder ein friedensmaessiges Bild. Diese ausreichende Versorgung mit Lebensmitteln aller Art wurde nur dadurch moeglich, dass durch das ERP Lieferungen im Gesamtwert von 166 Millionen Dollar nach Oesterreich kamen.

US 20.784-B (ECA 119/7)
The purchase of shoes for her daughter is not a problem anymore. Shoe shops offer a great variety again, the Austrian shoe manufacturers having been supplied with 6,000 tons of hides and leather through the ERP.
Die Anschaffung von Schuhen fuer die Tochter bereitet kein Kopfzerbrechen mehr. Die Auswahl in den Schuhgeschaeften ist wieder gross, da im Rahmen des ERP fast 6000 Tonnen Felle, Haeute und Leder fuer die osterreichische Schuhindustrie geliefert wurden.

US 20.785-B (ECA 119/8)
Gardening is a pleasure again as 12 million dollars worth of shipments of insecticides and fertilizers were granted by the ERP.
Die Arbeit im Garten macht wieder Freude, da durch die Marschallplan-Lieferungen von Schaedlingsbekaempfungs- und Duengemitteln im Wert von 12 Millionen Dollar Obst- und Gemueseernten gesichert sind.

Notes

1 For a detailed presentation, see Hans Petschar, *Die junge Republik: Alltagsbilder aus Österreich 1945–1955* (Vienna: Ueberreuter, 2005). For U.S. information policy in Austria, see Oliver Rathkolb, "Politische Propaganda der amerikanischen Besatzungsmacht in Österreich 1945 bis 1950: Ein Beitrag zur Geschichte des Kalten Krieges in der Presse-, Kultur- und Rundfunkpolitik (1. 2.), Ph.D. diss., University of Vienna, 1981.

2 We want to thank Oliver Rathkolb for his information on this important document. National Archives Record Group 260.11.2. Okamoto to Hopman, Memorandum 31 August 1950.

3 Ibid., 1.

4 A copy of the staff photo files was sent to Washington after August 1946 when the Library of Congress requested a copy of all staff photo files for their archives. National Archives Record Group 260.11.2. Howard R. Hollem: History of the Pictorial Section,2.

5 Okamoto, Memorandum, 2.

6 The ISB Pictorial Section as of 31 August 1950, 2.

7 A transcript of the speech and an audio file have been published on the U.S. Department of State website; see George C. Marshall, "Marshall Plan Speech," 5 June 1947, America.gov http://www.america.gov/st/texttrans-english/2007/May/20070521153224MVyelwarC0.4675867.html, accessed 28 May 2009.

8 Ibid.

9 Marshall, George Catlett: Assistance to European economic recovery. Statement by George C. Marshall, Secretary of State, before Senate Committee on Foreign Relations, 8 Jan. 1948. The President (Harry S[hippe] Truman)'s Message to the Congress, 19 Dec. 1947, Washington, 1948 (Economic Cooperation Series 2) (Dept. of State Publication 3022), 1.

10 The text accompanying the photos is an exact replication of that found in the archive.

11 Ibid.

12 Ibid.

13 Ibid.

Section IV:

The Memory of the Marshall Plan

Dieter Stiefel

"Thanks, Yank":

The Propagandistic Success of the Book *Zehn Jahre ERP in Österreich* in the U.S. Media[1]

The Book *Zehn Jahre ERP in Österreich*

In 1958, the Austrian government published a 368-page document titled *Ten Years of ERP in Austria, 1948–1958: Economic Aid for the Benefit of Understanding among Nations*. Published by the Austrian State Press with the collaboration of the Federal Press Office and the use of documents from the Federal Chancellery's Section for Economic Coordination, its dedication read: "To the unknown American taxpayer, to whose contribution the Austrian economy is indebted for the millions invested toward its reconstruction."

Why did the government make this effort? The book is written in German and would, therefore, have primarily addressed Austrians. It served as proof of Austria's successful reconstruction with U.S. aid and was, therefore, meant to strengthen Austria's self-confidence by supplanting the legacy of the small country's economic inability to survive in the interwar years. On the other hand, it may have also intended to document a closed chapter in Austria's economic and political development. With the success of the reconstruction and the 1955 State Treaty, Austria's special relationship with the United States belonged to the past. Neutral Austria was not part of the North Atlantic Treaty Organization, and economic aid was discontinued with the end of the Marshall Plan. Economically and politically, Austria had become independent, and the book showed how this had happened. Also, Austria was no longer an issue for the United States after the State Treaty: it was a politically and economically stable country, which no longer required foreign aid. An ulterior motive may have been the release of counterpart funds, which in 1958 were still under U.S. control. The initiative of the Austrian Ambassador in Washington supports this view: "On the occasion of the presentation of the work to Mr. Dillon, Ambassador Dr. Platzer also mentioned the question of the release of counterpart funds. Mr. Dillon agreed to take care of this question personally. His intervention led to the competent American offices subjecting the question of the release of counterpart funds once more to a thorough examination."[2] In 1962, these resources were awarded to the Austrian European Recovery Program Fund.

The Reaction in the United States

On 5 March 1959, thirty copies were sent to the United States, twenty-eight of which were destined for the International Cooperation Administration (ICA) in

Washington. On 11 March, the first ten copies had arrived, but no special significance had been attached to their presentation. Despite this initial lack of response, things turned out differently. "Originally, Ambassador Dr. Platzer had intended to present this work personally only to the Under-Secretary for Economic Affairs, Mr. Dillon, who acted as a representative of Secretary of State Dulles during his illness. Mr. Dillon, however, encouraged spontaneously that the Ambassador should present this work personally to President Eisenhower."[3] The presentation of the book to the President took place on Wednesday, 18 March 1959 at 8:45 a.m. in the White House, and subsequently he also presented it to Under-Secretary of State for Economic Affairs Dillon. The presentation to the President was photographed. On this occasion, the Austrian Ambassador stressed the significance of U.S. economic support and expressed his gratitude.

> President Eisenhower declared that the United States has willingly helped Austria in the years after the War and that it is proud to have been able to offer a contribution to the economic reconstruction of Austria. He said he had very closely followed the economic development of Austria in the course of the last years and that he was extraordinarily satisfied with the country's economic progress and political stability. President Eisenhower then stressed that Austria enjoyed great favor in America and exhorted the Ambassador to express his gratitude to the Austrian federal government for the publication of this book and its presentation to him. He added that he had particularly liked the dedication to "the unknown American taxpayer."[4]

This was not just a courtesy. The signing of the Austrian State Treaty—for which the United States had been a mediator—dated back only four years; therefore, Austria was still a household name for the U.S. government and administration.

Image 1: *Presentation of the book Ten Years of ERP in Austria to President Eisenhower, Washington, D.C., 18 March 1959*
Source: *Dwight D. Eisenhower Library, Abilene, Kansas.*

The President's satisfaction, however, was for another reason of which the Austrians were unaware. The timing could not have been better. In the Senate and in the House, the President's foreign aid program was being discussed, and Austria offered a well-documented example of the politically and economically efficient deployment of aid in a country which was also thankful for it: "The work was very well received," wrote the Austrian embassy:

> and the dedication "to the unknown American taxpayer" had caused enthusiasm in the competent American government offices. From an American perspective, this moment is particularly favorable for the presentation of the work to the President and for the publication of the relative press release, since at the moment the debate about the budget and the foreign aid is taking place in the Congress.[5]

The Ambassador himself observed:

> The State Department was pleased with the publication of the book, especially because the American government is currently experiencing considerable difficulties in the Congress in having its foreign aid program accepted for the coming fiscal year. The fact that Austria not only used the aid granted to it with extraordinary efficiency but also expressed gratitude years later, is for the administration a very appropriate argument in its effort to carry the aid program in the Congress [...] Also, in the view of our friends at the State Department, Austria has never since the days of the Hungarian uprising found such general approval as through this friendly gesture of gratitude towards the American people.[6]

The unique political circumstances the United States was facing made the receipt of *Ten Years of ERP in Austria* an event that could be used to for the administration's benefit: "The Press Secretary of the White House and the Press office of the State Department were, therefore, also very accommodating in helping the embassy to publicize the work in the media."[7] Press releases were prepared, and an English abstract was distributed to journalists. This seven-page abstract in English was written by the AP Business News Analyst Sam Dawson (New York). The Austrian embassy completed the preparation of the press resources in collaboration with the information service in New York and the public relations company Curtis J. Hoxter, Inc. The public relations expert Curtis J. Hoxter, with the collaboration of the Embassy and the information service of the Consulate General of Austria in New York, prepared a commentary for columnists. In addition, the Austrian Consulates General in Los Angeles (Dr. Friedrich E. Waller), Miami, Atlanta (Robert M. Bunzl), and Detroit were in charge of placing the articles.

The limited number of copies of the book available in the United States, however, was a problem about which the embassy complained several times. "With regard to the great interest for this book in American circles, the fact that the economic liaison office has hitherto received only *one* copy of the work is an extremely unpleasant obstacle to its promotion in the media."[8] At the beginning of April, another five copies had arrived in Washington; they could, however, satisfy only the most urgent need. Even the director of the ICA was left without a copy. Therefore, an urgent request for at least five more copies was sent.[9] In order to reduce expenses, it was suggested that "individual copies should be successively added to an airfreight carrier, which, as is known from experience, rarely reaches the weight limit of the minimum fee, in order to take advantage of the free weight available."[10] It was also a considerable lacuna that, given the display of interest, there should be no English-speaking edition. "With regard to the question of an English edition of the work, nothing definitive can as yet be said on its prospects of success," the embassy observed, cautiously adding that "it would be essential to know which intentions Vienna has with regard to the financing of such an English version."[11] This edition was, however, never produced.

Despite its scarcity, the book's success in the media was stunning. No one in Austria could have imagined such a success, which was achieved as if by miracle. U.S. newspapers published 191 articles, which were essentially based on the report written by Dawson: "Mr. Dawson's report about Austria's gratitude towards the American taxpayers can be regarded as a special success in U.S. publicity about Austria [...] The 191 newspapers are spread across almost all of the States of the USA and have a total circulation of 4 to 5 million."[12] Radio and television also reported on the Austrian initiative. The Austrian trade commissioner in Chicago proffered one of the rare copies to the mayor and, on the initiative of the Chamber of Commerce in Chicago, appeared on a television program during the first week of April. As a result, the Embassy spoke of very satisfying reporting in the media and was especially delighted that an article with a photo of the Federal Chancellor appeared in the *Times*. In a speech in the Senate on 20 March, Democratic Senator Richard L. Neuberger (Oregon), expressed his particular satisfaction with the publication of the book, and Democratic Representative Paul Rogers (Florida) expressed his congratulations to Ambassador Platzer over the telephone. Republican Senator Jacob K. Javits (New York) requested a copy of the book, as did the Spanish ambassador, who also recommended a similar initiative to his government; the Turkish and Greek ambassadors equally requested copies for their governments. As a result, the Austrian embassy could observe that, after its presentation to the President, the work "has found a durable echo in all sectors of the population of the USA," as witnessed from magazines and conversations with public figures. Not only did members of Congress request a copy of this work, but members of various professional groups (for example, primary school teachers, lawyers, university professors, and housewives) also "spontaneously wrote to us expressing their satisfaction with the dedication of the work."[13] "The embassy also received a series of letters in which American citizens expressed their satisfaction with Austria's attitude."[14]

The Press Releases

Sam Dawson's Report of 17 March 1959

This seven-page text constituted the basis for virtually all other broadcasts and newspaper articles. It quotes the dedication to the "unknown American taxpayer" and introduces the book as a summary of the foreign aid for Austria. "The Marshall Plan has been an effort of worldwide significance. The magnanimous aid of the American people has put an end to the seemingly inevitable decline of the old continent. Today, there can be no doubt about the fact that without this aid Europe would have been engulfed by poverty, suffering and chaos." The prefaces of Federal Chancellor Julius Raab and Vice-Chancellor Bruno Pittermann are quoted, although they occupy substantially more space in the other broadcasts.

Then the content of the book is described: the economic decline after World War I, the disintegration of the Hapsburg monarchy, the inflation of the 1920s, and the world economic crisis of the 1930s. The Corporate State is not mentioned. "Thus, the subsequent worldwide economic crisis hit Austria with full force, a fact that greatly contributes to the development leading to the annexation of Austria by Hitler in 1938. This time, the Austrian economy was rapidly—if somewhat brutally—readjusted to fit into the economic concept of Hitler's Germany." Clearly, the report espouses the so-called victim theory (*Opferthese*), which U.S. newspapers partly adopted. Subsequently, the book focuses on the destruction brought about by World War II and the situation in 1945 when the Austrian population had to live on 800 calories a day. "Even in this dark hour of her history and despite the occupation of the country by foreign armed forces, the Austrian population did not waver in its firm determination to attain full independence and to live again as a free people in a free world. It was obvious that such independence could not be attained—much less maintained—without first establishing sound economic conditions." The report stresses that Austria was unable to reconstruct its economy on its own, which had been the case after World War I, but was true to an even greater extent after the Second World War. Dawson's dramatization of the economic consequences of World War I for Austria as unable to survive is simply an exaggeration which attempted to paint Austria as a country with a thirty year economic decline from 1914 to 1945. In reality, the economic problems of the interwar years were due largely to Austrian politics and economic policy itself.

The report then deals with the "historic merit of the United States" after 1945, which is described in the chapter "The USA Rectifies History." The United States "has recognized the vital importance of creating healthy economic conditions as an essential prerequisite for a lasting peace." This led to the Marshall Plan, without which Austria would have had few chances of survival. There follows a two-page description of the Marshall Plan in Austria, and the Counterpart Funds in 1954; the press primarily mentioned the total amount of U.S. aid, which amounted to \$1.4 billion:

> As a result of the effort of her population, assisted by the generous aid received from the United States, Austria was able to raise her standard of living to a Western European level, to reconstruct and expand her industry, and subsequently to remove gradually the restrictions on imports and invisible transactions within a short period of time, thus complying with the obligations established by the OEEC [Organization for European Economic Cooperation], of which Austria has been a founding member. In 1953, only five years after the Marshall Plan had been put in operation, Austria could proudly announce that she would require no further aid. Foreign aid actually was discontinued at the end of the same year.

Austria's balance of payments had remarkably improved, the full convertibility of its currency had been largely achieved, and the country was already able to grant loans to other countries within the framework of the European Payments Union. "Austria became a creditor in the European Payments Union and was now even in a position to grant loans and commodity credits to other countries, among them Israel, Poland, Yugoslavia and Turkey." Although the U.S. media especially mentioned the granting of loans to Israel, numerous press reports would equally observe that foreign aid was also a psychological boost for Austria in seemingly hopeless years:

> One realizes throughout the book that all that has been achieved through the ERP [European Recovery Program] was made possible solely by the sacrifices of the American taxpayer to whom the book is dedicated. Consequently, the purpose of this book is to give not only an account of how the aid had been put to use and to express once more the deep gratitude of the Austrian people to those who had made it possible.

The book also aims to convince American taxpayers that their money was sensibly invested, not only in a visible reconstruction, "but also invisible, in the heart of a grateful nation, which having regained her liberty with the signing of the State Treaty in 1955 has resumed her place among the family of free nations."

Department of State for the Press, No.197, 18 March 1959, Austrian Book on United States Is Presented to President

This press release mentions the dedication and the scope of the book before dealing with its prefaces. Federal Chancellor Julius Raab writes: "Wherever and however we celebrate the anniversary of Austria's rescue from economic collapse we should be mindful of the fact that the means for our reconstruction were contributed by the American taxpayer [...] To him, America's man in the street, Austria owes its thanks." This press release also quotes Vice-Chancellor Bruno Pittermann, who compared the Marshall Plan to a "life-saving blood transfusion made at a crucial moment of economic decline." Beside a general overview over Austria's financial progress during the course of ten years, the book also sheds "[...] light on the psychological effects of the ERP and how it mobilized the psychological energies of the Austrian people and helped them regain their national self-confidence." Foreign Minister Leopold Figl is also quoted in this context: "None of the political steps which Austria took in the past decade would have been possible without the economic help of the United States within the framework of the European Recovery Program. Austria's gratitude has manifested itself in its clear intervention for all peaceful goals and in its maintenance and protection of the dignity of the human individual." The press release briefly mentions the chapter "The Hole in the East" and the problems with the Soviet Union before dealing with the final chapter:

> If one reviews the accomplishments of the European Recovery Program in Austria despite the stringent economic conditions of the year 1958, if one contemplates the great crises of the last ten years in the economy and the communication of Austria from the viewpoint of its proven ability to resist a crisis in the economy, if one measures the confidence which the Austrian people have in the stability and the capabilities of their economy and its rising standard of living in spite of continued unsettled international conditions, and if one takes into calculation the sound currency, then we come to the inevitable conclusion that the American taxpayer invested his money successfully in the stabilization of Austria.

Curtis J. Hoxter, Austria—Editorial News Notes, New York, 20 March 1959

Hoxter also quotes the book's dedication: "Dedicated to the unknown American taxpayer to whose contribution the Austrian economy is indebted for the millions invested toward its reconstruction, producing equal millions in the good will for the U.S." He mentions the presentation to President Eisenhower with the quote of the unknown American taxpayer "whose generosity, right after World War II, enabled the Free World to work and live in freedom again." The book is "in essence a report to the American people on how their taxes through Marshall Plan programs have revitalised Austria as well as a heartfelt 'thank you'." In the preface, the major representatives of the Austrian government have "[...] paid homage and tribute to America for providing a helping hand to a friend in need and thus enabling Austria to survive as a free and economically healthy nation. Equally, it was stated that a free Austria meant important strength to the entire Free World." The press release also quotes Federal Chancellor Julius Raab: "The Marshall Plan has been a deed of world importance. The magnanimous aid of the American people has brought an end to the seemingly inevitable decline of the Old Continent. Today, there can be no doubt about the fact that without this aid Europe would have been engulfed by poverty, suffering and chaos and with it the free world has been dragged into ruin." This is followed by Vice-Chancellor Bruno Pittermann's words: "The people of Europe, Austrians among them, have recognized Marshall Plan aid as a life-saving blood transfusion made at a critical moment of economic decline. We Austrians shall always remember this aid with deep gratitude." In a "touching chapter," "The USA Rectifies History," the book observed "that there can be little doubt in the critical post-war period the population of Austria had but a slim chance for survival without the generous foreign aid granted under the Marshall Plan. $1.4 billion in total aid was granted from 1948 to 1953, when Austria was able to announce that she would require no further outside assistance. As a result of these five years of aid, Austria has been able to raise herself from the dust, rubble, and destruction of war by reconstructing and expanding her industry amidst Allied occupation." After a short description of the functioning of the Marshall Plan (counterpart funds and so forth), it concluded:

> As a result of these financial infusions plus the ingenuity and hard work of the Austrian people, Austria in a comparatively short period of time made a remarkable economic comeback. The book further shows that the help Austria received during her troubled, seemingly hopeless years also had a deep psychological effect on the people. Marshall Plan aid was proof that they had not been forgotten and abandoned, but that the people of the United States—although geographically remote—did not hesitate to lend a helping hand to a friendly nation in need. It is underscored throughout the book that the sacrifices of the American taxpayer were instrumental in establishing Austria's current healthy economic condition. To Austria the Marshall Plan program was essential seed money, a development which will be recorded in the history books of the country and recognized in its importance for generations to come.

The Speech of Senator Neuberger (D-Ohio)[15]

Senator Neuberger stressed that he had been one of the few members of the Senate—from Harry S. Truman and George C. Marshall to Dwight D. Eisenhower and John Foster Dulles—who had always supported the foreign aid program:

> Most of my mail from Oregon criticizes me for supporting the administration on foreign aid. Much of this mail charges that other nations are ungrateful, that they never appreciate what America has done for them. Today, I note with satisfaction that the Austrian Government has published a 368-page volume telling how the Marshall Plan enabled Austria to rebuild from the ruins and devastation after the bombings of World War II.

He cites the dedication to the unknown taxpayer and quotes from the book: "It is to the historic credit of the United States to have recognized the vital importance of creating healthy economic conditions as an essential prerequisite for a lasting peace." He then quotes the *New York Times* article of 18 March 1958 about the Austrian book as well as a (Portland) *Oregon Daily Journal* article of 17 March 1959, which stressed the general significance of the economic foreign aid for the

United States itself, saying the United States is as safe as "the weakest of our allies or other friendly nations [...] We have reached a condition of world affairs when this country cannot, in its own interest, allow other nations to be swallowed by the Communist world conspiracy by political, economic or military means."

The Print Articles

Of the above-mentioned 191 articles in the press, fifty-one are preserved as copies in the Archive of the Austrian Republic (*Archiv der Republik*). They show the functioning of the media at that time, documenting how a piece of information spread across the U.S. continent. The articles cover the time between 18 March until the beginning of May, a period defined by the date on which the regional Austrian representatives took the initiative to place the articles and the time required to publish the stories in newspapers and magazines (daily, weekly, or monthly publications). Normally, newspapers extracted passages from the press releases, depending on the length of the article. Worth noting is not only what was chosen, but also the comment which usually introduced or concluded the report. A detailed description of Austrian reconstruction as documented in the book is virtually never given, above all because the book was not available for journalists and, even if it had been, most of them would have been unable to read the German text. The dedication "to the unknown American taxpayer" was always mentioned. Whoever created this dedication has been proven to have great political intuition and effective words that touched a nerve in the U.S. media. The ungratefulness of many countries that accepted U.S. money but nonetheless were anti-American was often stressed. Thus the articles show the attitude of Americans towards their foreign policy and their astonishment, even bewilderment, regarding the anti-Americanism in the Western world that was present as early as the 1950s. Instead, the little country of Austria is put forward as a praiseworthy example, which should serve as a model for the others. Most articles are related to the discussion about future U.S. foreign aid which took place in Congress at that time. In this context, Austria demonstrated that the Marshall Plan funds had been put to good use in a politically and economically efficient way. In addition, Austria's political and economic stability is portrayed as an American success in the Cold War.

- *Miami Herald* (Florida), 18 March 1959, "Austria Is Thanking U.S. For Aid by Marshall Plan": "The American Taxpayer quickly becomes the forgotten soul in too much of our foreign aid program. But here is an instance where our aid paid off and where we are not forgotten. Little Austria, once the greatest empire in Europe, is paying tribute to the U.S. taxpayer [...]."
- *Baltimore Sun* (Maryland), 18 March 1959, "Expressed Gratitude": "How at least one of this country's European friends feels about the aid America has given it was expressed today [...]."
- *Washington Post*, 19 March 1959, "Thanks—A Billion: Austria Honors American Taxpayer for Foreign Aid that Brought Nation Back": "The ordinary American taxpayer, sometime called the 'man in the street' is a hero—in Austria anyway."

- *New York Times*, 19 March 1959, "Austria Thanks U.S. Taxpayers": "Americas 'man in the street' was thanked by the Austrian Government today [...]." The newspaper chose the dedication of the book as Quote of the Day.
- *Rochester Times-Union* (New York), 20 March 1959, "To the "Unknown Taxpayer": "The little country of Austria finally gave credit where credit is due."
- *Cleveland Plain Dealer* (Ohio), 20 March 1959, "At Last, Some Gratitude": "Gratitude is such a rare commodity in international relations, that when it finds expression, as it does in a book which was presented to President Eisenhower by Dr. Wilfried Platzer, Austrian Ambassador to the United States, it is noteworthy [...] it is the first time in our recollection that a people has expressed gratitude for American help."
- *Herald Tribune* (New York), 21 March 1959, "To America with Thanks": "The American taxpayer, who pays the bills for foreign aid but rarely gets any thanks, had a book dedicated to him this week [...] In a case of this kind the principle of foreign aid, so often questioned by legislators and taxpayers, is justified many times over [...] As taxpayers, we thank Austria and wish her long life."
- *Washington Post*, 21 March 1959, "Music from Vienna": "At a time when appropriation requests are again stirring grumpy complaints in Congress about foreign aid, there is something especially timely about Austria's gracious gesture to the unsung American taxpayer."
- *Watertown Times* (New York), 21 March 1959, "Tribute to Taxpayers": "America's forgotten man has been remembered—in Austria. Our taxpayers have been cited by the highest officials of Austria for their part in the reconstruction of that nation through the Marshall Plan aid [...] Taxpayers about this time of year really do begin to feel they are definitely the man in the street, or that they soon will be there, but they have rarely felt that anyone else knew or cared. They are wrong, for in fact millions of people in many other countries are profoundly aware of their contributions, but, as with most gratitude, theirs usually goes unexpressed. Austria has been particularly gracious about U.S. aid [...]."
- *Troy Times-Record* (New York), 21 March 1959, "Timely Thanks": "We are given over to wonder how the critics of America's foreign aid program will react to the 'thank you' which has been compiled by the government of Austria. It would be nice if other countries, recipients of the same opportunities and benefits, would show the same appreciation [...] We don't expect effusive thanks for our help, but we like to know that it is appreciated and that something worth while has been accomplished. Austria has seen fit to give us this accounting and a public 'thank you.' And in reply we cannot help but say 'You are welcome.'"
- *Philadelphia Bulletin* (Pennsylvania), 21 March 1959, "Austria's Thanks": "Not all European governments and peoples have given thanks in such a cordial way for the help they received for the Marshall plan [...] Politeness is also rather exceptional in international relations these days [...]."
- *Trenton Times* (New Jersey), 22 March 1959, "Austria Is Grateful": "Austria, in its own unique way, has made important international history and in doing so has heightened the respect in which this enlightened land and its people are held by Americans [....] What touches the heart of America with a peculiar

intimacy, however, is the Austrian government's sincere tribute to America's 'man in the street' for his contribution to the nation's reconstruction through the Marshall Plan."

- *Buffalo Courier-Express* (New York), 22 March 1959, "America's Taxpayers Get Austria's Thanks": "'Thanks, Yank' being hardly as prevalent a phrase these days as 'Yankee, Go Home,' it's pleasant to hear words of gratitude from some of the people to whom we have extended economic aid. One such beneficiary is Austria [...] As we said, such words are pleasant to hear. They carry the impression that in at least one instance American contributions not only have done some good but are appreciated. To the Austrians America's man in the street may well say: 'Glad to have been of service.'"
- *The Christian Science Monitor*, 23 March 1959, "Thanks for the Thanks": "The evil that nations do tends to get the big headlines; the good is often interred with the drier bones of unread history. The Austrians appear to have noticed this, and they have done something about it [....] The book is useful in reminding Americans that their country's aid to other free nations is appreciated. Of course, no one will ever quite forget Sir Winston Churchill's reference to Marshall Aid as the 'most unsordid act in history.' And sometimes expressions of thanks which should have been heard in America have been blanketed by more spectacular news from the aided areas [...] Among ways in which the book says that Austrians have shown they merited aid is this: Austria has proved this attitude towards hundreds of thousands of refugees."
- *Syracuse Post-Standard* (New York), 23 March 1959, "Thanks from Austria": "American taxpayers are not accustomed to thanks from beneficiaries of our foreign aid. More often we are attacked for not providing additional funds or told that no strings must be attached. But Austria acknowledges her debt handsomely in a book reviewing 10 years of her recovery program [...] Such acknowledgements are appreciated because of their rarity. U.S. taxpayers, who sometimes wonder about the effectiveness of their contributions to mutual security, have evidence here that it is paying dividends."
- *New York Long Island Star-Journal*, 23 March 1959, "Grateful Austria": "Critics of our foreign aid program like to call attention to spots on the globe which seem to love us less after we have sent them generous allotments of American dollars. Well, Austria has just prepared a report [...] Other nations dwelling in the shadow of Red domination, undoubtedly feel as grateful. The trouble is that the voices of agitators and the malcontents too often are more noisy and more widely heard."
- *Pittsburgh Post-Gazette* (Pennsylvania), 23 March 1959, "The Priceless Ingredient": "There was a story, told in the old days when pipe organs were hand-pumped, about the elegant virtuoso and his shirt-sleeved assistant who manned the pump. 'For my next number,' the virtuoso told his audience one day, 'I shall play Bach's Toccata and Fugue in D minor.' No sound issued when he touched the keyboard. Then came a hoarse whisper form the unseen pumper: 'Say we, dammit, say we!' The unseen American taxpayer is grateful to the Austrian government for its gratitude."

- *Parsons Sun* (Kansas), 24 March 1959, "Appreciative Austria": "The idea that foreigners are a pretty ungrateful lot has gained circulation through anti-American demonstrations in various spots on the globe. While billions have been spent for foreign aid in different forms, opponents of that program in this country have played on the theme that it's impossible to buy friends and that the American taxpayer is a sucker to permit continued spending of this kind. A different note is sounded by Austria [...] The bad usually outweighs the good in the news and the public's mind. Riots in South America and the Middle East that were directed at the United States will linger longer than the kind words form Austria, but proper note should be made of the latter. There are appreciative people to be found in the world after all."
- *Greensboro Record* (North Carolina), 24 March 1959, "Unknown Taxpayer": "It's not a monument, but the American taxpayer should be gratified at the recognition he has received from the government of Austria [...] The unknown taxpayer should be grateful for this recognition, especially with April 15 fast approaching." The day of 15 April was the deadline by which Americans had to submit their tax returns.
- *Danville Commercial-News* (Ohio), 24 March 1959, "Unknown Taxpayer": "The little country of Austria finally gave credit where credit is due."
- *Utica Press* (New York), 25 March 1959, "To the 'Unknown Taxpayer'": "The little country of Austria finally gave credit where credit is due."
- *Wichita Falls* (Texas), 25 March 1959, "Appreciation from Austria" questioned the timing of the book, since foreign aid was being discussed in Congress at that time: "Nonetheless, the 'thank you' message addressed to the taxpayers of this country is appreciated [....] Can anyone remember a similar expression to have come from any other country, large or small, since the aid program initiated with the Marshall Plan started pouring out some $60 billion into the far and near corners of the globe? The gesture puts Austria in a class by itself [...]."
- *Clarksburg Telegram* (West Virginia), 25 March 1959, "Where Thanks Are Due": "There's a word of thanks for the American taxpayer. It comes from the Austrian government [...] This shines out in a world where Americans are more used to being criticized than thanked. In several parts of the world, of late, there have been anti-Yankee rioting and some instances of mobs trying to attack American embassies and wrecking American information centers. Most of these countries have been recipients of U.S. foreign aid and in at least one recent instance this American aid was a major factor in the nation's economy. But Austria says it is pleased with our aid program [...] The Austrian gesture comes—unwittingly or not—while Congress is debating next year's foreign aid spending."
- *Scranton Times* (Pennsylvania), 25 March 1959, "Our Generosity Appreciated": "Many critics of our foreign aid program complain that not only do the American taxpayer receive no thanks for their generous shelling out of their dollars to overseas nations but that the people of the recipient countries frequently become downright ungrateful, if not openly hostile, to their benefactors. Austria has provided a shining exception."

- *Bethlehem Globe-Times* (Pennsylvania), 25 March 1959, "One Nation Views Foreign Aid": "The American hand which helped feed less fortunate countries has often been bitten in return. That is why the rare and heart-warming expression of appreciation received from Austria last week deserves more than passing notice [...] Americans can have the warm feeling of knowing that their foreign aid has helped save the national life of a nation of 10 million who are grateful."
- *Cincinnati Enquirer* (Ohio), 26 March 1959, "Austrian Gratitude": "Because, as the fellow said, gratitude usually is a lively appreciation of favors to come, the Austrian government's book-length report to President Eisenhower on how American assistance restored that country's economy and insured its independence is a refreshing phenomenon [...] Without help from this country, one is moved to inquire, would the government at Vienna have reached the state of independence enabling it to stand off Moscow's protest over its generous welcome to the refugees fleeing the Red army's Hungarian terror? A thriving Austria, healed of the wounds inflicted by the Nazi occupation, World War II and Soviet Russia's brutal looting, is indeed a monument to American good will and it is gracious of Vienna to mention it."
- *Pontiac Press* (Michigan), 26 March 1959, "Austria's 'Thank You' to American Taxpayer": "At a time when foreign aid requests are meeting with complaints in and out of Congress, it is pleasant to note a gracious gesture of the Austrian government." The article then quotes Leopold Figl: "that Austria in turn has been able to help others including thousands of Hungarian refugees [...] If we had refused our help after the devastations of World War II, Austria today could very well be a Russian satellite or at least dominated by that country. It would lack the economic stability so vital to its independence from pressure."
- *Providence Bulletin* (Rhode Island), 26 March 1959, "A Testimonial to Foreign Aid": "The much-burdened and grumbling American taxpayers probably never have received such a gracious tribute as they did this week from the Government of Austria. In a rare and heart-warming expression of hands-across-the-sea gratitude, Austria has published a book [...] It would be easy to be cynical and to dismiss the publication of the book and the ceremonious presentation of a copy to President Eisenhower as diplomatic apple-polishing. But to do so would be to ignore the record and to do rank injustice to the governments and peoples of both Austria and the United States. Indeed, the sincerity and the sentiments expressed in the book merely reflect the remarkable harmony that characterized Austrian-American relations on both the optical and personal levels and made operation of the Marshall Plan in Austria virtually a model performance [...] Americans can have the warm feeling of knowing that a nation of nearly 10 million is able to hold up its "head and still say thanks to American taxpayers for having saved its national life.
- *Dayton News* (Ohio), 27 March 1959, "Foreign Aid Brings Dedicated Thanks": "A falsehood perpetrated by foes of American foreign aid programs is that other nations take every opportunity to bite the hand helping to feed them. There have been instances of ingratitude, but they are outweighed by the acts

of kindness and reciprocity by the recipients of help from the United States. One recent example, from Austria, illustrates the attitude of many Europeans and others who could not have regained economic and political stability in the post-war years without outside assistance."

- *Beaumont Journal* (Texas), 27 March 1959, "Austria Is Thankful": "It's about time. A foreign nation has finally got around to expressing thanks for U.S. aid, and to the proper people—the American Taxpayer [...] Who will be next? Or should we ask WHAT does Austria want next?"
- *Charleston Mail* (West Virginia), 27 March 1959, "A Word of Thanks Never Hurt a Bit": "The Austrians have done a gracious and tactful thing. They have addressed a 'thank you' note, not to the American government, but to the American taxpayer for the generous assistance [....] This is not quite the whole story, of course. The American taxpayer—and whether or not he knows it—has his own good reasons for investing in Austrian recovery. For one thing it keeps the Soviets out of Middle Europe where they do not belong. But it helps a lot to know somewhere among the millions who have shared in this program there is someone who recognizes that every last cent of it came from American taxpayers' pockets."
- *Portland Express* (Maine), 28 March 1959, "Welcome Thanks from Austria": "That is very gracious—and almost unprecedented. It is, or should be, reckoned somewhat heartwarming, for most of the American taxpayers have felt the pinch which our generosity is meant [...] Nobody thanks the average taxpayer for all this money that is taken from him. Nobody but the Vice Chancellor of Austria. It is gratifying to have this recognition."
- *Time Magazine*, 30 March 1959, "A Word for the Taxpayer," as a caption to a picture of the Austrian Federal Chancellor Julius Raab.
- *St. Paul Dispatch* (Minnesota), 30 March 1959, "The American Taxpayer Gets a Thank You Note": "No longer can the American taxpayer complain that no one ever thanks him for money which has gone toward the reconstruction of some phase of the postwar world [...] If that [the book *Ten Years of ERP in Austria*] doesn't wrap it up for even the most critical of America's citizens who have vaguely known that they were helping Austria to get on its feet [...] It may be a rare instance where the American taxpayer has been singled out and called by name as the generous guy who reaches down into his pocket to help stricken nations to rise again, but his expression is genuine and inspiring. The American taxpayer has been thanked officially."
- *Omaha World-Herald* (Nebraska), 31 March 1959, "Some Welcome Sentiments Whatever the Motivation": "Even taken with enough cynical salt to sweeten what must be, a fairly gamey pitch for continued foreign aid, the Austrian Government has handed President Eisenhower a document that should give Americans some satisfaction [...] Even though the timing is, as previously mentioned, probably intended to bolster the President's fight for foreign aid, the dedication is unusual [...] In an era when too many countries grab our money with both hands and kick us with both feet, such sentiments, however motivated, are welcome."

- *Greensboro News* (North Carolina), 31 March 1959, "'Thanks'—A Billion": "'You can't buy friends.' The usual complaint heard in Washington at foreign aid consideration time is being aired again. No serious supporter of the Mutual Assistance Program believes that foreign aid buys friends, nor are they deterred when recipients don't thank the U.S.A. in the warm, polite way in which a personal gift might be welcomed. Economic and military assistance should be extended for its value to American foreign policy and defense, as well as in altruism to help people raise their living standards. The hope is that this too ultimately will benefit our international objectives. Austria's action in thanking the American taxpayer—'America's man in the street'—for Marshall Plan money is a delightful surprise [...] So often the American taxpayer feels he is the world's unsung hero. So these kind words from Austria are music to his ears."
- *Schenectady Union Star* (New York), 31 March 1959, "Foreign Aid Good Side: Austria's Gratitude": "We had some comments here the other day about the sordid side of foreign aid—or at least charges there is such a side. Now we'd like to show the reverse of the coin."
- *Haverhill Gazette* (Massachusetts) 31 March 1959, "Thanks from Austria": "So it is the American people, who finance a huge foreign aid program that goes on year after year, hardly know how the peoples who receive the benefits really feel about it. Occasionally we are led to believe that America is hated abroad despite the country's good intentions and we are mystified and somewhat shocked at this. And the every now and then there is a glimmer of news that suggests quite the opposite is true [...] At a time when a small voice saying 'thank you' could be—and was—all but lost amid the outcries over Berlin and other crises in Tibet and the Middle East, Austria's gesture of appreciation should strike a particularly responsive chord in the United States."
- *Dothan Eagle* (Alabama), 2 April 1959, "Thanks to the Unknown Taxpayer": "Not the least of arguments being advanced for reductions in President Eisenhower's proposed foreign aid request is the one that the beneficiaries of this largess have seldom seemed fit to interrupt the spending thereof to say "thank you" or otherwise make appreciative acknowledgments. Perhaps this silence, or looking the other way, could be due to the fact that the recipients of foreign aid believe, as do some American advocates, that the assistance is in the United States' interest in that it strengthens them to resist and fight communism. In other words, it's America's self-interest. That, at least, is a charitable observation. At any rate, it's refreshing to learn that one country is in a 'thank you' frame of mind and unabashedly saying so. The little nation of Austria [...]."
- After discussing the facts in the book that prove Austria had invested American money sensibly, the article continues: "This isn't likely to whip up a substantial number of votes for foreign aid because it seems to be an isolated instance. However, it's conceivable that opponents of aid might suggest to their colleagues: 'Well, if you're going to vote for the money, be certain that the Austrians are taken care of in good fashion.'"

- *Memphis Commercial Appeal* (Tennessee), 4 April 1959, "Unexpected and Welcome": "Such generous words of thanks to the men and women of this country are unexpected and welcome. The graceful gesture will go far toward strengthening the good opinion we in this country have held in respect to Austria and its people."
- *Butte Montana Standard*, 5 April 1959, "Americans Are Thanked for Foreign Aid": "The U.S. Taxpayer finally has won a little recognition. And at the same time foreign aid has been given a boost. This came to pass recently in Washington, D.C. [...] This sort of thing will be cheerful news to the American people. Americans may be generous, but they like to have appreciation, also. It is almost the first official thank you Americans have received for some 70 billion dollars given away."
- *Shreveport Times* (Louisiana), 9 May 1959, "A Nation Thanks the U.S. Taxpayer": "Throughout the history of the present type of American foreign aid—launched originally in the Truman administration as the Marshall Plan—there have been far too many instances of overseas nations gladly grabbing America's millions—of even billions, cumulatively—and then telling this nation to jump in the lake when we needed their friendship. So it is especially gratifying to find one nation that seems to understand truly what the United States dollars have done for it and to be deeply appreciative. This nation is Austria [...] This is, so far as is known, the only time that a people expressed gratitude for American help."

Conclusion

Sometimes chance plays a key role in events; it certainly did for the success of this book in the American media in 1958. Austrian politicians were unaware of the perfect timing of the presentation of the book in the United States. At that time, Austrian politics was focused on Europe, above all the normalization of Austria's relationship with Germany and its Eastern European neighboring countries. The 1956 Hungarian crisis, with its large number of refugees, had revealed the instability of the political order after the war. The Marshall Plan was history, the book was hard work, and the importance of the United States was constantly decreasing. The United States had regarded Austria, at the time of its occupation from 1945 until 1955, as an essential front in the Cold War; the retreat of Allied troops after the 1955 State Treaty was regarded as a victory of the Western world. But by 1958, Austria meant nothing to most Americans—Vienna perhaps, for cultural reasons, but certainly not Austria. The U.S. government was well informed about Austria until 1955. At the National Archives in Washington, a large number of documents are available for this period, but their quantity decreases steadily for the decades after 1955 because Austria was a politically and economically stable country which no longer required foreign aid, and with regard to its size, it was virtually immaterial. The global interests of the United States had shifted. The promotion of the Austrian book about the Marshall Plan in the media was not, therefore, the expression of a special relationship between both countries; instead, it revealed the United States' slightly naive fear of being regarded as the "ugly American" despite its considerable financial and military foreign aid.

Notes

1 All documents and newspaper extracts are preserved at the Österreichisches Staatsarchiv, Archiv der Republik, 05, BKA ERP, Gr.Zl. 3095159.
2 Austrian Embassy, Washington, Economic Liaison Office to the Federal Chancellery, Section for Economic Coordination, Vienna, Washington, 18 March 1959.
3 Austrian Embassy, Washington, Economic Liaison Office to the Federal Chancellery, Section for Economic Coordination, Vienna, Washington, 11 March 1959.
4 Enderl, to the Federal Minster of Foreign Affairs, to the Federal Chancellery Section V, Vienna, 6 April 1959.
5 Austrian Embassy, Washington, Economic Liaison Office to the Federal Chancellery, Section for Economic Coordination, Vienna, Washington, 11 March 1959.
6 Platzer to the Federal Minister, Washington, 23 March 1959.
7 Platzer to the Federal Minister, Washington, 23 March 1959.
8 Austrian Embassy, Washington, Economic Liaison Office to the Federal Chancellery, Section for Economic Coordination, Vienna, Washington 26 March 1959.
9 Austrian Embassy, Washington, Economic Liaison Office to the Federal Chancellery, Section for Economic Coordination, Vienna, Washington, 2 April 1959.
10 Austrian Embassy, Washington, Economic Liaison Office to the Federal Chancellery, Section for Economic Coordination, Vienna, Washington, 2 April 1959.
11 Austrian Embassy, Washington, Economic Liaison Office to the Federal Chancellery, Section for Economic Coordination, Vienna, Washington, 18 March 1959.
12 Austrian Information Service in New York to the Federal Chancellery, Foreign Affairs, Vienna, New York, 8 April 1959.
13 Austrian Embassy, Washington, Economic Liaison Office to the Federal Chancellery, Section for Economic Coordination, Vienna, Washington, 26 March 1959.
14 Platzer to the Federal Minister, Washington, 23 March 1959.
15 S.4231 Congressional Record, Volume 105 No. 46, 20 March 1959.

Eric and Linda Christenson*

The Making of *The Marshall Plan:*

Against the Odds

A Long Gestation

In 1990, when my wife, Linda, suggested that we create a documentary for U.S. public television on the Marshall Plan, I thought it was a wild idea. Neither of us had had experience or academic training in television, film, or history. I was a public high school English teacher nearing retirement and, on the side, a production potter. Linda had been a French and Spanish teacher, church organist, and freelance photo researcher. The likelihood of success for such a project was rather like the Marshall Plan itself, "against the odds." How would the two of us, completely inexperienced in the world of television production, ever manage to do such a thing? The answer is that, by ourselves, we could not and did not. It took a team made up of many friends and a network of helpful and encouraging people on both sides of the Atlantic to realize this goal.

The idea sprang from the photo research for one of Linda's jobs in 1984. She had contracted with the United States Information Agency (USIA) to do research for an exhibit destined to travel around France illustrating with photographs and minimal text the story of French participation in the 1948–1951 European Recovery Program (ERP)—the Marshall Plan. The ERP's scope, boldness, and farsightedness had inspired Linda, as had the 30,000+ photographs in the Marshall Plan collection (Record Group 286-MP) at the U.S. National Archives. "Picture stories"—invaluable photo essays accompanied by written summaries—describe various Marshall Plan projects in all of the seventeen participating countries.

Those picture stories must have come to mind that evening in 1990 while Linda was watching a stirring PBS documentary that relied on old photographs. She turned to me and said, "The fiftieth anniversary of the Marshall Plan will be in June 1997. Someone should make a PBS documentary on it, and I know where the pictures are." So it began.

Finding a producer was our first step. Our introductory letter to the local PBS station, WETA, brought an exciting hour-long discussion with two producers. But it also brought our first reality check: all fundraising would be our responsibility,

* The authors wish to thank the members of their Academic Advisory Board: Professors Volker Berghahn, David Ellwood, Richard Kuisel, Thomas Schwartz, Reinhold Wagnleitner, and Imanuel Wexler, who helped to make their envisioned documentary a reality.

and WETA would take a percentage of the funding for general overhead in addition to the costs of making the documentary. Other producers in Washington and New York professed interest. Luckily, a friend in the business advised us to watch a film by each producer before making a choice. We did, but none felt right. Because each of my weekdays consisted of working on the potter's wheel from 5:00 to 6:30 a.m. and then teaching high school English from 7:00 a.m. to 3:00 p.m., Linda plunged ahead on most fronts, researching, reading, networking, and continuing the search for the right producer.

A former Marshall Plan staff member urged her to call Ira Klugerman, executive producer of the Educational Film Center (EFC), a production company in a nearby Washington suburb. Because the Marshall Plan had been an economic program with political implications and humanitarian overtones, we needed someone who could make abstractions come alive. Not only had Ira created a successful and long-running series, *Economics U$A*, he also felt comfortable with the post-World War II era, having recently produced a ninety-minute historical documentary about Harry Hopkins, a high government official during the Depression and the war. Linda met with him and brought home a copy of the show, hoping we would like it. Due to my early-morning pottery production, I always retired early. But the show captivated us so completely that my bedtime passed unnoticed. We had our producer.

Linda spent most of 1991 and 1992 researching further, delving deeper into the Marshall Plan, securing academic support, and networking. Every available book on every related subject became required reading. We both needed not only to become better informed, but also to gain the balanced point of view necessary for both a broadcast on PBS and possible funding from the National Endowment for the Humanities (NEH). With the complexities of the Marshall Plan in mind, we needed a scholarly advisory board comprising several disciplines. Linda gathered a team of six highly respected advisors kindly willing to read and discuss a succession of grant proposal drafts to the NEH.

She also gathered names of prospective interviewees, primarily "Marshall Planners," as the program's staff members tended to refer to themselves. Fortunately, many lived near us, and many, having been communicators in the Information Division, had stayed in touch with each other. Both the magnitude and the urgency of our task—given the Marshall Planners' advancing age—were becoming apparent.

Most Marshall Planners had been young and idealistic when they signed up in 1948 to "change the world," as one interviewee put it. Many described their experience as "the best years of my life." Their enthusiasm for the documentary project fired our commitment to take their stories to young adults, sadly ignorant of this era. Linda asked one university student, the daughter of two U.S. Foreign Service officers, what she knew. Confusing the name "Marshall" with its homonym, she asked, "Did it have something to do with martial law?" Clearly, we had a mission.

Needed: Persistence, Persistence, and More Persistence

Riding high on our enthusiasm, we dismissed warnings about the difficulty of finding funding. Armed with a first-rate scholarly board and the respect NEH officials had for Ira and the EFC, we felt growing confidence that our project would be funded. After months of work, we submitted the proposal in September 1992.

While waiting for the NEH's decision, we sought other funding sources as well. Wouldn't it be natural, we thought, for international companies such as Caterpillar and Mobil, which had themselves benefited from the Marshall Plan, to sponsor a documentary about such a celebrated international undertaking?

Acquiring the art of proposal writing was, however, a slow process and never fully mastered. Our early efforts mistakenly centered on requesting funds for the entire project, painting the Marshall Plan in general terms without having yet found an overarching theme—a necessity for the NEH grant proposal. As researchers, we were discovering many details and individual stories. However, it would take Ira and a scriptwriter, whom we could afford to hire only much later, to bring the central and compelling story into focus. So during these early efforts, we could not offer corporations and other funders a clear and logical connection between a documentary on the Marshall Plan and their own aims. None stepped forward to help.

Even more discouraging, in March 1993, the NEH turned down our proposal, citing insufficient European perspectives. Shortly afterward, Linda saw a call for grant proposals from the Virginia Foundation for the Humanities (VFH) and submitted a slightly modified version. Ironically, the VHF panel not only awarded it $8,000, their maximum, they also called it one of the best they had ever received. Though small, the award carried prestige and validation for subsequent grant applications, buoying both the project and us.

Networking

Meanwhile, having retired in January 1993 from full-time teaching, I began reading interview transcriptions, books, and articles. Linda returned to the Marshall Plan photo collection at the National Archives to find prospective European interviewees. One picture story caught her attention: Austrian fabric manufacturer Willi Steiner smiling in front of a huge bale of soft Italian merino wool, the preferred raw material for his famous *Schladminger Loden* cloth. ERP aid had helped Steiner get the wool. Photos and captions told the story—a surprise to Willie Steiner, Jr. He and his brother Herbert, now running the business, had had no idea of the Marshall Plan's involvement in its history.

The search began for similar stories in Europe. Linda recorded telephone interviews with people in many of the Marshall Plan countries, including a farmer in The Netherlands who had spent two years in the United States under the Technical Assistance Program and an engineer who had designed a Marshall Plan-financed hydroelectric plant in Luxembourg.

Innocents Abroad

The telephone interviews were a good beginning; now we needed to know how interviewees would look on camera. An interview trip to Europe in the fall was the next step. The press attaché of the German Embassy and Dr. Martin Eichtinger, then director of the Austrian Press and Information Service in Washington, provided invaluable help in locating and contacting some of the interviewees. However, we had no funding for travel. Helpful friends suggested SERVAS, an international peace organization that provides friendship, lodging, and meals. As new members, we took off with our family video camera and Ira's light kit. Our first SERVAS host was Clara Fuhr of Wiesbaden, Germany, who told us such compelling stories about fleeing from Eastern Germany into the Western sector that she appeared in the documentary.

In nearby Mainz, the historian of the Schott Glassworks recounted the company's long history and involvement with the ERP, and we interviewed a retired worker who had been in the company in the postwar period. We visited other German industries affected by the ERP, including the Paulaner Brewery in Munich, where we filmed bottles rattling along the assembly line. At the Faber-Castell factory in Stein, we met the former sales manager, who spoke excellent English after having been a POW in Louisiana, and we filmed [slices of] California cedar—made available in the postwar era by the Marshall Plan—as it joined graphite and a little glue to become pencils.

Many European interviewees shared vivid memories of the postwar years. In Linz, Austria, retired steel worker Max Grabner remembered patching the soles of his only shoes with cardboard and trying to survive on 900 calories a day while working fifty-two hours a week to repair the severely bomb-damaged VOEST, the United Steel Works. He recalled the thriving black market, with people trading valuables for vegetables and scarce meat. The town's postwar population was increasing dramatically, he recalled, but wartime bombing raids had created an enormous housing shortage. "The need was very great," he said. But he also spoke of their postwar optimism for a better life and the rumored hope for help from the United States—the former enemy.

Near Plambach, Austria, a farm family related how their father, a refugee from the Südtirol, had received a loan through the Marshall Plan to repair the dilapidated barns of his family's formerly abandoned farmstead. In Lech, we met the hotelier who had distributed Marshall Plan funding to hotels and ski areas. The University of Salzburg's Professor Reinhold Wagnleitner, one of our cultural advisors, helped us interview two farmers in Pöchlarn about the new agricultural techniques promoted by the Marshall Plan's 4-H (*Landjugend*) program.

In Vienna, Professor Heinz Jankowsky, then director of the Österreichisches Gesellschafts- und Wirtschaftsmuseum, supplied us with information and photos. Mr. Erich Eibl, of the Eibl & Wondrak Tractor Company in Vienna, described his father's struggle to keep the factory going in the Soviet zone and the ERP aid he received to improve the factory's productivity after the war. Visiting Willi Steiner, Jr., in Mandling, we fingered the dense, warm garments made with the mill's

Loden cloth. Feeling steeped in the pervasiveness of Marshall Plan aid throughout the economies of the participating countries, we flew home, energized to get even more interviews and to find serious funding.

The Best and the Brightest

Back in Virginia, Linda continued to talk to Europeans and Americans involved in any way in the Marshall Plan. Although aging, they remained vigorous, writing books and speaking at conferences, some playing tennis well into their eighties. When we interviewed him in 1996, British economist Lord (Eric) Roll, born in 1907, was president of an investment bank in London and active at the bank until his death in 2005. In 1948, he had been one of the European "Committee of Four" responsible for recommending the division of the first U.S. aid allotments to the participating countries—an unexpected, daunting, and critical task.

Another was economist Dr. Ernst van der Beugel, a Dutch representative who had to defend The Netherlands' requests for as large a share of that aid as possible. Similarly, many American interviewees who worked with the Marshall Plan in their youth later served with distinction in government and the private sector. Many joined the U.S. Foreign Service, some eventually serving as ambassadors, such as Lincoln Gordon, Arthur Hartman, Paul Nitze, John Tuthill, and Vernon Walters. Ambassador George Ball had served as aide to Jean Monnet, a French economic planner deeply involved with the Marshall Plan.

All interviewees, the eminent as well as the not-so-famous, were articulate and able men and women who informed the overall story. They included a journalist who had promoted the Marshall Plan to the American public, a U.S. labor attaché who believed the Marshall Plan's success was won on the factory floor, an oil expert who had urged a Congressional committee to pass the enabling legislation, and a woman who had created radio broadcasts promoting Marshall Plan goals and projects in Italy.

More Money Matters

Eventually, we learned to research granting institutions' particular objectives and to shape requests more precisely, thereby obtaining support for specific elements of the project. The George C. Marshall International Center at Dodona Manor contributed toward interview travel in New England and Utah and interview transcriptions. The German Marshall Fund of the United States later supported interview travel in Germany and an advisory board meeting required by the NEH.

However, by 1994 the project was becoming seriously hobbled by insufficient funding. My pottery sales, educational consulting, and pension were still financing most expenses, including the 1993 European trip. Far more money would be needed for the production and post-production phases of the project. In an effort to professionalize a second grant request to the NEH, we hired a professional proposal writer in early 1994. Unfortunately, Linda failed to inquire about his experience in writing a proposal with the "balanced" viewpoint that we wanted and that the NEH and PBS required. Despite many discussions and piles of material we provided to the contrary, he produced a flag-waving, nationalistic story devoid of the European viewpoint and international cooperation we had intended to stress. Gloom enveloped us.

But at least his proposal crystallized for us what we did *not* want to say. Working frantically toward the September 1994 NEH submission deadline, we revised our own draft to reflect much more emphasis on European participation in the Marshall Plan.

Then an even more severe setback arrived. Days before the deadline, our previously-supportive lead scholar faxed his resignation from the project; he had not liked the direction of the professional's proposal, nor did he think at this point that the project would ever be funded or produced. We were devastated. However, regardless of their own doubts, our remaining advisers remained loyal and generous with their time and wisdom. Filled with gratitude, we were confident of a good outcome of this second major grant request.

Alas, once again in March 1995, another rejection arrived. Half of the NEH panel had faulted our new funding proposal because it showed too little emphasis on the Cold War. The other half had faulted it for showing too *much* emphasis on the Cold War.

Abroad Again, Home Again, and Carrying On

Meanwhile, smaller grants enabled us to carry on. The George C. Marshall International Center at Dodona Manor, the German Marshall Fund of the United States, and the RIAS Berlin Commission provided much-appreciated support toward another European interview trip later that month. With the assistance of cultural and press attachés in the embassies of Germany, The Netherlands, Belgium, and Luxembourg, Linda and I developed a full schedule to interview former government ministers, engineers, diplomats, economists, and officials in local governments and industry. For thirty days we roared through those countries, laying our heads on different pillows nearly every night and meeting new and interesting people every day.

After returning, we continued preliminary interviews with American scholars, Marshall Planners, and observers. Ira's steady support and cooperation, contributing his time during weekly lunches while we pursued interviews and funding, was immensely helpful. Film and photo researcher Elisabeth Hartjens, a crucial ally, helped Linda find inexpensive footage at the National Archives, and the staff of its Motion Picture Division went to great lengths to help Linda find, view, copy, and later order footage for the film editor, a scriptwriter, and Ira to sift through.

"The Break above the Habsburg Empire"?

A scriptwriter would need paper copies of interviews, but we could afford only amateur transcribers with scant experience and little familiarity with the subject matter or foreign accents. Errors abounded. One interviewee had said that Charlie Kindleberger was "a famous economist," but the transcriber wrote, "Charlie Kindleberger was a famous Communist."

Another interviewee had said, "The question was, would the Europeans cooperate?" Instead, the transcriber wrote, "The question was, would the Europeans copulate?" Yet another transcription puzzled Linda when she read "The problem was the break above the Habsburg Empire." In fact, the Austrian interviewee had said, "The problem was the breakup of the Habsburg Empire." Editing became critical.

Funding at Last

In the spring of 1996—just in time—the suspense was over. Sharing part of a grant from Germany, the George C. Marshall Center at Dodona Manor pledged enough to cover the remaining phases of the project. It *would* be a PBS documentary! Now we could hire a professional cameraman, begin to conduct final interviews, and work with a scriptwriter to make it all happen.

Our new writer, Louis Barbash, began to work his magic, using old newsreels, footage from films created by the Marshall Plan itself, some photographs, and transcribed interviews of witnesses and academics. Ira, video editor Dan Rose, Linda, and I all campaigned for our favorite bits and pieces of the narrative—an untidy but necessary process. Remarkably, the preliminary script took shape.

The final script would be quite different from this first draft. One interviewee froze before the big camera. Another had died, and we wondered if PBS would allow the inferior footage from Linda's and my preliminary camcorder interview with him (they did). Although two refused to allow their wrinkled faces to appear on television, most others were happy to tell their stories on camera.

We flew some interviewees to Washington and drove with Ira and a cameraman to videotape others in their homes. Lord Roll was in Washington for a business meeting, so we taped him in his hotel room. Local interviewees—at least ten or twelve—were taped in either our home or the homes of nearby friends.

In October, four of us flew to Europe for a final, professional, two-week interview trip—a German-speaking cameraman (Pascal Dieckmann), soundman (Ira, the producer), project director and keeper of the interview log (Linda), and interviewer (me). We videotaped in Linz and Mandling (Austria), Munich, Bonn, and Stein (Germany), Swifterbant and Rotterdam (The Netherlands), and Paris.

Paris presented logistical problems: how to move all the video equipment on the hotel's tiny elevator and into our van parked in a barely accessible garage behind the hotel and then to find our way to two or three interviews a day. The solution: all interviews but one were taped in the same hotel room. With new shelf paper taped to the wall for background, altered lighting in the room, different books on the shelves, and fresh flowers in a different vase, each set appeared new.

Back Home to Make the Movie

With transcribed and edited interviews, photographs, and footage in hand, we had everything we needed to meld the myriad stories into a compelling one-hour documentary—everything except the story. According to Ira, most of the "information" viewers get from television documentaries derives visually, not verbally. A good television documentary is a story, not an illustrated lecture. Good stories with suspense, emotion, pathos, and humor stir the heart and engage the mind. They are about someone who wants to *do* something. But who was that someone? The answer would become the job of the production team. Making sure everything was correct became the job of the "accuracy police," Linda and me. Production began with all of us noisily contributing to Louis's final script and Ira and film editor Dan creating the video.

Then in February, just weeks before the finished product was due to PBS, production came to a sudden halt. With faint hope of a positive reply, Linda had once again phoned her favorite storyteller, Dr. van der Beugel, to inquire about his health. The Dutchman, a gentleman of keen insight and droll stories, had been too ill for us to interview while filming in Europe the previous fall. He was feeling better, he said. Would he be willing to be interviewed? Yes.

Ira listened attentively as Linda insisted that Dr. van der Beugel's stories offered not only insight into relevant and significant issues, but also some much-needed humor for the script. So with a little money lifted from another part of the budget, Pascal, Ira, and I flew to Amsterdam the next week, rented a car, and rang Dr. van der Beugel's doorbell at exactly the appointed hour. Then the trouble began. Mrs. van der Beugel greeted us by warning that it was "forbidden to move the furniture"; she must have had some unpleasant experiences with film crews in the past, we assumed. We then discovered that the camera, which had become cold during the flight, had developed condensation and refused to operate. While it dried out, my task as interviewer for an hour or two was to keep Dr. van der Beugel engaged. That was not difficult; he held forth on his favorite subject, opera. Once the interview began, he looked at his watch and startled us by saying he could not give us more than ten or fifteen minutes. Miraculously, however, he got into his story, forgot the time, and provided one of our best interviews, both insightful and humorous. Louis happily worked him into the script.

With the program nearly finished, we still had no narrator. Fortunately, Roger Mudd, formerly with the CBS and ABC networks, agreed to help and to do it for a lower-than-usual fee. A stickler for historical accuracy and good grammar, he approved the script after a painstaking three-hour meeting.

Was It Worth the Effort?

The entire project was a voyage into kindness and cooperation, both in Europe and the United States. It also had a steep learning curve and was not without its frustrations. We learned that George C. Marshall's biographer Dr. Forrest Pogue was right: we had to leave a lot out.

But we look back with pleasure on all phases of the experience—an adventure fraught with uncertainty and excitement, requiring enterprise, enthusiasm, and, above all, persistence. Later awarded a Cine Golden Eagle, the documentary has been at least modestly successful. Ken Ringle of *The Washington Post* had this to say when it premiered on 6 June 1997:

> Someone once described George C. Marshall, unkindly and probably unfairly, as the most boring great man of the 20th century. The same might be said of the majestic foreign aid program that bears his name. Yet tonight at 9 on Channel 26 [PBS] an important hour-long film achieves the impossible by making the Marshall Plan not only understandable but fascinating—as important and engaging a history lesson as you're likely to get this year. "The Marshall Plan: Against the Odds" deserves its title in more ways than one [. . .]."

In addition to the satisfaction of actually finishing the show, it was a great pleasure to interview so many remarkable people, to collaborate with the team at Educational Film Center, and to work with world-class journalist Roger Mudd. In the years since the 1997 broadcast, related projects have presented themselves, including work for the U.S. Embassy in Paris, the George C. Marshall Foundation in Lexington, Virginia, the George C. Marshall International Center at Dodona Manor in Leesburg, Virginia, and, of course, the Marshall Plan conference in Vienna in May 2008. The documentary experience was also a great adventure in conjugal collaboration. Even this article, first drafted by me, has been revised and edited by the both of us. It is Linda's as much as it is mine.

List of Authors

Günter Bischof, Mag. Phil., M.A., M.A., Ph.D.; born 1953; Marshall Plan Professor of History and Director of CenterAustria, University of New Orleans; principal field of research: twentieth-century international history, World War II, Cold War, biography.

Mark Carson, Ph.D.; born 1963; presently adjunct professor, Loyola University of New Orleans, formerly visiting Assistant Professor in American History at Tulane University; principal fields of study: the Vietnam War, Cold War History, American Southern Political History.

Eric Christenson, M.A. (Education), M.A. (English); born 1937; educator, writer, consultant on writing and on Marshall Plan, co-executive producer of PBS Marshall Plan documentary.

Linda Christenson, B.A., born 1937; Marshall Plan historian, researcher, writer, project director and co-executive producer PBS documentary on Marshall Plan, creator/editor Marshall Plan Filmography.

Helge Danielson, Ph.D. (Dr. art), born 1968; currently senior researcher at the Norwegian Institute for Defence Studies, previously a post-doctoral fellow at the Forum for Contemporary History at the University of Oslo; main fields of research: modern and contemporary Scandinavian and Norwegian history, U.S. public diplomacy, Norwegian-American relations.

Victoria de Grazia, Ph.D.; born 1948; Moore Collegiate Professor of History, Columbia University; before joining the Columbia faculty in 1994, she taught at Rutgers University; she is the author of *Irresistible Empire: America's Advance Through Twentieth-Century Europe*; her research interests lie in contemporary history, with longstanding commitments to studying western Europe and Italy from a gendered perspective and to developing a global perspective on commercial revolutions.

David Ellwood, Ph.D.; born 1946; associate professor in International History, University of Bologna, and Adjunct Professor, Johns Hopkins University, SAIS Bologna Center. First major book *Italy 1943–1945: The Politics of Liberation* (1985), then *Rebuilding Europe: Western Europe, America, and Postwar Reconstruction* (1992). Currently in production large-scale work on *America and the Politics of Modernization in Europe* for Oxford University Press.

Herbert Friedlmeier; born 1952; key researcher on photography and contemporary history at the Austrian National Library; author of books on Austrian history in photographic documents and USIS photography in Austria.

George Fujii, B.A. (History), B.A. (English), M.A. (History); born 1980; Ph.D. candidate, University of California, Santa Barbara; principal field of research: twentieth-century history of foreign relations, Cold War, economic foreign policy (U.S., U.K., Canada).

Christoph Höllriegl, Ing., Mag. (FH), M.A., M.A.S., Ph.D. candidate in behavioral economics; born 1970; public relations consultant, freelance journalist, filmmaker, Austrian Marshall Plan film scholar, research scientist.

Hans Petschar, Dr. Phil.; born 1959; Director of the Picture Archives at the Austrian National Library; senior researcher in European Research Programs on digitalization of European cultural heritage; author of books on library history and Austrian History; principal field of research: contemporary history and visual studies, media history.

Michaela Pfunder, Mag. Phil.; born 1965; key researcher on Austrian Contemporary History at the Austrian National Library; adjunct lecturer at the University of Vienna and the Donauuniversität Krems; projects on the history of photography.

Helge Ø. Pharo, Cand. philol., Ph.D. (Dr. philos.); born 1943; Professor of International History and Co-Director of Forum for Contemporary History, University of Oslo; principal field of research, 20th century international history, Norwegian foreign policy, development aid, Cold War, European integration.

Ramón Reichert, Mag. Phil., Ph.D.; born 1966; Professor of Film and Media Studies at the University of Vienna Institute of Theatre, Film and Media Studies and Key Researcher at the Ludwig Boltzmann Institute for European History and Public Spheres; research interests include the historiography of media and technology, the impact of new media and communication technologies such as the Internet, film history and film analysis, history of science and identity politics. He is the author of *Im Kino der Humanwissenschaften: Studien zur Medialisierung wissenschaftlichen Wissens* (2007).

Hannes Richter, M.A., Ph.D.; born 1966; is the co-founder of *Campaign Digital, Inc.* a non-profit corporation based in Washington D.C., where he specializes in the research and application of new media. He is a Fellow of CenterAustria at the University of New Orleans and teaches American politics at the John F. Kennedy Institute, Freie Universität Berlin; he specializes in public opinion and American voting behavior.

Hans-Jürgen Schröder, professor (em.) of Contemporary History; born 1938; Justus-Liebig University Giessen, principal fields of research: twentieth-century international relations, World War II, U.S.-German relations, the reconstruction of Western Germany after the Second World War.

Barbara Stelzl-Marx, Mag., Ph.D. (Phil.); born 1971; deputy director of the Ludwig Boltzmann-Institute for Research on War Consequences, Graz – Vienna – Klagenfurt; fields of research: Soviet occupation of Austria, Cold War, social and cultural history of Stalinism; Prisoners of War.

Dieter Stiefel, Mag. and Dr. rer.soc.oec, Dr. Phil.; born 1946; Professor for Social and Economic History at the University of Vienna; Executive Director of the Vienna Schumpeter Society and the Schumpeter Program Harvard/Austria. Research Fellowships at Cambridge University (England), Harvard University, and UC Berkeley. Author of books on European. economic history, the Great Depression, business and banking history, nationalization and privatization, history of bankruptcy, Marshall Plan, de-Nazification, and Holocaust era assets.

Stelios Zachariou, B.A. (History & Communications), M.A. (History), Ph.D.; born 1969; expert counselor for the Hellenic Ministry of Foreign Affairs on Disarmament related matters, principal field of research: twentieth-century history of foreign relations, Cold War, economic foreign policy, and Greek-U.S. relations.

Klaus Eisterer/Günter Bischof (Editors)

Transatlantic Relations

Austria and Latin America in the 19th and 20th Centuries

Transatlantica, Volume 1
332 pages
€ 34.90/sfr 60.40
ISBN 978-3-7065-4213-5

Starting with the diplomatic relations in the 19th and 20th centuries, the contributions focus on exile, culture, film, and literature studies. Especially migration runs along very different patterns when looking at the Nazi period compared to the decades after 1945. Scientific relations are described as well as solidarity movements' cooperations regarding Chile and Nicaragua. The volume also contains abstracts in German and Spanish.

With contributions by Katrin Achrainer, Rudolf Agstner, Herbert Berger, Günter Bischof, Gerhard Drekonja-Kornat, Klaus Eisterer, Margit Franz, Franz Grafl, Stefan A. Müller, Ursula Prutsch, Claudia Reichl-Ham, Christa Riedl-Dorn, Erwin A. Schmidl, Eva Maria Stehlik, and Gerald Steinacher.

Reinhold Wagnleitner (Editor)

Satchmo Meets Amadeus

Transatlantica, Volume 2
328 pages
€ 33.90/sfr 57.90
ISBN 978-3-7065-4150-3

"Satchmo Meets Amadeus" examines the close encounters between classical music, the soundtrack of the Europeanization of the world, and jazz, the classical music of globalization. This collection of essays by renowned experts in the history of European and American music, African American culture, international cultural encounters, the political, economic, and cultural histories of New Orleans and Salzburg, the political exploitation of music during the eras of National Socialism and the Cold War, the economic utilization of art by music and tourism industries, bypasses the artificial crevice between classical music and jazz, the new world and the old. "Satchmo Meets Amadeus" analyzes the cultural, economic, social, and political structures shaping or hindering the creation of music as well as the construction of popular images and myths about (and against) these seminal musical figures – in short, the creation of SatchmoTM and AmadeusTM – from the 18th to the beginning of the 21st century.

The collection is enhanced by the insights of noted musicians Joe Muranyi (the last surviving member of the Louis Armstrong All Stars), Tom McDermott, Wolfgang Pillinger, Abi von Reininghaus, and S. Frederick Starr. Other authors include Connie Atkinson, (University of New Orleans), John H. Baron (Tulane University, New Orleans); Erwin Giedenbacher (University of Salzburg), Hubert Giesinger (Salzburg), Christian Gruber (University of Salzburg), Rainer Gstrein (University of Innsbruck), Robert Hoffmann (University of Salzburg), Tad Jones (New Orleans), Kurt Luger (University of Salzburg), David Nelson (University of North Carolina at Greensboro's School of Music), Berndt Ostendorf (Ludwig Maximilians University Munich), Clemens Panagl (Salzburg), Gilda Pasetzky (Université de Franche-Comté, Besançon), Lawrence N. Powell (Tulane University, New Orleans), Oliver Rathkolb (University of Vienna), Jack Stewart (New Orleans), Penny Von Eschen (University of Michigan, Ann Arbor), and Reinhold Wagnleitner (University of Salzburg).